DESEXUALISATION IN LATER LIFE

The Limits of Sex and Intimacy

Edited by
Paul Simpson, Paul Reynolds and
Trish Hafford-Letchfield

With a Foreword by
Ketki Ranade

D1613241

P

First published in Great Britain in 2023 by

Policy Press, an imprint of
Bristol University Press
University of Bristol
1-9 Old Park Hill
Bristol
BS2 8BB
UK
t: +44 (0)117 374 6645
e: bup-info@bristol.ac.uk

Details of international sales and distribution partners are available at
policy.bristoluniversitypress.co.uk

© Bristol University Press 2023

British Library Cataloguing in Publication Data
A catalogue record for this book is available from the British Library

ISBN 978-1-4473-5546-5 hardcover
ISBN 978-1-4473-5547-2 paperback
ISBN 978-1-4473-5549-6 ePub
ISBN 978-1-4473-5548-9 ePdf

Cover design: Robin Hawes
Front cover image: iStock / 4FR

Bristol University Press and Policy Press use environmentally responsible
print partners.

Printed in Great Britain by CMP, Poole

Sex and Intimacy in Later Life

Series Editors: **Paul Simpson**, Independent Academic,
Paul Reynolds, International Network for Sexual
Ethics and Politics and The Open University and
Trish Hafford-Letchfield, University of Strathclyde

Older people are commonly characterised as non-sexual, or their sexuality
is considered a superficial concern in comparison to health, public services
and pensions. This is despite evidence of an increase in sexual engagement
amongst older people. Little academic attention has been given to this
subject, or to the impact that this may have, such as increased rates of
sexually transmitted infections or the implications for healthy sex lives
in care institutions.

This new, internationally-focused series will build on, extend and deepen
knowledge of sexual practice amongst older people. Pulling together work by
established and emerging scholars across a range of disciplines, it will cover
the experiential, empirical and theoretical landscapes of sex and ageing.

Also available

Sex and Diversity in Later Life: Critical Perspectives

Edited by **Trish Hafford-Letchfield, Paul Simpson and Paul Reynolds**

Forthcoming in the series

HIV, Sex and Sexuality in Later Life

Edited by **Mark Henrickson, Casey Charles, Shiv Ganesh, Sulaimon Giwa,
Kan Diana Kwok** and **Tetyana Semigina**

Find out more at
**policy.bristoluniversitypress.co.uk/
sex-and-intimacy-in-later-life**

Sex and Intimacy in Later Life

Series Editors: **Paul Simpson**, Independent Academic,
Paul Reynolds, International Network for Sexual
Ethics and Politics and The Open University and
Trish Hafford-Letchfield, University of Strathclyde

International Advisory Board

Jill M. Chonody, Boise State University, US and
University of South Australia, Australia

Mark Henrickson, Massey University of New Zealand, Auckland, New Zealand

Ricardo Iacub, University of Buenos Aires, Argentina

Diana Kwok, The Education University of Hong Kong, Hong Kong

Ketki Ranade, Tata Institute of Social Sciences, Mumbai, India

Marjorie Silverman, University of Ottawa, Canada

Suen Yiu Tung, The Chinese University of Hong Kong, Hong Kong

Find out more at
policy.bristoluniversitypress.co.uk/
sex-and-intimacy-in-later-life

We would like to thank the contributors whose critical scholarship and hard work have made this volume possible. Thank you to the international advisory board for its help and support concerning this book series. Paul Simpson would like to thank his husband, Gordon Blows. Trish Hafford-Letchfield would like to dedicate this book to her daughter Katie Letchfield who has worked so hard to support older people as an Occupational Therapist during the pandemic. Paul Reynolds would like to thank J.S., L.C., A.M., B.B. and P.V. for their continued support in a less than easy time, and S.G. for her patience and fortitude in the first fruits of our writing collaboration – not an easy assignment for her!

Contents

Notes on editors and contributors

Editors

Paul Simpson was awarded a PhD in Sociology in 2011 and has lectured in Sociology at the University of Manchester, UK, and at Edge Hill University, UK, where he was a Senior Lecturer in Health and Social Wellbeing. He has published extensively on gay male ageing (including a monograph, *Gay Men, Ageing and Ageism: Over the Rainbow?*), and on disadvantaged men and health and also on sexuality and intimacy in later life. Since 2012, he has had 21 journal articles published, in *Ageing & Society*, *The British Journal of Sociology*, *Men and Masculinities*, *Qualitative Research in Psychology*, *Sociological Research Online*, *Sociological Review* and *Sociology of Health and Illness*.

Paul Reynolds taught across Northern British Universities for over 30 years, attaining the position of Reader in Sociology and Social Philosophy. He currently tutors on courses for the Open University, UK. He is currently Co-Director of the International Network for Cultural Difference and Social Solidarity, Co-Convenor of the International Network for Sexual Ethics and Politics and a member of the Editorial Board of *Historical Materialism: Research in Critical Marxist Theory* among other commitments. His current research interests are sexual ethics and literacy; kink and the construction of perversion; Marxism, sexuality, subjectivities and collectivities; and the role and responsibilities of the intellectual.

Trish Hafford-Letchfield is Professor of Social Work and Social Policy and Head of School at the University of Strathclyde, Glasgow, Scotland. Trish is a qualified social worker and nurse. Her research interests lie in the experience of marginalised groups in aged care, sexuality and gender identity issues in social work and social care, leadership, management and organisational development in public services, and art-based pedagogies. Trish has more than 100 publications on topics relating to care services.

Contributors

Clare Anderson completed her PhD in 2015, which is a language-based study examining discourses concerning gender and ageing. Her book *Discourses of Ageing and Gender: The Impact of Public and*

Private Voices on the Identity of Ageing Women was published by Palgrave Macmillan in 2018. Clare continues her research and teaching interests as an Associate Tutor at the University of Birmingham, UK, Visiting Lecturer in Media, Culture and Representation and Academic Guidance Tutor at the University of Roehampton, UK, and Visiting Lecturer in Language and Gender at Goldsmith's, University of London, UK. Clare is also Assistant Editor of *Discourse, Context & Media*. Clare combines her academic interests with consulting. Her consulting work focuses on diagnosing the 'language gaps' which can appear between organisations and their target audiences and between brands and their consumers. Clare's passion for understanding language runs through her academic and business activities, and this combines with her core purpose: to empower women (and ageing women in particular) to reclaim confidence and visibility in all domains of their lives.

Josep Fabà has a PhD in Psychology and is Adjunct Professor in the Department of Cognition, Development and Educational Psychology at the University of Barcelona, Spain. He also works as a psychologist in a nursing home. His research interests lie in the areas of the gains that caregivers of individuals with dementia ascribe to their roles, and how sexuality is addressed in residential aged care settings. He has published multiple papers in peer-reviewed international journals, such as the *European Journal of Ageing*, the *Journal of Clinical Nursing*, the *Journal of Homosexuality* and the *Journal of Advanced Nursing*.

Susan Gillen has a master's degree by research in Sociology and has been lecturing in the social sciences and in health and social care for over 20 years, currently working for Edge Hill University, UK, and the Open University, UK. Susan has a varied employment background; as well her experience of teaching and training adults in a variety of settings, including higher education, further education, workplaces and prisons, she has specialist knowledge in the areas of housing and dementia. She also has significant expertise in various issues affecting older people, which have been gained from academic study and employment in the voluntary sector. In addition to a focus on older people, Susan's research interests include ageing across the life course, dementia, health inequalities, and identity and place. Her master's degree thesis, based on qualitative methods, focused on the impact of care workers' constructions of the sexuality of older people resident in care homes, which was motivated by concern with the impact of stereotypes on citizenship status.

Ricardo Iacub has a PhD in Psychology and is Professor of Psychology of Ageing at the University of Buenos Aires, Argentina. He teaches various courses relating to narrative and critical gerontology and has published extensively on the subjects of identity, empowerment and erotics in later life.

Linn J. Sandberg is Associate Professor (docent) in Gender Studies at Södertörn University, Sweden. Her research interests are in the field of gender and sexuality in ageing and later life. Linn has contributed to numerous international scholarly publications in this field: for example, she has published chapters in *Routledge Handbook of Cultural Gerontology* (eds. Twigg and Martin, Routledge, 2015), *Introducing the New Sexualities Studies* (eds. Fischer and Seidman, 3rd edition, Routledge, 2016), *Addressing the Sexual Rights of Older People* (eds. Barrett and Hinchliff, Routledge, 2018) and *Ageing and Everyday Life: Materialities and Embodiments* (ed. Katz, Policy Press, 2018); and peer-reviewed articles in journals such as the *Journal of Aging Studies*, *Sexualities, Men & Masculinities* and the *International Journal of Ageing and Later Life*. Linn's research is interdisciplinary and encompasses qualitative methodologies but primarily in-depth interviews. Her most recent study investigates sexuality and intimacy among couples with Alzheimer's disease. Linn is the co-founder and convenor of a recently launched international network on critical dementia studies, https:// memoryfriendly.org.uk/programmes/critical-dementia-network/, founded by the Swedish Foundation for Humanities and Social Sciences.

Feliciano Villar has a PhD in Psychology and is Professor in the Department of Cognition, Development and Educational Psychology at the University of Barcelona, Spain. He directs the master's degree programme in Psychogerontology and coordinates the research group on Gerontology. He is interested in the implementation of person-centred care in long-term residential settings and in the policies and practices that concern opportunities for resident social participation and rights, particularly among people living with a dementia. Feliciano has published extensively on sex and intimacy in later life in care settings, using qualitative, quantitative and mixed methods, and often as lead author in a research team. More recently, he has published in *Dementia*, the *European Journal of Ageing*, *Sexuality Research and Social Policy* and the *Journal of Advanced Nursing*.

Jane Youell is a Chartered Psychologist and qualitative researcher with particular interests in dementia, autism, learning disability, end-of-life care, death and dying, and family and relationships. She has a PhD in Psychology. Jane's doctoral work addressed the issue of intimacy, sexuality and dementia. She is a Senior Research Fellow at the University of Leeds, UK. Jane has previously been commissioned to work with Dementia UK to develop a training programme to enable Admiral Nurses to better support couples living with dementia, particularly in relation to intimacy and sexuality, and to create a community dementia hub in Leicestershire (East Midlands, UK). Jane was a Dementia Lead at Milton Keynes University Hospital and continues to work directly with patients and carers in her consultancy work. She is also a 2017 Winston Churchill Memorial Trust Award Fellow, which enabled her to conduct the research in Australia on which her chapter is based.

Series editors' introduction

Paul Reynolds, Paul Simpson and Trish Hafford-Letchfield

This *Sex and Intimacy in Later Life* book series will explore, interrogate and enlighten on the sensual, sexual and intimate lives of older people. The motivation for launching this series was a concern with the relative lack of attention in public, professional and academic/intellectual spheres to sex and intimacy in later life (indicatively, Hafford-Letchfield, 2008; Simpson et al, 2018a, 2018b). The series is intended to contribute to and enrich the development of the field of studies composed of the intersections of age, sex, sexuality and intimacy as a critical and important area of scholarship. It is only beginning to be recognised as an important social, cultural and political domain of study within and beyond the 'Western' academy, from which it has emerged. Its earliest contributions, of which this volume is a part, are motivated by a desire to recognise and reject the pathologies and prejudices that have infused this intersection – what Simpson has termed 'ageist erotophobia' (Simpson et al, 2018b, p 1479) – and fuel the failure to acknowledge older people as sexual agents. This is both an intellectual and a political agenda, to question and evaluate the impact of real rather than assumed losses of cognitive, physical, social and sexual capacity, and to recuperate older people as sexual agents from dismissal, ridicule and trivialisation.

If the latter half of the twentieth century was characterised by challenges to the pathologies of social identities – particularly gender, ethnicity and race, disability, sexuality – and struggles for recognition, rights and liberties, more intersectional struggles and recognitions characterise the twenty-first century (on intersectionality, see indicatively Hancock, 2016; Hill Collins and Bilge, 2016). Significant among these has been the re-evaluation of what it is to age and to be an older agent in contemporary societies. Older people have historically experienced both veneration and respect and neglect and pathology, largely based on differing cultural stereotypes of the value of age (Ylanne, 2012). The most common characterisation is that older people are not sexual, past being sexual or represent a problematic sexuality – or their sexuality is a superficial concern and secondary to concerns of health, care, life course and support by public services and engagement and pensions/resources. Such concerns are mainly those of 'Western' cultures and reflected in the 'Western' influence across the globe in respect of state intervention and provision, but elsewhere they have been subsumed and often rendered invisible into family and kinship structures.

Older people's intimate and sexual lives and experiences have transformed in the last 40 years, as a consequence of a number of significant social changes: new technologies – digital, mechanical and pharmaceutical – and their interventions; the recognition of older people as exploitable markets for consumption; healthier lifestyles, changes and extensions to life course and life expectancy; the erosion of social and sexual pathologies around age and recognitions of different intersections and their importance (LGBTQI older people, older people of different ethnicities, older disabled/neurodiverse and 'able-bodied/minded' people; older men and women).[1] These transformations demonstrate evidence of increase in the sexual relations and intimacies of older people and their impacts, such as increased rates of STD transmission, or implications for healthy sex lives for older people in care institutions (indicatively, Drench and Losee, 1996; Lindau, 2007; Bodley-Tickell et al, 2008; Chao et al, 2011; Simpson, 2015; Age UK, 2019).

The scholarship exploring these developments has only recently begun to catch up. A small but growing literature has focused on age and sexuality (represented in the sources authors draw from in this series), with a principal focus on the erosion of easy pathologies and stereotypes of older people's heteronormativity and heterosexuality. Particularly as the 'baby boomers' of the 1950s and 1960s move into old age, changed sexual attitudes, wants and needs require changed political, cultural and institutional responses. The older generation of baby boomers in the late 1940s and 1950s may have remembered Vera Lynn (an iconic British wartime singer singing patriotic songs during World War 2) and post-war society – retaining traditional stereotypes of older people. However, their horizons will have been formed and broadened more by influences from the 1960s' pop and rock culture (notably with such artists as the Beatles, Rolling Stones, Jimi Hendrix and Janis Joplin), women's and lesbian, gay and bisexual liberation struggles, the proliferation of accessible public representations of sex and the 'pornification' of society in the digital age.

Ageing and becoming 'older', intimacy, sexual identity, relations and practices and sexual pleasure are all contested concepts and subject categories. They are understood as being constituted by different demarcations, distinctions and understandings arising from different intellectual disciplines, conceptual approaches, cultures, geographical contexts and historical conjunctures. While it is neither desirable nor credible to preclude critical and constructive debate on the meanings and demarcations of these intersections, it is necessary to draw some broad conceptual boundaries rather than hard-and-fast definitions.

'Ageing' and 'older' are broad categories that are attached to people considered in their 'third age' or 'later life' – in more affluent countries/ regions of the mainly Global North, the threshold is often seen as the age of 50+. This reflects common practice in the literatures of social gerontology, psychology and the sociology of ageing (see Zaninotto et al, 2009; Cronin and King, 2010; Stenner et al, 2011). It is after that, and into their sixth decade, that older people experience a process of de-eroticisation that could be called 'compulsory non-sexuality' (taking our cue from feminist theorist Adrienne Rich [1981], who articulated pressures on women's sexuality towards 'compulsory heterosexuality').

Ageing and being older can be understood mainly in two ways. First, the terms describe ageing as a chronological and physiological process involving key changes, which become particularly marked (and can be stigmatised) in the later stages of the life course. This raises questions around the differential impact of life course experience and physiological change – which *may* include loss and/or reduction of physical and mental capacities for *some* people at different stages in the life course. It is structured both by physiological change and by the (often imperceptible) internalisation and normalisation of orthodoxies describing ageing and being older in cultural and social discourse, and the everyday practice and experience of how older people are perceived and how older people see themselves – often as lacking – and in relation to younger people (Foucault, 1977, 1978). Such is the means by which older people (as much as younger people or social and cultural institutions) both produce and accept the discursive limits to ageing.

Second, ageing and being older could be described as an attribution constituted by ideology and discourse, structural-hierarchical and cultural-discursive influences and material contexts, such as the structure of organisations, public spaces, cultural representations and spaces of connection (for example, labour markets). Ageing is usefully regarded as a product of intersections between the symbolic/discursive and structural/material dimensions of existence. The attribution of a particular age – young, mature or older – is an ideological construct suffused by power relations and composed of cultural attributions, instantiated in material processes and practices. These structural factors impose all manner of constraints on older people's sexual agency (though these can be questioned, challenged and resisted). Put simply, age is a social, cultural and political construct and how older people are perceived and valued – whether prejudicially or with respect – is constituted in the wider character of social values and dominant discourses. While age is an experienced and embodied phenomenon, its meaning is socially, culturally and politically mediated.

'Sex' and 'sexuality' are often distinguished by the former being focused on practices and behaviour, and the latter being focused on identities, relations and orientations. The terms are nevertheless porous and intertwined (Weeks, 2010). Sexuality describes the processes of being sexual (or not) in the world and through self-recognition, expressing (or not) sexual choices and preferences and enjoying (or not) sexual pleasures. It involves the expression of emotions, desires, beliefs, self-presentation and how we relate to others. It most commonly relates to sexual identity – for example hetero, lesbian, gay, bisexual, queer, asexual (Rahman and Jackson, 2010). Sexuality is multidimensional, being co-constituted by the biological (for example bodily sensations interpreted as 'sexual'), the psychological (for example emotions and reasoning) and cultural and socio-economic influences such as dressing up and flirting and so on (Doll, 2012). It is often understood narrowly as genitocentric, itself tied to the heteronormative relationship between genital sex and reproduction. Yet it encapsulates a range of practices that bring sensual pleasure and fulfil wants and desires, such as the agglomeration of practices that are subsumed under the umbrella term BDSM (Bondage and Discipline, Domination and Submission, Sadism and Masochism) (indicatively Weiss, 2011; Ortmann and Sprott, 2013).

'Intimacy' refers to involvement in close and interpersonal relations. It can be a feature of diverse relationships, from those that are sexual, or with strong close personal friendship bonds, or characterised by physical and emotional closeness, to those where a particular relation or facet of life is shared closely, such as close work relationships. It encompasses a spectrum of emotions, needs and activities ranging from feelings of caring, closeness and affection (that can go with long-term companionship) through to 'romance', where an individual 'idealizes' a person(s) (Ehrenreich et al, 1997). Intimacy is to a degree conceived in gendered terms: if men tend to define it more in physical terms, women usually emphasise more its emotional content (O'Brien et al, 2012). It is often conceived as two people sharing intimacy rather than a larger number and is constituted subjectively as a value that is owned or shared with others, although equally it is sometimes seen as an arena that reinforces oppressive conventions of private–public divides and 'compulsory monogamy' (Bersani and Phillips, 2008; Heckert, 2010; Musial, 2013).

These three conceptualisations – age/older, sex/sexuality and intimacies – intersect in complex ways. For example, the prevailing assumption that sexual relationships involve shared intimacy fails to recognise 'fuck buddies' or so-called casual relationships for mutual sexual gratification, though intimacy is sometimes used to describe a particular event without relationship – 'they were intimate' (Wentland and Reissing, 2014). Likewise, sex and age often enmesh in complex ways, though these linkages too often involve mutually reinforcing negative representations. Decline in sexual capacity – often reduced to coital/genital function – is associated with ageing and later life as a standard correlation as opposed to a graduated contingency. Drawing in other intersections, the relationship between sexual capacity and potency is a significant feature of masculinity and therefore sexual capacity is considered more challenging for men, given fears of loss of status and greater reluctance than women to seek help concerning sexual and relationship problems (O'Brien et al, 2012). This reflects gendered assumptions that male sexuality is more active and women's more passive that is rooted in classical sexology (indicatively Davidson and Layder, 1994; Bland and Doan, 1998).

Nevertheless, the sexuality of older women could be constrained by biological changes, understood through cultural pathology as decline and loss of attractiveness. As female sexuality tends to be more associated with youth-coded beauty, older women become excluded from the sexual imaginary (Doll, 2012). In addition, women face the moral constraints of being a good wife/mother/grandmother, where being non-sexual is seen as a virtue and not a deficiency, whereby older women face moral censure for transgressing an approved ageing femininity when not acting their age (Lai and Hynie, 2011). As such the narrative of decline is perpetuated. Since the 1970s, however, women now over 50 will have encountered the countervailing influences of feminism and might challenge such culturally constituted assumptions (Bassnett, 2012; Westwood, 2016).

Even where the idea of older sexual agents meets with approval because of its contribution to well-being and self-esteem, their sexuality has been subject to a medicalised, book-keeping approach that disregards emotions and pleasures and focuses on who is still 'doing it' (Gott, 2004), in the context of declining physical capacity for genitocentric penetrative sex (see Trudel, Turgeon and Piché, 2000, as an example). However, more encouragingly, we perceive the beginnings of challenge to these negative discourses in European, Australian and US contexts and writing, which attempt to recuperate older people, including the oldest citizens (commonly care home residents) and across the spectrum of genders and sexualities, as legitimate sexual/intimate citizens (see Gott, 2004; Hafford-Letchfield, 2008; Bauer et al, 2012; Doll, 2012; Simpson et al, 2016, 2017; Villar et al, 2014).

The purpose of elaborating these brief examples is to underline that a focus on sex and intimacy in later life involves the recognition of intersections both within and beyond the conceptual constituents of the series focus. Lives are not lived in sexual, intimate or aged-based singularities, but in complex differentiated yet overlapping and intertwined experiences with myriad intersections, such as class, race/ethnicity, gender, disability, embodiment and affect (Simpson, 2015). It is this rich patina of experience and knowledge creation that this series seeks to elucidate, working outward from a critical focus on the core concerns of sex/sexuality, intimacy and ageing, and providing the space for innovative and high-quality scholarship that can inform institutions, policy, professional practice, current and future research and older people encountering this focus as lived experience and not simply a subject of inquiry.

The vision behind the series is that it will:

- put the *sex* back in sexuality (and into ageing). This arises from the observation that while sexuality studies has progressed considerably over the last 40 years (Fischer and Seidman, 2016), its development as an intellectual field of enquiry has to some extent dampened the subversive character of a focus on the 'messy physicality' of sexual pleasure. Put simply, there is lots of scholarship about sexuality, but less focus on the pleasures of sex. There is an aspiration that this series might be one avenue by which that can in a small way be corrected. Putting the 'sex' back into 'sexuality' is part of an agenda to enable older people to continue to be recognised as sexual citizens (or more specifically to have the choice to be sexual agents or not). As such, this series can support the vanguard of an intellectual project that will establish sex in later life as a serious yet neglected political issue and thus stimulate and advance debate. If what is at stake in understanding current experience are the impediments and constraints to choice and pleasure, embodied sensual practice and agency must constitute part of the site of scholarship;
- promote and offer an avenue for *critically engaged* work on the subject matter, whether it is empirical and theoretical-philosophical, from across the social sciences, humanities and cultural studies, incorporating scientific and aesthetic insights. An essential part of the project is that assumptions, claims and received knowledge about sex and intimacy in later life are always questioned, challenged and subject to critical review. This is the means by which both extant knowledge is tested, refined and strengthened or rejected, and new knowledge is produced. A critical frame also offers the opportunity

to move beyond traditional academic frames – insofar as a book series allows – in presenting new ideas, evidence and conjectures;

- emphasise the value of *multidisciplinary and interdisciplinary* approaches to sex and intimacy in late life. Though the series is open to critical research studies from specific disciplinary positions, such as sociology, psychology or gerontology, it recognises the value of multidisciplinary studies that draw on more than one discipline or field, and interdisciplinary studies that cut across and suture together different disciplines, perspectives and approaches in understanding the complexity of older people and their sexual and intimate lives. This extends to recognising the value of the interweaving of science, aesthetic and critical approaches across paradigm and disciplinary boundaries;
- recognise the value of different approaches that foreground the *experiential* and/or *empirical* and/or *theoretical* landscapes of sex and intimacy in later life, whether they form layered responses to a question or are presented as discrete levels of analysis;
- have an *international* focus, recognising global differences and inequalities; there is value in both the specificity and depth afforded regional, national and locally based studies but there should be acknowledgement of supranational, international and global contexts to phenomena, trends and developments and political, cultural and social responses. It should be acknowledged that the emergent knowledge on sex, intimacy and later life has been generated mostly within academies of the Global North, but it does not follow that this necessarily implies progress in comparison to other parts of the globe. It also recognises that there are inherent difficulties of resourcing and organisational and common conceptualisation in the development of international projects with a global reach, and these difficulties are unevenly distributed across the globe. In some parts of the globe, researching this focus is not simply difficult but inherently risky to those who might research, be subjects of research or researched with through intolerance, hostility and lack of recognition. Genuine attempts at a global research agenda require properly distributed and balanced strategies for collaboration to meet relevant constraints and challenges. There should be both attention to the seeds of emergent scholarship in the Global South, and sensitivity to the tendency of western scholarship to reflect a bias towards a 'colonial' approach to knowledge production. Notwithstanding the tendency for scholarship to focus on the Global North and particularly North America, Europe and Australasia, the series seeks – in a small way – to promote *international* understandings. This is achieved through the conviction that cross-cultural and spatial perspectives, drawing

from insight and evidence across the globe, can contribute to better understandings of experience and avenues for research, policy and practice and reflection;

- allow for *language, labels and categories* that emerge from particular geographical and cultural contexts in the development of scholarship to be questioned, adapted, resisted and brought into relief with alternatives and oppositions in how age, sex, sexuality and intimacy are conceived;

- recognise and explore the constraints on and complications involved in *expressions of sexual/intimate citizenship as an older person* and across a spectrum of sexual and gender identities, interrogating and challenging stereotypes of older people as prudish or sex-negative and post-sexual. Equally, the series seeks to explore, examine and advocate sex-positive approaches to sex and intimacy in later life that can help empower, enable and support older people's sexual and intimate relations;

- be accessible to readers in order to inform *public understanding, academic study, intellectual debate, professional practice and policy development.*

This is an ambitious agenda to set for any enterprise, and the series hopes only to make modest contributions to it. Nevertheless, the series has been born of a conviction that unless this sort of agenda is adopted, the experience everyone shares of growing old will always be unnecessarily impoverishing and incapacitating. At the core of this series, and what it should exemplify, is the flourishing that arises from older sexual agents making choices, giving and enjoying pleasure and recognising options and experiences that are open to them as they age.

The Editors
March 2021

Note

[1] The long, full version of what has been called the 'alphabet soup' of sexual identities is LGBTIQCAPGNGFNBA ('Lesbian', 'Gay', 'Bisexual', 'Transgender', 'Intersex', 'Questioning', 'Curious', 'Asexual', 'Pansexual', 'Gender Nonconforming', 'Gender-Fluid', 'Non-Binary' and 'Androgynous'). This list is neither exhaustive nor does it take in non-western sexual identities and cultures that should not be assumed to be equivalent in their conception.

References

AgeUK (2019) *AS STIs in older people continue to rise Age UK calls to end the stigma about sex and intimacy in later life* https://www.ageuk.org.uk/latest-press/ articles/2019/october/as-stis-in-older-people-continue-to-rise- ageuk-calls-to-end-the-stigma-about-sex-and-intimacy-in-later-life/

Arber, S. and Ginn, J. (1995) *'Only Connect:' Gender Relations and Ageing*, in Arber, S. and Ginn, J. (eds), *Connecting Gender and Ageing*. Buckingham: Open University Press.

Bassnett, S. (2012) *Feminist Experiences: The Women's Movement in Four Cultures*. London: Routledge.

Bauer, M., Fetherstonhaugh, D., Tarzia, L., Nay, R., Wellman, D. and Beattie, E. (2012) 'I Always Look Under the Bed for a Man.' Needs and Barriers to the Expression of Sexuality in Residential Aged Care: The Views of Residents with and without Dementia', *Psychology and Sexuality*, 4(3): 296–309.

Bersani, L. and Phillips, A. (2008) *Intimacies*. Chicago, IL: Chicago University Press.

Bland, L. and Doan, L. (1998) *Sexology in Culture: Labelling Bodies and Desires*. Cambridge: Polity.

Bodley-Tickell, A.T., Olowokure, B., Bhaduri, S., White, D.J., Ward, D., Ross, J.D.C., Smith, G., Duggal, H.V. and Gould, P. (2008) 'Trends in Sexually Transmitted Infections (Other than HIV) in Older People: Analysis of Data from an Enhanced Surveillance System', *Sexually Transmitted Infections*, 84: 312–17.

Chao, J.-K., Lin, Y.-C., Ma, M.-C., Lai, C.-J., Ku, Y.-C., Kuo, W.-H. and Chao, I.-C. (2011) 'Relationship Among Sexual Desire. Sexual Satisfaction and Quality of Life in Middle-Aged and Older Adults', *Journal of Sex and Marital Therapy*, 37(5): 386–403.

Cronin, A. and King, A. (2010) 'Power, Inequality and Identification: Exploring Diversity and Intersectionality Amongst Older LGB Adults', *Sociology*, 44(5): 876–92.

Davidson, J.O. and Layder, D. (1994) *Methods, Sex, Madness*. London: Routledge.

Doll, G.A. (2012) *Sexuality and Long-term Care: Understanding and Supporting the Needs of Older Adults*, Baltimore, MD: Health Professions Press.

Drench, M.E. and Losee, R.H. (1996) 'Sexuality and the Sexual Capabilities of Elderly People', *Rehabilitation Nursing*, 21(3): 118–23.

Ehrenfeld, M., Tabak, N., Bronner, G. and Bergman, R. (1997) 'Ethical Dilemmas Concerning the Sexuality of Elderly Patients Suffering from Dementia', *International Journal of Nursing Practice*, 3(4): 255–59.

Fischer, N.L. and Seidman, S. (eds) (2016) *Introducing the New Sexuality Studies* (3rd edition). London: Routledge.

Foucault, M. (1977) *Discipline and Punish: The Birth of the Prison*. London: Penguin.

Foucault, M. (1978) *The History of Sexuality Volume 1: An Introduction*. London: Penguin.

Gott, M., (2004) *Sexuality, Sexual Health and Ageing*, London: McGraw-Hill Education.

Hafford-Letchfield, P. (2008) 'What's Love Got to Do with It? Developing Supportive Practices for the Expression of Sexuality, Sexual Identity and the Intimacy Needs of Older People', *Journal of Care Services Management*, 2(4): 389–405.

Hancock, A.-M. (2016) *Intersectionality: An Intellectual History.* Oxford: Oxford University Press.

Heckert, J. (2010) *Love without Borders? Intimacy, Identity and the State of Compulsory Monogamy* http://theanarchistlibrary.org/library/ jamieheckert-love-without-borders-intimacy-identity-and-the-state-ofcompulsory-monogamy

Hill Collins, P. and Bilge, S. (2016) *Intersectionality.* Cambridge: Polity.

Lai, Y. and Hynie, M. (2011) 'A Tale of Two Standards: An Examination of Young Adults' Endorsement of Gendered and Ageist Sexual Double Standards', *Sex Roles*, 64(5–6): 360–71.

Lindau, S.T., Schumm, P., Laumann, E.O., Levinson, W., O'Muircheartaigh, C.A. and Waite, L.J. (2007) 'A Study of Sexuality and Health among Older Adults in the United States', *New England Journal of Medicine* 357: 762–74.

Musial, M. (2013) 'Richard Sennett and Eva Illouz on Tyranny of Intimacy. Intimacy Tyrannised and Intimacy as a Tyrant', *Lingua Ac Communitas*, 23: 119–33.

O'Brien, K., Roe, B. Low, C., Deyn, L. and Rogers, S. (2012) 'An Exploration of the Perceived Changes in Intimacy of Patients' Relationships Following Head and Neck Cancer', *Journal of Clinical Nursing*, 21(17–18): 2499–508.

Ortmann, D. and Sprott, R. (2013) *Sexual Outsiders: Understanding BDSM Sexualities and Communities.* London: Rowman and Littlefield.

Rahman, M. and Jackson, S. (2010) *Gender and Sexuality: Sociological Approaches.* Cambridge: Polity Press.

Rich, A. (1981) *Compulsory Heterosexuality and Lesbian Experience.* London: Onlywomen Press.

Simpson, P. (2015) *Middle-Aged Gay Men, Ageing and Ageism: Over the Rainbow?.* Basingstoke: Palgrave Macmillan.

Simpson, P., Brown Wilson, C., Brown, L., Dickinson, T. and Horne, M. (2016) 'The Challenges of and Opportunities Involved in Researching Intimacy and Sexuality in Care Homes Accommodating Older People: a Feasibility Study', *Journal of Advanced Nursing*, 73(1): 127–37.

Simpson, P., Horne, M., Brown, L.J.E., Dickinson, T. and Torkington, K. (2017) 'Older Care Home Residents, Intimacy and Sexuality', *Ageing and Society*, 37(2): 243–65. DOI: 10.1017/S0144686X15001105

Simpson, P., Almack, K. and Walthery, P. (2018a) 'We Treat Them all the Same': the Attitudes, Knowledge and Practices of Staff Concerning Old/er Lesbian, Gay, Bisexual and Trans Residents in Care Homes', *Ageing & Society*, 38(5): 869–99.

Simpson, P., Wilson, C.B., Brown, L.J., Dickinson, T. and Horne, M., (2018b) ' "We've Had Our Sex Life Way Back": Older Care Home Residents, Sexuality and Intimacy', *Ageing & Society*, 38(7): 1478–501.

Stenner, P., McFarquhar, T. and Bowling, A. (2011) 'Older People and "Active Ageing": Subjective Aspects of Ageing Actively', *Journal of Health Psychology*, 16(3): 467–77.

Trudel, G., Turgeon, L. and Piché, L. (2000) 'Marital and Sexual Aspects of Old Age', *Sexual and Relationship Therapy*, 15(4): 381–406.

Villar, F., Celdrán, M., Fabà, J. and Serrat, R. (2014) 'Barriers to Sexual Expression in Residential Aged Care Facilities (RACFs): Comparison of Staff and Residents' Views', *Journal of Advanced Nursing*, 70(11): 2518–27.

Weeks, J. (2010) *Sexuality* (3rd edition). London: Routledge.

Weiss, M. (2011) *Techniques of Pleasure: BDSM and the Circuits of Sexuality*. Durham, NC: Duke University Press.

Wentland, J.J. and Reissing, E. (2014) 'Casual Sexual Relationships: Identifying Definitions for One-night Stands, Booty Calls, Fuck Buddies, and Friends with Benefits', *The Canadian Journal of Human Sexuality*, 23(3): 167–77.

Westwood, S. (2016) *Ageing, Gender and Sexuality: Equality in Later Life*. London: Routledge.

Ylanne, V. (ed) (2012) *Representing Aging: Images and Identities*. Houndsmill: Palgrave Macmillan.

Zaninotto, P., Falaschetti, E. and Sacker, A. (2009) 'Age Trajectories of Quality of Life Among Older Adults: Results from the English Longitudinal Study of Ageing', *Quality of Life Research*, 18(10): 1301–9.

Foreword

That older people are seen as asexual or post-sexual and that this is true for many societies and cultures across the world is a widely known and uncontested proposition. A book that explores the how and why of the desexualisation in later life and puts forth an academic (theoretical and empirical) inquiry and policy analysis, as well as narrative and case study reporting of the complex processes that produce and maintain this desexualisation, is a welcome addition to an emerging field – the sexuality of older people.

Ageing conceptualised solely as a biological phenomenon and the associated decline-deficit-loss narrative leading to the pathologisation and medicalisation of the ageing body-mind is known; and so is the burgeoning of medical/health industries selling the idea of 'restoring' health, capacity and wellbeing or 'postponing' decline. The major contribution of this book is to show us the links between these dominant narratives of ageing and the (im)possibilities of sexual agency or rights that these produce. By dwelling on socio-cultural constructs of ageing, i.e. what are the socially and culturally sanctioned milestones/scripts for older people?, this book pushes its readers to think about the unviability of the idea of a sexually thriving older body – rendered unviable in a material sense of access to resources, opportunity, privacy and sexual autonomy. Also made unviable in a discursive sense is the absence of a sex-positive imagination and representation of sex and intimacy among older adults. Such issues pose major obstacles to the aspiration of sexual agency, desire and pleasure for older adults.

The editors of this book (and the series Sex and Intimacy in Later Life) and its contributors are mindful of avoiding homogenisation of older people or presenting a singular narrative of sexuality in later life. The book does not restrict its commentary to cisgender, heterosexual, marital sexuality of old age, but instead includes a focus on older LGBT older persons, older women, older people in care homes, older disabled people and those affected by a dementia such as Alzheimer's disease.

Researchers, scholars, educators, social workers and policy makers who are engaged with the discourse of ageing and care about the needs, concerns and rights of older adults would benefit immensely by thinking about the many invisible and erased aspects of the ageing person that this book calls attention to. As a researcher working on non-normative gender-sexualities in India, I find this book to be of immense value, as it expands the boundaries of inquiry of ageing research and sexuality rights discourse by placing the two side by side.

Ketki Ranade
Chair, Centre for Health and Mental Health,
Tata Institute of Social Sciences, Mumbai

Introduction to volume two: themes, issues and chapter synopses

Paul Simpson, Paul Reynolds and Trish Hafford-Letchfield

Older people's sexual and intimate lives represent an emerging field of study that fuels demands for change across public, private and voluntary services and holds some promise for representing age as positive change (see the volume edited by Barrett and Hinchliff, 2017). Yet, there remain significant constraints on older individuals' sexual expression and limitations in knowledge on sexuality in later life (Reynolds et al, 2021). Constraint on sexual and intimate self-expression and practice, operating in diverse, intersectional modes, was a key motif that emerged in the first volume addressing diversity in this book series on Sex and Intimacy in Later Life. Older people (defined as aged 50 and over in the series introduction in this volume) remain the subject of stereotyping as non-sexual or 'post-sexual' (Simpson et al, 2018). Such a concept broadly refers to the process of desexualisation of older people that appears endemic in late modern societies and marks limits to who counts, age-wise, as a legitimate sexual being (Gatling et al, 2017).

Indeed, representations of age stress unsexy, sagging flesh, tarnished bodies, sexual dysfunction and absence of eroticism (Moore and Reynolds, 2016). More specifically, Gilleard and Higgs (2011) talk of how the leaky, less continent bodies of the oldest old are contrasted with the vital performances of younger adults, and Moore and Reynolds (2016) draw attention to a negative aesthetic that equates older people with ugliness *and* dearth, if not death, of desire. In light of such endemic pathologies and prejudices, it is tempting to believe that older people are generally not only thought of as no longer interested in engaging in sexual activity and pleasure but also are probably not even expected to think of it (Simpson et al, 2018; Bauer et al, 2016). Given the absence of more validating images of ageing sexuality, older people themselves can come to think of themselves in this way (Simpson et al, 2018). It is also quite likely that older people are excluded from the many and varied practices that constitute the 'sex industry', though ironically DIY porn sites indicate that older women can be fetishised in a niche way.

Key terms that populate this volume – later life, ageing, ageism, sex, intimacy and ageist erotophobia – were defined in the book series introduction in this volume. The latter concept bears some repetition, as it invokes widespread subconscious fear and/or denial of older people as sexual beings, which is central to desexualisation (Simpson et al, 2016). In addition to the constraints that ageist erotophobia can impose on older people, there is a tendency to fall back on naturalised developmentalist fallacies (Moore and Reynolds, 2018) that represent ageing as a desexualising process, which also represent a persistent pathology. Older people's sexuality and sexual lives, notwithstanding this recognition, are still generally regarded with disdain, ignored or else seen as requiring interventions focused on health and risk rather than pleasure and quality of life (Garrett, 2014; Gott, 2004; Hafford-Letchfield, 2008; Villar et al, 2014).

Ageism, with its associated stigmas (commonly referring to wrinkles, changing body shape, loss of physical capacity and lack of interest), prejudices and pathologies, over-associates age with loss and misery (Calasanti and King, 2019). Along with the underlying developmentalist assumptions noted, the factors just noted work together to feed a range of devaluing reactions. These reactions can range from feelings of disgust at the thought or sight of frail bodies to the infantilisation of older people's sexuality and a complete conceptual disconnect between ageing and sex (Gott, 2004; Hockey and James, 1993; Simpson et al, 2018). Yet, the literature exploring ageing sexuality that seeks to distinguish the challenges to older people who wish to enjoy sex from the desexualising discursive nexus that is imposed upon them appears relatively limited (DeLamater, 2012).

Further, this volume is based on the premise that it is not enough simply to describe desexualisation and pathologisation of later life sexuality with due evidence. It is also necessary to understand how these factors occur in and across different contexts, across different identities, relationships and practices, if we are to bring about change. Such is the intent of this volume, which is designed to provoke debate on a neglected issue to encourage readers to think about how to challenge ageist erotophobia and thus widen the discourse to acknowledge and value the legitimate sexual status of older people who wish to continue their erotic lives.

In effect, this volume builds on and extends the limited academic and policy- and practice-related knowledge of how desexualisation works in relation to older people. With such a purpose in mind, established and emerging scholars across a range of disciplines that include the social sciences, health and social work studies, and the humanities have been brought together to highlight the different voices that help constitute much contemporary enquiry. Nevertheless, and to add to current knowledge, the book provides an overview of research concerned with the intersections of ageing and desexualisation, through different examples. Drawing on a range a conceptual-theoretical analysis and theoretically- or practice-informed studies, this volume seeks critically to engage with the various challenges that constitute the desexualisation of older people.

Desexualisation

Before we outline the chapters in this volume, it is worth detailing some of the contours of desexualisation, which can function in diverse, cross-cutting ways (which inform and are evident in this book), and that are indicative of socio-economic, political and cultural influences.

To begin with, and as shown by Simpson (2021) in the first volume of this book series, social class (in terms of income and status), strongly influences ability to participate in aspects of socio-sexual life and pleasure (just to get out and about to meet others) and the ability to present and legitimate oneself as an attractive being worthy of being considered sexy and sexual in later life. At a basic material level, class can affect ability to afford sex toys and fantasy paraphernalia, but this also correlates with cultural capital – capacity to mobilise the know-how and the self-permission to develop knowledge of and experience the enjoyment that they can bring. It may just be, then, that older, middle-class white men are generally better positioned than other older people to claim ongoing validity as sexual agents.

Desexualisation is also heavily influenced by gender ideology. For instance, loss of sexual capacity in later life is considered more challenging for men, given the fear of loss of masculine status (O'Brien et al, 2012). Older heterosexual men can find their sexuality limited, even excluded, by youth-coded discourses that exert pressure to maintain penetrative sex, especially given the availability of pharma-technologies like Viagra (Lee and Tetley, 2021). In contrast, older women not only tend to favour the intimacy involved in emotional closeness, sharing, caressing and cuddling (O'Brien et al, 2012), they also face a different set of problems. Older women have reported experiencing desexualisation more intensely because of the harsh, exacting aesthetic standards of consumer societies that equate youth with female beauty (Doll, 2012). Some women might well invoke the double-standard that has followed them through the life course, that has encouraged male experimentation while policing women's sexual self-expression, and which now demands that they behave age-appropriately (Kaklamanidou, 2012). If older males expressing desire can be stereotyped as a 'chip-off-the-old-block' (or sometimes 'dirty old men'), sexually assertive older women fear being seen to breach a legitimate ageing femininity that demands decorum and passivity (Kaklamanidou, 2012). That said, 'baby-boomer' women now in middle age will have encountered sex-positive feminist thought, which has helped articulate women's (continued) right to sexual enjoyment (Hinchliff and Gott, 2008), though we might speculate that other older women could appreciate respite from male scrutiny and 'conjugal duties'.

Differences in desexualisation also occur within and between non-normative ageing identity categories, that is referring to older gay, lesbian bisexual and trans (LGBT) individuals, though, for brevity, we focus here mainly on experiences reported in relation to gay men and trans people. The main motif in the literature addressing older gay men draws attention to how experience of desexualisation might be different for them compared to lesbian-identified women and heterosexual men. Mirroring older heterosexual women's experience, older gay men report being subjected to harsh bodily aesthetics that result in judgement of their putative loss of sexual/physical capital (Green, 2011; Simpson, 2015). A perennial feature of this body of literature concerns the idea that ageing is 'accelerated' in gay male cultures or 'scenes' where one is seen as old and beyond desirability at a relatively young age, for example, around the age of 40 (Bennett and Thompson, 1991; Hostetler, 2004; Simpson, 2015) as a common cultural marker of middle age. Although 'early' exclusion from sexual status is keenly felt by older gay men, the concept has been critiqued because it obscures diverse responses to sexual expression among gay men that include continuity and celebration as well as resistance to gay ageism (Hughes and King, 2018; Simpson, 2015).

There is very little scholarship on sexuality, intimacy and older trans individuals, though the process of trans ageing appears subject to a range of cultural, psychological, material, legal and health-related constraints and disadvantages and not least access to sexual health support that would involve sexual pleasure (Donovan, 2002). Older trans individuals especially seem far less legible as sexual and intimate subjects than any other social group. This failure of recognition may have much to do with their over-association with gender rather than sexuality and that, when acknowledged, their sexuality can be read as unreal and pathological for being old *and* trans (Simpson, 2016). It could be argued that their putative abnormality causes older trans individuals to be excluded from intimacy and sexual opportunity or else misread as sexually desperate/indiscriminate or as appealing to very 'niche markets' that relate, for example, to the fetishisation of some transwomen as 'chicks with dicks'.

Chapter synopses: biological, legal, relational, cultural, structural and policy/practice constraints on older people as sexual agents

This section provides a survey of the terrain within which ageist erotophobia, desexualisation and pathologisation are constituted and manifest. Such matters, inevitably, involve consideration of embodiment and the older body as identical with physical loss, decline and incapacity. One might even argue that these narratives provide a baseline from which theorising about diverse forms of desexualisation could proceed.

As the chapters in this book will show, however, there is much more to the story of ageing sexuality than biological reductionist thinking that equates bodily age with loss of capacity and status. Indeed, we theorise that ageism and ageist erotophobia are produced through the complex interarticulation of various influences. Specifically, such influences involve embodiment, social structures (of class and institutions), cultures and ideological framings. Together these intersecting influences can inform and maintain discourses and reinforce dissonances that characterise and can constrain thinking about age and sex. In particular, they invoke 'pedagogisation'/didactic developmentalist orthodoxies (see Foucault, 1979 and Moore and Reynolds, 2018 in relation to child development). Such an intellectual project requires examination of how developmentalism underpins medical, cultural, legal and policy developments and constitutes a bio-politics that penetrates the body and characterises the biological occupation of the ageing body as incapable, frail and undesirable (Moore and Reynolds, 2016).

The reader is also asked to note the logic to the order of chapters. Essentially, they proceed from general, macro-level, theoretical issues, such as consent, relationality and aesthetics, to particular issues of ageing femininity, disability and dementia, and policy and practice. Although all chapters ramify in terms of ideas for care policy and practice, the last three substantive chapters, 9, 10 and 11, can be grouped thematically because they discuss head-on, and in a theoretically-informed way, such issues that concern LGBT individuals, care homes and their residents, and the role of healthcare professionals in denying or enabling older people's sexuality.

Consent and constraint

Underlying all discussions of sex is the subject of consent and sexual agency (autonomy) or the lack thereof. In Chapter 2, Paul Reynolds offers a critical-theoretical ground-clearing of the complexities of consent and highlights particular concerns for sex and intimacy in later life. Sexual consent involves a complex process of communication between competent sexual agents that are informed about their choices and free from coercion. This becomes more complicated with older people who may be vulnerable, ill-informed of contemporary norms and conventions, or experiencing cognitive decline that can affect their capacity to consent. Issues of consent can be exacerbated within a context of desexualisation, which in different ways limits the cultural and communicative space in which older people's consent decisions are made and issues and concerns are raised and discussed by older people themselves and those who care for and support them. In the context of generations who have not benefited from a more nuanced focus on sexual consent than has developed over the past two decades, where heteronormative values and assumptions might constitute orthodoxy, and where there may be critical impediments to legally recognisable consent decisions, such as early onset dementias or frailty, the focus on consent can be overwhelmed by notions of risk (see also the point made later in this chapter) and protection. While these are important considerations, in a desexualised context they become barriers to older people's sexual intimacies. Older people with sexual desires can find themselves in a hostile terrain, where the limited representation of their sexuality is negative. In exploring these complexities and decoding the pernicious impact of desexualised terrain that amplifies these problems, Reynolds recognises the importance of enabling quality consent decisions. However, for that to be assured, there needs to be substantive culture change and change in how knowledge and understandings of diverse sexual and intimate needs and wants are to be considered and satisfied. This requires more substantive cultural change, and Reynolds advocates a more comprehensive, political and critical approach to this task in the shape of 'sexual literacy.'

Relational constraints

If consent informs all manner of relationships, older people (including those with fewer relations or contacts) are involved, unconsciously or otherwise, in complex webs of relationships at the macro- and meso-levels with unknown others and at the everyday or micro-level with those known to them to a greater or lesser degree. As Judith Butler (2004) has famously remarked: 'Let's face it. We're undone by each other. And if we're not, we're missing something.' Such words suggest the value of relationships in (inevitably) challenging and unsettling each other's taken-for-granteds, which have the power to occasion re-thinking of the meanings of our individual and collective vulnerability. With relational vulnerability in mind, Paul Simpson's theoretical Chapter 3 critically examines literature bearing on how older people, and especially the oldest citizens resident in care homes, can be desexualised by relationships at macro-, micro- and meso-levels. In particular, this chapter considers how 'ageist erotophobia' can undermine at all levels and in various ways the opportunities for sexual and intimate expression available to older people. The latter may find their sexuality restricted by wider discursive-cultural and structural-institutional influences, which enmesh with interpersonal lives that involve relatives and significant others. To avoid homogenising older people as lacking in agency, the chapter also briefly draws attention to some of the ways in which (different) older people challenge ageist erotophobia.

Aesthetic(s) of eroticism in later life

In Chapter 4, Ricardo Iacub and Feliciano Villar explore how negative aesthetics of old age contribute to or even construct a stigmatised sexuality that arouses feelings of disgust or else prompts ridicule. Such stigma naturalises and limits critical and political thinking about the mechanisms of social control over eroticism in later life. In addition to examining how older-body-selves are desexualised, this chapter also discusses images of more recent vintage that defy conformity to traditional ageing stereotypes and which have emerged especially in the gay world, such as 'bears' (older, bigger/fatter, hairier men), 'daddies', mature men, and grand-daddies. Essentially, this chapter critically examines the mechanisms that regulate the aesthetics of eroticism as they relate to old age from fragments of historical accounts, exploration of social trends and by using insights from psychological studies, in Buenos Aires, Argentina, of younger people's perceptions of young and old people about sexuality and older bodies. Such a focus enables an analysis that accounts for in-depth understanding of the 'politics of age' (Iacub, 2002) and how the 'aesthetics of the erotic in old age' can work differently for different individuals and social groups (Iacub, 2002).

Discourses of ageing femininity and the menopausal body

Simone de Beauvoir wrote that women 'of a certain age constitute a "third sex" ... while they are not males, they are no longer females' (1949/1997: 63). This statement pinpoints what continues to be the uneasy reciprocal relationship between culture, age and gender. In Chapter 5 on older, menopausal women, Clare Anderson examines how the cultural as well as the subjective gaze continues to characterise the process of female ageing as one of loss, in which the female body is both desexualised and degendered. In exploring the relationship between the two problematic concepts, the author draws on a range of menopause discourses generated by the lifestyle media and advertising industries, and the growing sub-genre of semi-autobiographical midlife narratives. Further, the chapter compares such public voices with the private voices of a group of women's individual accounts of the menopause, taken from a series of qualitative interviews. The analysis here is informed by the contention of theorist of age Margaret Gullette that the menopause is culturally constructed and that the profusion of menopause discourses, or 'the menoboom' (Gullette, 1997: 98), artificially conflates menopause with inevitable decline, creating a single narrative of loss that variously refers to physical strength, emotional stability and sexual attractiveness.

The chapter concludes that the notion of an older female body, which can still be sexual, remains too challenging for the narrow ideological, visual and linguistic repertoire of a prevailing culture unable to accommodate a notion of ageing that permits sexual desirability and a notion of sexual desirability that can encompass the ageing female body. Given the increasing visibility of older women on the public stage, this work has important implications: for gender and linguistic studies; for the message-makers in the public domain – the influential voices of the media and advertising industries; but, most importantly, for the women they target.

Constraints on older disabled people

While physical disability creates conditions that make 'healthy' sex lives somewhat more difficult and complex in their performance, the intersection of the conditions of ageing and disability create a terrain of desexualisation that distorts, amplifies and augments such complexities. Such a proposition undergirds the argument made in Chapter 6 by Susan Gillen and Paul Reynolds that surveys the intersectional terrain of age and disability. The authors observe that ageing and disability connect two characteristics of the person that are traditionally desexualised, to which can be added the assumption that ageing involves a progressive process of disability, all of which becomes self-reinforcing in propagating pathology and prejudice. This chapter reviews the social construction of disability and recent developments in 'crip'/'queer' studies that resist the normalising of desexualised older disabled people. It explores the desexualising discourses within the intersection of age, sex and intimacy and physical disability, elaborating how common medicalised and developmentalist orthodoxies provide the framings for pathology and prejudice, and how such a process bleeds into cultural and political discourses that discourage seeing the intersection of age and disability as one that can be sexual. Finally, the authors consider what needs to change at conceptual, policy and individual levels to begin to change this state of affairs.

Constraint and older people with an intellectual disability

Following discussion on physical disability, in Chapter 7, Gillen and Reynolds move to discuss the sexual and intimate lives of intellectually disabled people where a twofold pathology is observed. First, intellectually disabled people are invariably assumed to be unreliable, lacking competence and therefore lacking meaning and risk-laden (see also later in this chapter) in their sexual and intimate expressions. Equally, they are regarded as not sexual, either in their subjectivities but also as subjects of other's desires. While both of those representations are false, they have a powerful cultural impact on how sex and intimacy are regarded: by the person themselves, by the family, workers and professionals who provide care and support, and by wider policy and representational structures. In this chapter, Gillen and Reynolds seek to survey the diversity of intellectual disabilities and point out the slipperiness of this identifier, label and appellation. The discussion recognises an emergent and important crip/queer/neurodiverse cluster of approaches that rejects the assumptions and paradigmatic values of medicalisation or standard socio-cultural positions. It also surveys some recent studies to tease out how the institutions, policy and professional practice are both products of and reinforce desexualising discourses. From such a focus, they identify the personal, policy/political and conceptual frame from which the beginnings of a rejection of desexualisation might emerge.

Constraints: the need to go beyond dementia and sexuality as a problem

It is only quite recently that the sexual rights of older people have started to be addressed, and although both scientific and popular discourses are increasingly pointing to sexuality as lifelong and asexuality in later life as a 'myth', stigmas around older people's sexualities persist in various ways (Barrett and Hinchliff, 2017; Sandberg, 2015). With this context in mind, and based on research conducted in Sweden, in Chapter 8 Linn J. Sandberg considers people with dementia as an example of a particular group of older people whose sexualities are commonly deemed problematic. As the author shows, the problematisation of the sexuality of older people with a dementia is clearly reflected in the scientific literature, where their sexuality is commonly discussed in pathologising terms such as 'hypersexuality' or 'inappropriate sexual behaviours'. The author also draws attention to research indicating that nursing staff tend to experience discomfort with, and try to suppress or redirect, sexual expressions among residents with dementia (Mahieu et al, 2011; Dupuis et al, 2012). For such reasons, this chapter goes beyond the narrow conceptualisation of sexual activity as a problem by turning to experiences of the sexual and intimate relationships as narrated by people with dementia themselves and their partners. It also draws on existing research and, in particular, the author's in-depth interview-based study on heterosexual couples' experiences of sexuality and intimacy when living with Alzheimer's disease (AD). The chapter points to how sexual relationships must be understood in terms of the influences of dementia overall on them, and not least a couple's gendered subjectivities. In particular, the themes of *reciprocity, recognition and responsibility* are discussed as influencing how the sexual relationship is experienced. By bringing out the detailed narratives of people with AD and their partners, the author articulates the entanglements of pleasure, joy, comfort, grief and sorrow that shape sexual experiences of people living with dementia.

Constraints on older people living in long-term care facilities

In Chapter 9, and drawing on knowledge generated in Spain, Feliciano Villar and Josep Fabà observe that sexuality is not only a fundamental human experience but can also be maintained among the oldest citizens, who are likely to be affected by significant illness and dependency. Despite this possibility, the sexual needs of older residents are often ignored in long-term care facilities (L-TCFs) and, when they are manifest, are considered more a problem or a potential source of conflict to be managed than the expression of a human need and a question of rights. Therefore, this chapter discusses the barriers that older care home residents commonly face with regard to the expression of sexual interests, emphasising the key role of staff's attitudes and practices to support or repress residents' sexual needs. Further, the authors examine how sexual expression can be especially challenging among specific populations of older adults living in institutions, such as people with a dementia and LGBT residents. These sets of concerns are illustrated with examples extracted from two research projects, one qualitative and the other quantitative. Finally, the authors consider some practical implications to facilitate sexual expression and guarantee sexual rights of older people living in L-TCFs.

Ageing LGBT individuals and sex

Sexuality and intimacy have largely been seen as a domain of the young and 'attractive' in contemporary (consumerist) societies, especially. For older LGBT+ individuals (that takes into account categories like intersex, asexual, queer/questioning), there is an even greater invisibility, particularly concerning sexuality and intimacy. In Chapter 10, Jane Youell explores actions taken by the Australian Government, care providers and LGBT+ activists to push inclusive care up the political agenda. In response, the academic community, in conjunction with local care providers and strategic partners, have developed the 'Rainbow Tick Accreditation'. The 'Rainbow Tick Standards' are applicable to any organisation, but the initial focus has been predominantly in care of older people. This chapter will also consider how perceiving the LGBTI+ community as a homogeneous group is particularly problematic in general, and in dementia care in particular. Concerns about coming out again or having to go back in the closet, lack of advocacy, few LGBTI+ facilities and the impact on identities and relationships are all concerns that are articulated and are discussed here.

Sex and intimacy in later life: the role of professionals in overcoming desexualisation

The transformation of intimacy and sexuality within care institutions is challenging established views about ageing. Chapter 11 by Trish Hafford-Letchfield draws on scholarship from both sexuality and workforce development on how health and social care providers have yet to respond to the growing empirical evidence on what contributes a meaningful life for older care recipients in relation to their sexuality, sexual identities and meeting sexual needs. It is argued that there is an urgent need to transcend established views about the role of all professionals involved in the provision of care to people in later life and to recognise new opportunities for responding to the complexity of sexuality in such contexts. This involves developing and promoting professional practice on theoretical and empirical standpoints that are inclusive of older people's own voices. The chapter also provides examples of how we might recognise the complexity of older people's relationship situations. These involve making sure within the assessment and the provision of care to supply information and give support that would also recognise different relationships and creating conditions for them to flourish. Finally, the author calls for older people's sexuality to be included in professional education, care practices and evaluation of services, and for care facilities to work towards a culturally competent, enquiring and authentic approach to workforce development.

The concluding Chapter 12 synthesises some of the broader themes signalled across the chapters and identifies an agenda for further research on ageing sexuality and intimacy. It is also worth noting that most, if not all, chapters suggest risk as a structuring condition of ageing/older sexuality. Such thinking is particularly evident in Chapters 2 (as noted earlier) and 3, 6, 7, 8 and 10 in terms of surveillance and control over sexual and intimate lives of older people, whether via interpersonal relationships or professional care and support.

Conclusion

This edited volume variously addresses themes and complexities relating to constraints on the autonomy of different older people concerning possibilities for sexual and intimate lives. Inevitably, it illuminates the key relational barriers which undergird desexualisation and pathologisation of older people's sexuality, occurring at the wider cultural discursive and structural levels and in ways that permeate personal and institutional experiences. Taking our cue from Pryzbylo (2021), we can see how desexualisation is produced at the intersections of ageism, sexism, racism, classism and ableism. We would also factor into this mixture a kind of 'healthism' that would require 'good health' as a condition of sexual activity as well as heteronormative and cisgender discourses. Following the chapters of Villar and Fabà, of Youell and of Hafford-Letchfield in this volume, welfare structures and the structure of care home environments also require consideration.

The volume also highlights and critically examines differences in desexualisation that concern: menopausal women (metonymic with loss, who also find themselves degendered); older disabled people; those identifying as LGBT; and those with a dementia, whose sexuality is medicalised and seen as problem to be contained, managed or even prevented. It has been observed that the most common first response to the sexuality of old people affected by a dementia (and especially those 'in care') is to safeguard rather than to think about enabling (Simpson et al, 2018). The situation can become even more complex for old care home residents (whether or not affected by a dementia) identifying/identifiable as LGBT, who can find their identities/differences erased because of a failure of recognition by care homes and staff (Hafford-Letchfield et al, 2017).

While the contributors to this volume have described and analysed complex processes of desexualisation and pathologisation, readers may well ask, what about human agency in questioning, challenging and even resisting such processes? One might ask, what might be the grounds for *resexualisation* of older selves? Thus, contributors to this volume are also keenly aware of the power and necessity of forging intimacies on terms more convivial to older people. Contributors are also aware of avoiding reduction of later life sexuality to a single, dominant story of loss (of capacity and value), rejection and misery. Despite the volume's rightful emphasis on desexualisation, the chapters offer some insights into the possibilities that older people, perhaps courtesy of the epistemic, emotional and cultural-political resources of ageing (Simpson, 2015), could question and challenge ageist erotophobia to assert rights to sexual expression and bodily and relational autonomy. This story of agentic capacity itself offers a challenge to later life identities (including sexual ones) as rendered abject. The theme of self-resexualisation, in the face of considerable obstacles and forms of control, will be explored in a forthcoming volume in this book series.

References

Barrett, C. and Hinchliff, S. (eds) (2017) *Addressing the Sexual Rights of Older People: Theory, Policy and Practice*. London: Routledge.

Bauer, M., Haesler, E. and Fetherstonhaugh, D. (2016) 'Let's Talk about Sex: Older People's Views on the Recognition of Sexuality and Sexual Health in the Healthcare Setting', *Health Expectations*, 19(6): 1237–50.

Bennett, K. and Thompson, N. (1991) 'Accelerated Ageing and Male Homosexuality: Australian Evidence in a Continuing Debate', *The Journal of Homosexuality*, 20(3–4): 65–75.

Bildtgard, T. and Oberg, P. (2017) *Intimacy and Ageing: New Relationships in Later Life*. Bristol: Policy Press.

Butler, J. (2004) *Precarious Life: The Powers of Mourning and Violence*. London: Verso Books.

Calasanti, T. and King, N. (2019) 'Firming the Floppy Penis: Age, Class and Gender Relations in the Lives of Old Men', in Valentine, G., Trautner, M.N. and Spade, J.Z. (eds) *The Kaleidoscope of Gender: Prisms, Patterns and Possibilities*. London/Thousand Oaks: SAGE, pp 246–56.

De Beauvoir, S. (1949/1997) *The Second Sex*. London: Vintage.

DeLamater, J. (2012) 'Sexual Expression in Later Life: A Review and Synthesis', *Journal of Sex Research*, 49(2–3): 125–41.

Doll, G.A. (2012) *Sexuality and Long-term Care: Understanding and Supporting the Needs of Older Adults*. Baltimore: Health Professions Press.

Donovan, T. (2002) 'Being Transgender and Older: a First Person Account', *Journal of Gay and Lesbian Social Services: Issues in Practice, Policy and Research*, 13(4): 19–22.

Dupuis, S., Wiersma, E. and Loiselle. L. (2012) 'Pathologizing Behavior: Meanings of Behaviors in Dementia Care', *Journal of Aging Studies*, 26(2): 162–73.

Foucault, M. (1979) *History of Sexuality, Volume 1: An Introduction*, trans. by R. Hurley. London: Allen Lane/Penguin.

Garrett, D. (2014) 'Psychosocial Barriers to Sexual Intimacy for Older People', *British Journal of Nursing*, 23(6): 327–31.

Gatling, M., Mills, J. and Lindsay, D. (2017) 'Sex After 60? You've Got to be Joking! Senior Sexuality In Comedy Film', *Journal of Aging Studies*, 40: 23–8. DOI: 10.1016/j.jaging.2016.12.004

Gilleard, C. and Higgs, P. (2011) 'Ageing Abjection and Embodiment in the Fourth Age', *Journal of Aging Studies*, 25(2): 135–42.

Gott, M. (2004) *Sexuality, Sexual Health and Ageing*. London: McGraw Hill Education.

Green, A.I. (2011) 'Playing the (Sexual) Field: The Interactional Basis of Systems of Sexual Stratification', *Social Psychology Quarterly*, 74(3): 244–66.

Gullette, M. (1997) *Declining to Decline: Cultural Combat and the Politics of the Midlife*. Charlottesville: University of Virginia Press.

Hafford-Letchfield, T. (2008) 'What's Love Got to Do with It? Developing Supportive Practices for the Expression of Sexuality, Sexual Identity and the Intimacy Needs of Older People', *Journal of Care Services Management*, 2(4): 389–405.

Hafford-Letchfield, T., Simpson, P., Willis, P. and Almack, K. (2017) 'Developing Inclusive Residential Care for Older Lesbian, Gay, Bisexual and Trans (LGBT) People: An Evaluation of the *Care Home Challenge* Action Research Project', *Health and Social Care in the Community*, 26(2): e312–e20.

Hinchliff, S. and Gott, M. (2008) 'Challenging Social Myths and Stereotypes of Women and Aging: Heterosexual Women Talk about Sex', *Journal of Women & Aging*, 20(1–2): 65–81.

Hockey, J. and James, A. (1993) *Growing Up and Growing Old: Ageing and Dependency in the Life Course*. London: SAGE.

Hostetler, A. (2004) 'Old, Gay and Alone? The Ecology of Well-Being Among Middle-Aged and Older Single Gay Men', in de Vries, B. and Herdt, G. (eds) *Gay and Lesbian Aging and Research: Future Directions*. New York: Springer.

Hughes, M. and King, A. (2018) 'Representations of LGBT Ageing and Older People in Australia and the UK', *Journal of Sociology*, 54(1): 125–40.

Kaklamanidou, B. (2012) 'Pride and Prejudice: Celebrity versus Fictional Cougars', *Celebrity Studies*, 3(1): 78–89.

Lee, D. and Tetley J. (2021) 'Sex and Ageing in Heterosexual Men', in Hafford-Letchfield, T., Simpson, P. and Reynolds, P. (eds) *Sex and Diversity in Later Life: Critical Perspectives*. Bristol: Policy Press.

Mahieu, L., van Elssen, K. and Gastmans, C. (2011) 'Nurses' Perceptions of Sexuality in Institutionalized Elderly: A Literature Review', *International Journal of Nursing Studies*, 48(9): 1140–54.

Moore, A. and Reynolds, P. (2016) 'Against the Ugliness of Age: Towards an Erotics of the Ageing Sexual Body', *Inter Alia: A Journal of Queer Studies*, 11a: 88–105.

Moore, A. and Reynolds, P. (2018) *Childhood Sexuality: Contemporary Issues and Debates*. Basingstoke: Palgrave Macmillan.

O'Brien, K., Roe, B., Low, C., Deyn, L. and Rogers, S. (2012) 'An Exploration of the Perceived Changes in Intimacy of Patients' Relationships Following Head and Neck Cancer', *Journal of Clinical Nursing*, 21(17–18): 2499–2508.

Pryzbylo, E. (2021) 'Aging Asexually: Exploring Desexualization and Aging Intimacies', in Hafford-Letchfield, T., Simpson, P. and Reynolds, P. (eds) *Sex and Diversity in Later Life: Critical Perspectives*. Bristol: Policy Press.

Reynolds, P., Simpson, P. and Hafford-Letchfield, T. (2021) 'Sex, Intimacy and Diversity in Later Life: A Survey of the Terrain', in Hafford-Letchfield, T., Simpson, P. and Reynolds, P. (eds) *Sex and Diversity in Later Life: Critical Perspectives*. Bristol: Policy Press.

Sandberg, L.J. (2015) 'Sex, Sexuality, and Later Life', in Martin, W. and Twigg, J. (eds) *Routledge Handbook of Cultural Gerontology*. London: Routledge, pp 218–25.

Simpson, P. (2015) *Middle-Aged Gay Men, Ageing and Ageism: Over the Rainbow?*. Basingstoke: Palgrave Macmillan.

Simpson, P. (2016) 'Ageisms and Lesbian, Gay, Bisexual, Trans and Queer Cultures', in *The SAGE Encyclopedia of LGBTQ Studies*. London/New York: SAGE. DOI: 10.4135/9781483371283.n24

Simpson, P. (2021) 'Older People Sex and Social Class: Unusual Bedfellows?', in Hafford-Letchfield, T., Simpson, P. and Reynolds, P. (eds) *Sex and Diversity in Later Life: Critical Perspectives*. Bristol: Policy Press.

Simpson, P., Brown Wilson, C., Brown, L., Dickinson, T. and Horne, M. (2016) 'The Challenges of and Opportunities Involved in Researching Intimacy and Sexuality in Care Homes Accommodating Older People: a Feasibility Study', *Journal of Advanced Nursing*, 73(1): 127–37.

Simpson, P., Brown Wilson, C., Brown, L, Dickinson, T. and Horne, M. (2018) '"We've Had Our Sex Life Way Back": Older Care Home Residents, Sexuality and Intimacy', *Ageing & Society*, 38(7): 1478–1501.

Villar, F., Celdrán, M., Fabà, J. and Serrat, R. (2014) 'Barriers to Sexual Expression in Residential Aged Care Facilities (RACFs): Comparison of Staff and Residents' Views', *Journal of Advanced Nursing*, 70(11): 2518–27.

2

Consent and sexual literacy for older people

Paul Reynolds

Consent is generally regarded as a problem for the young and the inexperienced. The focus of academic literature, sexuality education and legal and cultural debate is upon those who are entering the sexual world, rather than those who are mature within it (selectively, Archard, 1998; Cowling and Reynolds, 2004; Moore and Reynolds, 2016; Popova, 2019; Stryker, 2017). In part, this is a product of the naturalised and normalised developmental model of sex that identifies sexual risk and danger primarily around the young (Moore and Reynolds, 2018, pp 24–26). It reflects a minimalist notion of sexual learning, regarded as a part of child social development that is adequately completed with maturity. For older people, consent is principally seen as an issue accompanying concerns about diminished capacity. This reflects the desexualisation of older people, where mainstream cultural representations and articulations of sex and sexuality involve stereotypes of youthful, 'beautiful', vigorous bodies and acute and rational minds. Older people do not conform to those dominant representations and its stereotypes (Moore and Reynolds, 2016; Hafford-Letchfield et al, 2020, *passim*; and this volume). Underlying this is a hetero- (and more recently homo-) normative sexuality that is focused on genito-centric, penetrative sexual functionality and in phallocentric vigour and fecundity (in respect of men) (selectively, Beasley, 2005; Jackson and Scott, 2011; Weeks, 2016). This normativity frames older sexual desires as risk and problem oriented, whether the focus is on desexualised older bodies or dysfunctionality, and discourages approaches to older sexual agency that emphasise sexual experimentation and creativity, which might provide different pleasures and alternative and new forms of sexual learning and knowledge. Consent is not an issue because, *surely*, older people's sexual desires are diminished or absent?

The implications of this are that consent is not seen as a problem because it is *displaced* by desexualisation and the 'normal' conception of the sexual 'life course'. Older adults are assumed to understand consent (unless they transgress and commit an offence like rape or sexual assault, or they have problems of competence and are deemed as unable to consent).

This chapter will explore some of the relevant issues for older people's consent to sexual activity, both those factors that are shared with younger people and those factors that are more specific to older people. It will take as a starting point a digest of some recent research on older people's sexual activity, and the snapshot it gives of changing trends. The discussion of consent will explore issues of competence, informed consent and freedom from coercion, and suggest the need for careful consideration of the problems of residually and historically adverse sexual cultures. These considerations are best thought out within a broader conception of sexual literacy.

Older people's sexual activity, desires and impediments

It is commonly assumed that older people are unlikely to exercise new consent negotiations in the context of diminishing appetites and long-term relationships or single status (with existing consent negotiations deemed unproblematic). Contrary to these assumptions, older people are sexual, and not simply passively sexual, within long-term relationships. A snapshot of prevalent studies both illustrates the point and provides the basis for a nuanced discussion of consent and literacy, taking in issues of exposing desexualising stereotyping, the impact desexualisation has had on sexual agency, health and support services and the necessity of research and cultural change that enables rather than simply charts problems with older people's sex and intimacy.

When evidence is gathered, it contradicts the easy desexualisation of older people. Freak-Poli (2020), in an analysis of older Dutch adults, reported that partner availability and health were more important factors influencing sexual activity than age and diminished desire. Lee and Tetley's (2017) analysis of the English Longitudinal Study of Ageing (ELSA) reported that 80 per cent of people aged 75+ agree that satisfactory sexual relations are essential to the maintenance of a long-term relationship. They concluded that there was an urgent need to respond to this with four recommendations: the necessity of normalising debates around sex and older people as a public health priority; the need for health professionals to be open and proactive in responding to older individuals' and couples' sexual health and function; a positive approach to sexuality and intimacy in later life across the life course to promote happiness and wellbeing; and the right of older people to have good sexual healthcare (Lee and Tetley, 2017, p 6).

Lee et al (2015) surveyed 6,201 community-based participants (56 per cent women) who were part of the English Longitudinal Study of Ageing (ELSA). They noted the broad context of declining activity with older age and a relationship between diminished activity and ill health, though they noted a significant minority as still sexually active in their eighties and nineties. They noted a gender disparity in men being more focused on sex and engaged in more frequent sexual activity than women, but equally reporting more dissatisfaction and sexual health concerns. Men's concerns were erectile function (39 per cent), level of sexual desire (15 per cent) and erectile difficulties (14 per cent). Women's concerns were sexual arousal (32 per cent), achieving orgasm (27 per cent), level of sexual desire (11 per cent) and frequency of sexual activities (8 per cent). They also noted that dissatisfaction was not simply a product of health considerations but was influenced by partners' relations and disagreements about initiating and/or feeling obligated to have sex. Lee et al also noted a difference in the reporting of sexual health concerns with age, with men reporting more and women less as they got older.

Erens et al (2019) drew data on 3,343 people from 55 to 74 years old from the third British National Survey of Sexual Attitudes and Lifestyles (with 23 follow-up interviews) and reported that both men and women were increasingly likely to stay sexually active into later life, though their sexual activity and satisfaction decreased with increasing age, with ill health and medical treatments a factor. Importantly, however, they noted that a paucity of research meant it was difficult to gain a fine-grained understanding of how and why older people with health issues had differential responses in terms of sexual desire and activity. In the US, Lindau et al (2007) reported a prevalence of sexual activity in a study of 3,005 adults from 57 to 85 years old. There was a gender disparity, with men more active than women, and a gradiated decline overall – from 73 per cent (57 to 64), to 53 per cent (65 to 74) to 26 per cent (75 to 85). Women reported prevalent problems of low desire (43 per cent), difficulty with vaginal lubrication (39 per cent) and inability to climax (34 per cent). Men reported prevalent problems of erectile difficulties (37 per cent).

Issues of health are threefold. There is the general relationship between ill health and diminished sexual desire and activity that is illustrated across all studies. Then there are particular issues of sexual diseases and infections and sexual performance enhancement. Age UK (2019) reported a 13.9 per cent increase of new diagnoses of sexually transmitted infections (STIs) in men aged 45–64 between 2014 and 2018, against a 7.3 per cent increase in new STI diagnoses in men aged 20–24. Women's increase was a third of the men's infection rate (4 per cent). There was a 23 per cent increase in diagnoses among both men and women aged 65+ between 2014 and 2018. Summarising recent research on HIV transmission and older people, the Terrence Higgins Trust (2018) reported a 9 per cent increase in sexually transmitted diseases in people aged 45 between 2012 and 2016. HIV infections were increasing faster among the over-fifties than the under-forties. These trends were partly explained by a prevalent assumption that menopause and the end of reproductive fertility obviated the need for condoms. Taylor and Gosney (2011) examined the evidence of an 'asexual' old age and concluded that older people enjoy active sex lives but are impeded by the way in which older healthcare is set up on non-sexual grounds. This discourages disclosures, leaves health professionals ill-equipped, and results in limited support, though they also caution against a reaction that over-sexualises older people.

While it is difficult to quantify the use of performance-enhancing drugs like Viagra, they occupy a significant place in the space within which older people's sexual activity is conceived. Marshall (2008) surveyed the success of erectile drugs and the men's health 'industry' in dominating the conception of men's healthy ageing in a strongly medicalised context (Gott, 2006). Marshall (2015) summarised concerns with such a changed context: that an emphasis on performance comes with these drugs and can create its own stresses; that the new stereotype of the 'sexy senior' can be as pernicious as a desexualised stereotype; that such drugs have a gendered focus, reproducing a focus on male sexuality; that same-sex and trans older people are less likely to disclose sexual issues and enjoy less support; that there can be consequences in respect of the increased transmission of sexual diseases. Potts et al (2004) took a more nuanced view in appraising the 'quick fix' of Viagra, pointing out that it works under the assumption of the medicalised 'universal' body and sexual dysfunction, when their research showed more complex socio-cultural subjectivities within which the use of such drugs were situated. In one example of a wider analysis, Loe (2004) explored the socio-cultural impact of Viagra, focusing on how it allows the percolation of women's debates around pleasure and danger in sexualised masculinity, sexualised culture, the 'obligation' of sex in marriage and the identification and recognition of sexual health and pleasure.

Kleinplatz (2008), taking a broad approach to exploring sex and older people, focused on 'normal', rather than problem-centred, older people's sexual activity. It reflected the positive data produced by Beckman et al's (2008) reported increases in sexual activity and positive reporting of sexual activity and satisfaction in their study of sexual activity and satisfaction in 1,500 Swedish 70-year-olds in 4 comparable sets of cross-sectional data from 1971 to 2001. Kleinplatz notes the importance of the emergence of sexual performance drugs such as Viagra and of generational change. With generational change, Kleinplatz particularly draws out both changing popular culture and its impact on sexual visibility and freedom between, for example, the 1950s and the twenty-first century, and their implications in subjective terms, such as gendered expectations (men 'make the move') and older people's sexual expectations, where desexualisation may have been internalised and normalised. Kleinplatz articulates these changes in terms of health professionals being both sensitive to older people's concerns over sexual frequency, desire and satisfaction, and better trained and prepared to respond to older people's needs.

In considering these studies, and particularly the health data, it should be noted that they often reflect a focus on heteronormative, penetrative conceptions of sex, and fail to explore or treat as legitimate sexual intimacy non-penetrative and non-heteronormative sexual pleasure such as BDSM practices, of which there is a paucity of research. Additionally, there are important distinctions with gender/trans and sexual identity/orientation that are often not sufficiently explored (indicatively, see Fabbre, 2015 and Bouman and Kleinplatz, 2014).

In one reporting of Lee and Tetley (2017), Blair (2017) cites Denise Knowles, a sex therapist at Relate, as encouraging creativity, judicious use of performance drugs such as Viagra and supportive furniture, and considering other forms of intimacy than penetrative sex.

Four conclusions can be drawn from this snapshot. First, desexualisation has consequences for sexual health, the spread of STIs and diminished wellbeing. In this respect, as Lee (2015) concludes, this is a public health issue, and not simply a peripheral to medical care and health support through the ageing process. Second, the data suggests that older people are sexually active *despite* desexualisation. The problem this creates is that such sexual activity might be uninformed, in terms of safety, ethical awareness and conduct of self and with others, and exploring opportunities for changing forms of sexual satisfaction as ageing creates changes. One clear negative consequence of sexual agency in a culture hostile to it is increases in STIs.

Third, and allied to that, the increase of sexual agency is not simply an organic and agentic development. Many of those who seek to have satisfying sexual and intimate lives associate that with penetrative sex and issues of function and performance, which can create frustrations when sexual agents cannot fulfil penetration in a satisfying way. This signifies a need to move forward an approach to the sexual lives or older people that opens their thinking to adjustments to how they seek to satisfy their desires, and what constitutes sexual pleasure for them. Again, this is limited by the current sexual culture, but a significant issue for a population whose capacities may be different to younger people (but not lesser).

It is clear that an older population seeking enriched and satisfying sexual and intimate lives is increasing. This will have corresponding impacts on those who work with older people in care and support roles, and in how that support, community or institutionally based, is prepared (trained) to navigate existing cultural constraints and take a role in both supporting sexual health and enabling sexual agency.

Sexual consent is the beginning of sexual agency, where issues of desire, satisfaction, choice and orientation can be expressed and deliberated with those they wish to share sexual intimacies with. Older people therefore need to understand both the contemporary cultural constitution of sexual consent and the particularity of being older in a changing culture.

Understanding sexual consent

Sexual consent involves a complex process of communication and interaction between sexual agents. Modern societies are built upon the notion that autonomous (self-governing) individuals exercise freedom by their choices – their consent decisions – and the extent to which the choices are enabled or respected represents the balance of their agency in relation to cultural, economic, political and social structural constraints (Miller and Wertheimer, 2010, *passim*). Its absence leads to abuse, rape and exploitation, which is why a meaningful concept of consent is important to all sexual agents. Conceptually, sexual consent denotes free decision-making between individuals who conform to the model of the free, autonomous possessive individual (Macpherson, 1962). The most common formulation of consent is valid consent, comprising three criteria: that a person is adequately informed to make a decision; that they are competent and capable to make a decision; and that they are free from coercion in making a decision.

Sexual consent is particularly complicated because of its intimate context. The construction of intimacy and sexual relations has been within cultures of privacy and conventions of sexual modesty, where 'indecency' and 'obscenity' shrouds and restricts the transmission and sharing of sexual knowledge and understandings. In such cultures, extant sexual knowledge is either seen as pathological – subject to medico-moral discourses – or infused with naturalised assumptions of the riskiness and danger of sex (Mort, 2000; Weeks, 1985, 2017). Sex education is often risk-oriented, focused on health and protection, and focused on youth rather than across the life course (and very unevenly and deficiently with youth) (Moore and Reynolds, 2018). Public sexual knowledge is often fetishised, particularly pornography and reporting about sex crimes or sexual behaviour as 'entertainment', even 'educational' sex media (Hekma, 2014; Holmberg, 1998). Dominant sexual cultures are also a context within which intersectional sexual identities experience representations of both pleasurable sex and intimacy and negative sexual stereotypes differently. Even in the twenty-first century, the dominant heteronormative orientation that rewards male enterprise and female modesty pertains. Consent decisions as exercises in sexual agency are invariably context-sensitive as to the prevalent sexual culture.

Consent decisions are often made in private and with euphemism, 'body language' or gesture, which complicates what is being consented to and whether consent is being given. Pineau (1996) argued for a verbal consent standard being necessary for heterosexual consent, recognising a gendered power to sexual scripts (also, Moore and Reynolds, 2004). Husak and Thomas (1992) argued alternatively that contemporary sexual culture made such a standard, particularly in respect to enforcing law, problematic because the dominant culture produced imperfect, partial or non-verbal communication in sexual interactions (also see Cowling, 1997).

Sexual consent decisions, and scholarship, often focus on the early stages of intimate relationships, rather than within more established relationships, as if the terms of sexual consent and exchange remain a constant throughout the life course and within relationships. These can be characterised by still-tentative common grounds, rarely involving deliberated decisions around particular practices but more the umbrella framing of 'having sex', and often not involving extensive verbal communication about what sexual exchanges will involve. The 'language game' of consent, in Wittgensteinian terms, is complicated because consent is understood through such wide conceptual 'family resemblances' (Wittgenstein, 1978, p 32). Definitions invariably describe consent through other equivalent concepts. To give one example, the Merriam-Webster Online Dictionary provides the following terms to describe consent: assent, approval, agreement, in concord, compliance, approval, acquiescence, accede, come around, subscribe, allow, authorise, clear, concur, grant, licence, 'green light', permit, sanction, warrant, suffer(ance). Yet agreeing to something is not the same as complying or acquiescing or doing something under sufferance. This underlines the complexity of understanding consent.

Consent should be understood in two frames – the legal and the socio-cultural. In law, consent has very specific (if culturally influenced) meanings. Most contemporary law around sexual consent is framed around the notion of free agreement between individuals, with statutory restrictions as to who can be deemed to consent. For example, people under the age of consent or deemed mentally incompetent by the state are not regarded as being able to consent, even if they show a willingness (assent) to engage in sexual activity (this is taken further in the chapter on intellectual disability, Chapter 7).

The extent of both the cultural sensitivity and the complexity of consent decision-making can be illustrated with the medical example, where formal verbal consultation and written agreement are present. Medical studies of consent recognise that what constitutes being informed and understanding what is consented to are complex, difficult questions that are subject to power relations, imperfect and partial knowledge and situations where perceptions of choice may be influenced short of coercion, seem restricted or subject to a volition to conform (Manson and O'Neill, 2007; RCN, 2017).

Time, cultural change and consent issues for older people

Consent to sex provides a challenge to older people just as it does younger people. While there may be an assumption of a relationship between age, experience and knowledge, it is questionable. The generational and temporal nature of consent is an important variable. Prior to the 1960s, the strength of patriarchal ideology, reinforced by sexological assumptions about gendered sex roles, conceived male assertiveness and female modesty as a 'normal' mode of sexual conduct. In the UK, consent became part of sexual politics with the women's rights movement and the loosening of conservative sexual morality in the 1960s, and subsequent campaigns around consent were focused around rape and sexual violence (Ferris, 1993; Durham, 1991). Marital rape was only criminalised in 1992, and the first explicit definition of sexual consent came in the 2003 Sexual Offences Act. While #MeToo has been a powerful movement in the half-decade from 2015, it has the tendency to obscure from the contemporary gaze how marginal concerns about sexual consent were until the start of the twenty-first century (Fileborn and Loney-Howes, 2019).

In the context of past generations, who have not engaged fully or benefited from a more nuanced contemporary focus on sexual consent than has developed over the past two decades, complications are magnified. Traditional moral values and patriarchal, heteronormative assumptions may persist as orthodoxy, and act as critical impediments to legitimate consent, such as feelings of vulnerability, subservience or frailty. Older people with sexual desires find themselves in a hostile terrain, where the limited representation of their sexuality is either negative or, in the case of pornography, shrouded and problematic.

Even this cursory review of the complexities of consent demonstrates that there is a measure of judgement necessary to evaluate how each facet has been lived and experienced by successive generations. Criteria of necessity and sufficiency can be applied to all three. Framing necessity and sufficiency as measures draws from studies of philosophical logic, where a necessity is met only if there is a sufficiency to do so (selectively, see Brennan, 2017; Gomes, 2009). Therefore, if we regard consent as a necessary threshold for legitimate sexual activity, in law and in social values, then there must be sufficient grounds for consent to be regarded as valid. The problem might be framed as one of recognising necessity while the conditions of sufficiency are questionable.

What constitutes sufficiently informed? The implications are that the sexual activity is known to the person, has been clearly articulated and understood, and is agreed to. Older people are assumed to have had sexual experience, to know or be able to know what a sexual activity involves, to be able to articulate and understand the terms of their participation, and therefore to be able to agree to sex. However, many older people are not sexually experienced or have very narrow heteronormative sexual experience, particularly those with lifelong partners, where routine has set in, or those from backgrounds or within cultural contexts where sex was a 'taboo' subject for discussion when they were younger. They do not always have the means or wherewithal to learn or articulate sexual knowledge, whether they have got the skills to find sexual information or are culturally predisposed against seeking it, seeing sex as something 'decent people' do not learn about. This applies even more so to the idea that they might talk to others, whether existing or long-term partners or new partners, about their sexual appetites. Therefore, the sense in which they can agree to a sexual proposition in an informed fashion is a matter of concern.

Here, it is clear that blanket segmentations of age, such as 'third age' for 50+, are unhelpful. At the time of writing (2020), people who were teenagers in the mid-1960s or later (older people of 50–70) had a markedly different experience of sexual culture to those who are 75+ and whose youth was in the late 1940s or 1950s. Even those who were youth in the 1960s and 1970s may not have been domiciled in metropolitan cultures where sex was more open or may have seen it only as media representation, apart from their own experience. Just as assumptions that older people are desexualised should be challenged, so should the easy assumption that all older people are sexually experienced and have a confident and self-conscious approach to sex. While it may be that older people are informed about sex, the extent of that knowledge and the extent to which it can be mobilised in, for example, open sex communication, is questionable.

While it is necessary to have a clear legal and cultural line between consenting sex and sex without consent, elsewhere I have argued that the problem with this line is that all too often it is a minimalist conception (Reynolds, 2004). It operates within a sexual culture that is restrictive and limited in shared sexual knowledge outside of cultural forms that fetishise, reinforcing conventional notions of decency and obscenity. What is more critical is the quality of consent, and the extent to which sexual agents make consent decisions within an environment where they are not defensive, constrained or limited by the cultural tools and contexts within which they exercise their agency. For older people, time is a particular variable where there is no culture of the continual sharing and circulating of unencumbered knowledge, and limited opportunities for tentative experimentation and exploration.

In a previous reflection on the quality of consent, I conclude:

> The next stage of the emancipation of the sexual self – following on from the unfinished and partial sexual revolution of the 1960s and the subsequent legal, political and cultural changes towards greater openness and public discourse on sex, however sensational and fetishised – is to move from thinking about sexual 'problems' to thinking about sexual custom and practice ... the quality of sexual consent is also of critical importance if we are to think about and effect changes towards more ethical sexual communication, cultures, knowledge and understanding. A greater sense of ethical conduct in sexual pleasure will both encourage the setting of higher standards for consent decisions and encourage more open intolerance of those who engage in non-consenting sex. More simply and

immediately, reflection on the quality of sexual consent decisions begins the movement towards owning our sexual pleasure and demanding sexual ethics in everyday life. (Reynolds, 2004, p 108)

The question remains as to how that enhanced quality of consent is achieved, and particularly in the context of active discursive desexualisation displacing the ownership of sexual pleasure and building of ethically aware intimacies.

Sexual literacy and older people's sexual agency and lives

Against the focus of sexual learning on youth and the young, a focus on older people's learning and widening experience is restricted by their desexualisation. Consent issues are not seen as an issue – other than legally in respect of rape (non-consenting sex) – for the same reason that older people's sexual agency is neglected in general, despite the evidence – the dominant cultural discourses of desexualisation. While there might be relevant care/support training and adult learning opportunities at the margins, what is required to sustain sexual agency and a satisfying sexual and intimate life through the vagaries of the changes that ageing produces is a different and holistic approach to sexual knowledge.

One approach, building on the developments around sexual freedom, openness and experimentation that were part of the sexual revolution and the recognition of particularly lesbian and gay sexualities from the 1960s, is sexual literacy. Gilbert Herdt has championed the development of sexual literacy 'as the knowledge necessary to promote and protect sexual wellness and the rights of oneself and intimate others' (Stein and Herdt, 2005, p 1).

Earlier Herdt, through the National Sexuality Resource Centre (NSRC) stated:

> We focus on a positive, integrated and holistic view of sexuality from a social justice perspective. We believe that every person should have the knowledge, skills and resources to support healthy and pleasurable sexuality—and that these resources should be based on accurate research and facts. We examine how race, gender, culture, ability, faith and age intersect with and shape our sexual beliefs. We know that sexuality education and learning should be lifelong. We call this *sexual literacy*. (NSRC, 2003, cited in Moore and Reynolds, 2018, p 199)

The NSRC had a sex-positive mission to:

> build capacity to advance lifelong sexual literacy and foster
> healthy sexuality for all Americans.
>
> We do this by:
> - creating and disseminating trainings, research and
>   information that are accurate, research-based and
>   promote best practices
> - convening diverse communities of advocates, researchers
>   and academics to actively engage, shape and deepen the
>   concept of sexual literacy
> - mobilizing stakeholders to become activists, educators
>   and advocates for sexual literacy (http://cregs.sfsu.edu/
>   our-history-2/nsrc-history-and-mission).
>   (Cited in Moore and Reynolds, 2018, pp 198–9)

Sexual literacy offers a cohesive and comprehensive lifelong learning
project that combines a practice and skills oriented sexual knowledge
with the broader aptitudes of sexual communication and decision-
making, as a means of enabling sexual agency. Regardless of identity,
forms of relationships, desires or beliefs, sexual agents should have
the capacities to make free, informed choices and express their sexual
desires and wants (including what they do *not* want). Sexual literacy
is a project that seeks to enhance agency and self and mutual respect,
ensuring a balance of focus on safety and pleasure.

This approach builds upon a contemporary sexually diverse
and sex-positive approach that emphasises the space for learning,
open discussion and shared understandings, covering diverse non-
heteronormative, genito-centric and penetrative sexual practices, open
sexual negotiation, the legitimacy of diverse sexual pleasures (from same
sex to BDSM) with an ethical base (Barker, 2013; Barker and Hancock,
2017, 2018; Barker and Iantaffi, 2019; Comfort and Quilliam, 2011;
Hardy and Easton, 2018; Miller and Devon, 1995; Wiseman, 1996;
Stryker, 2017; Williams and Williams, 2019). It builds on a critical
pedagogy approach to learning, in which knowledge circulates and
is communicatively open and shared (Freire, 1996; hooks, 1994). It
can also be aligned with Plummer's (1995) exploration of the value
of 'telling sexual stories', first in groups who have suffered trauma
but relevant more widely, to demystify sexual discourse such as the
desexualisation of older people.

Sexual literacy, when taken seriously, presents a number of critical questions about how intimacy is organised within contemporary society. How are skills and information made available, communicated and circulated? How is a sexually literate culture developed as well as sexually literate individuals (the two being interlinked)? How can extant power/knowledge relations within sexual cultures be exposed and limited in a way that limits abuse but does not extend protection to unreasonable constraint? How can lack of practice and limited experience be addressed for some older people? What are the material implications – in time and economy – of a more enlightened and sexually open culture? (See Moore and Reynolds, 2018, pp 211–20 for a more elaborate discussion.)

Moore and Reynolds have observed:

> Sexual literacy is not simply a means by which a sexual subject takes charge of resources such as bodies of knowledge or means of understanding and engages in their own pleasures and desires. Nor is it simply an awareness and sensitivity of the rights of other sexual subjects; It involves an understanding of the agent as praxeological. Once practice is informed by thinking, and thinking with practice, the responsibilities, relationships and interactions between sexual subjects cannot return to ignorance. Sexual literacy may be hard work, as the sexual subject seeks to be informed, thinks through relations, make judgements, and becomes aware of the consequences and impacts of pleasures and desires. This is not necessarily an ethical or a regulatory obligation, but it is a condition by which sexual subjects enter into a sexually literate world of others. They cannot retreat to passive thinking on injustice, or to ill-considered action in relation to the pursuit of desires. (Moore and Reynolds, 2018, p 219)

The catch to this is that such a development is only possible with a changed sexual culture. Discreet developments in opening up sexual knowledge, however locally useful, are constrained by the sexual culture in which they reside. As the foregoing discussion has shown, consent decisions of themselves involve individual negotiations, but are very context sensitive. Where the context is desexualising older people, they are unlikely to feel secure entering into open discussions about their changing sexual needs, desires and satisfaction. The limited public sexual cultures of pornography or sex as 'entertainment' may only frustrate, discourage or trivialise openness about sex and intimacy among older people, who may find the cultural mediums of knowledge transmission, whether the technologies or the format, alienating and 'not for them'. It is, therefore, a political as well as a personal question, and requires political as well as interpersonal responses.

References

Age UK (2019) 'As STIs in Older People Continue to Rise Age UK Calls to End the Stigma about Sex and Intimacy in Later Life'. Available at: https://www.ageuk.org.uk/latest-press/articles/2019/october/as-stis-in-older-people-continue-to-rise-age-uk-calls-to-end-the-stigma-about-sex-and-intimacy-in-later-life/.

Archard, D. (1998) *Sexual Consent*. Oxford: Westview Press.

Barker, M. (2013) *Rewriting the Rules: An Integrative Guide to Love, Sex and Relationships*. London: Routledge.

Barker, M. and Hancock, J. (2017) *Enjoy Sex (How, when and if you want to)*. London: Icon Books.

Barker, M. and Hancock, J. (2018) *A Practical Guide to Sex: Finally, Helpful Sex Advice*. London: Icon Books.

Barker, M. and Iantaffi, A. (2019) *Life Isn't Binary: On Being Both, Beyond and In-Between*. London: Jessica Kingsley.

Beasley, C. (2005) *Gender & Sexuality: Critical Theories, Critical Thinkers*. London: SAGE.

Beckman, N., Waern, M., Gustafson, D. and Skoog, I. (2008) 'Secular Trends in Self Reported Sexual Activity and Satisfaction in Swedish 70 Year Olds: Cross Sectional Survey of Four Populations, 1971–2001', *British Medical Journal*, 337(7662): 151–4.

Blair, O. (2017) 'Using Supportive Furniture and Viagra: A Sex Therapist's Guide to Sex for the Elderly', *The Independent*, 17 February 2017. Available at: https://www.independent.co.uk/life-style/love-sex/sex-therapy-elderly-old-men-women-positions-viagra-support-aid-a7584366.html.

Bouman, W.P. and Kleinplatz, P.J. (2014) 'Moving Towards Understanding Greater Diversity and Fluidity of Sexual Expression of Older People', *Sexual and Relationship Therapy*, 30:1–3.

Brennan, A. (2017) 'Necessary and Sufficient Conditions', *Stanford Encyclopaedia of Philosophy*. Available at: https://plato.stanford.edu/entries/necessary-sufficient/ [Accessed 26 December 2019].

Carpenter, L. and DeLamater, J. (eds) (2012) *Sex for Life: From Virginity to Viagra, How Sexuality Changes Throughout Our Lives*. New York: New York University Press.

Comfort, A. and Quilliam, S. (2011) *The Joy of Sex* (revised edn). London: Mitchell Beazley.

Cowling, M. (1997) *Date Rape and Consent*. Aldershot: Ashgate.

Cowling, M. and Reynolds, P. (eds) (2004) *Making Sense of Sexual Consent*. Aldershot: Ashgate.

Durham, M. (1991) *Sex and Politics: The Family and Morality in the Thatcher Years*. Basingstoke: Macmillan.

Erens, B., Mitchell, K.R., Gibson, L., Datta, J., Lewis, R., Field, N. and Wellings, K. (2019) 'Health Status, Sexual Activity and Satisfaction Among Older People in Britain: A Mixed Methods Study', *PLOS*. Available at: https://journals.plos.org/plosone/article?id=10.1371/journal.pone.0213835.

Fabbre, V.D. (2015) 'Gender Transitions in Later Life: A Queer Perspective on Successful Aging', *The Gerontologist*, 55(1): 144–53.

Ferris, P. (1993) *Sex and the British: A 20th Century History*. London: Mandarin.

Fileborn, B. and Loney-Howes, R. (eds) (2019) *#MeToo and the Politics of Social Change*. London: Palgrave Macmillan.

Freak-Poli, R. (2020) 'It's Not Age That Prevents Sexual Activity Later in Life', *Australasian Journal of Ageing*, 39 (Sup 1): 22–9.

Freire, P. (1996) *Pedagogy of the Oppressed*. Harmondsworth: Penguin.

Gomes, G. (2009) 'Are Necessary and Sufficient Conditions Converse Relations?', *Australasian Journal of Philosophy*, 87: 375–87.

Gott, M. (2006) 'Sexual Health and the New Ageing', *Age and Ageing*, 35: 106–7.

Hafford-Letchfield, T., Simpson, P. and Reynolds, P. (2020) *Sex and Diversity in Later Life*. Bristol: Policy Press.

Hardy, J. and Easton, D. (2018) *The Ethical Slut: A Practical Guide to Polyamory, Open Relationships and Freedoms in Love and Sex*. New York: Ten Speed Press.

Hekma, G. (ed.) (2014) *A Cultural History of Sexuality in the Modern Age, Volume 6*. London: Bloomsbury.

Holmberg, C.B. (1998) *Sexualities and Popular Culture*. London: SAGE.

hooks, b. (1994) *Teaching to Transgress: Education as the Practice of Freedom*. London: Routledge.

Husak, D.N. and Thomas, G.C. (1992) 'Date Rape, Social Convention and Reasonable Mistakes', *Law and Philosophy*, 11: 95–126.

Jackson, S. and Scott, S. (2011) *Theorising Sexuality*. Maidenhead: Open University Press.

Kleinplatz, P.J. (2008) 'Sexuality and Older People', *British Medical Journal*, 337(7662): 121–2.

Lee, D. and Tetley, J. (2017) 'How Long Will I Love You? Sex and Intimacy in Later Life', The International Longevity Centre. Available at: https://ilcuk.org.uk/wp-content/uploads/2018/10/ILC-UK-How-long-will-I-love-you-1.pdf.

Lee, D.M., Nazroo, J., O'Connor, D.B. et al (2015) 'Sexual Health and Well-being Among Older Men and Women in England: Findings from the English Longitudinal Study of Ageing', *Archives of Sexual Behavior*, 45(1): 133–44. Available at: https://www.researchgate.net/publication/271594962_Sexual_Health_and_Well-being_Among_Older_Men_and_Women_in_England_Findings_from_the_English_Longitudinal_Study_of_Ageing.

Lindau, S.T., Schumm, L.P., Laumann, E.O., Levinson, W., O'Muircheartaigh, C. and Waite, L.J. (2007) 'A Study of Sexuality and Health among Older Adults in the United States', *New England Journal of Medicine*, 357: 762–74.

Loe, M. (2004) 'Sex and the Senior Woman: Pleasure and Danger in the Viagra Era', *Sexualities*, 7(3): 303–26.

Macpherson, C.B. (1962) *The Theory of Possessive Individualism: Hobbes to Locke*. Oxford: Oxford University Press.

Manson, N. and O'Neill, O. (2007) *Rethinking Informed Consent in Bioethics*. Cambridge: Cambridge University Press.

Marshall, B. (2008) 'Older Men and Sexual Health: Post-Viagra Views of Changes in Function', *Generations*, 1: 21–7.

Marshall, B. (2015) 'Senior Sex In A Post-Viagra World', *The Doctor Will See You Now*, 11 August 2015. Available at: http://www.thedoctorwillseeyounow.com/content/sex/art4742.html.

Miller, F. and Wertheimer, A. (2010) *The Ethics of Consent*. Oxford: Oxford University Press.

Miller, P. and Devon, M. (1995) *Screw the Roses, Send Me The Thorns: The Romance and Sexual Sorcery of Sadomasochism*. Fairfield: Mystic Rose Books.

Moore, A. and Reynolds, P. (2004) 'Feminist Approaches to Sexual Consent: A Critical Assessment', in Cowling, M. and Reynolds, P. (eds) *Making Sense of Sexual Consent*. Aldershot: Ashgate, pp 29–44.

Moore, A. and Reynolds, P. (2016) 'Against the Ugliness of Age: Towards an Erotics of the Aging Sexual Body', *Inter Alia*, 11a. Available at: http://interalia.org.pl/media/11A_2016/moore_reynolds.pdf.

Moore, A. and Reynolds, P. (2018) *Childhood and Sexuality: Contemporary Issues and Debates*. London: Palgrave Macmillan.

Mort, F. (2000) *Dangerous Sexualities: Medico-Moral Politics in England since 1830* (2nd edn). London: Routledge.

NSRC (National Sexuality Resource Centre) (2003) 'NSRC History and Mission', *Center for Research & Education on Gender and Sexuality*. Available at: http://cregs.sfsu.edu/our-history-2/nsrc-history-and-mission

Pineau, L. (1996) 'Date Rape: A Feminist Analysis', in Francis, L. (ed) *Date Rape: Feminism, Philosophy and the Law*. Pennsylvania: Pennsylvania State University, pp 1–25.

Plummer, K. (1995) *Telling Sexual Stories: Power, Change and Social Worlds*. London: Routledge.

Popova, M. (2019) *Sexual Consent*. Massachusetts: MIT Press.

Potts, A., Grace, V., Gavey, N., Vares, T. (2004) ' "Viagra Stories": Challenging "Erectile Dysfunction"', *Social Science & Medicine*, 59(3): 489–99.

RCN (Royal College of Nursing) (2017) *Principles of Consent: Guidance for Nursing Staff*. London: RCN.

Reynolds, P. (2004) 'The Quality of Consent: Sexual Consent, Culture, Communication, Knowledge and Ethics', in Cowling, M. and Reynolds, P. (eds) *Making Sense of Sexual Consent*. Aldershot: Ashgate, pp 93–108.

Stein, T.S. and Herdt, G.l. (2005) 'Editorial: Welcome to SRSP 2005 Sexuality Research and Social Policy', *Journal of the National Sexuality Resource Center*, 2(1): 1.

Stryker, K. (2017) *Ask: Building Consent Culture: An Anthology*. Portland: Thorntree Press.

Taylor, A. and Gosney, M. (2011) 'Sexuality in Older Age: Essential Considerations for Healthcare Professionals', *Age and Ageing*, 40(5): 538–43.

Terrence Higgins Trust (2018) 'Insight Briefing 2: Still Got It: Sexual Health of the Over 50s'. Available at: https://www.tht.org.uk/sites/default/files/2018-04/Still%20Got%20It%20-%20Over%2050s%20Insight%20Briefing.pdf.

Weeks, J. (1985) *Sexuality and Its Discontents: Meaning, Myth and Modern Sexualities*. London: Routledge.

Weeks, J. (2016) *Sexuality* (4th edn). London: Routledge.

Weeks, J. (2017) *Sex, Politics and Society: The Regulation of Sexuality since 1800* (4th edn). London: Routledge.

Williams, D. and Williams, D. (2019) *The Polyamory Toolkit: A Guidebook for Polyamorous Relationships*. Independently Published: eroticawakening.com.

Wiseman, J. (1996) *SM101: A Realistic Introduction* (2nd edn). San Francisco: Greenery Press.

Wittgenstein, L. (1978) *Philosophical Investigations*. Oxford: Basil Blackwell.

3

'At YOUR age???!!!': the constraints of ageist erotophobia on older people's sexual and intimate relationships

Paul Simpson

It is impossible to talk about sex without talking about relationships or modes of relating, yet sexual relations are assumed to be the preserve of the young. So it seems when older people's attempts to express sexuality or intimacy are commonly met with ridicule, condescension and infantilisation (Simpson et al, 2017). The quote in the chapter title, though fictional, is no less believable, but might seem incredible if not offensive to quite a few older people. Indeed, we can see the mockery of ageing and later life, and particularly of a presumed cognitive, aesthetic, physical and sexual decline, writ large in birthday cards for those aged 40 plus (Bytheway, 1995; Simpson et al, 2018b). This mockery reveals the casual, normalised nature of ageism in consumerist societies, where ageing can be seen as an individual pathology to be avoided (Biggs and Daatland, 2006). The anxieties occasioned by consumerist-driven ageism could well be responsible for the proliferation of sales of age-defying (denying?) cosmetics, as well as the increase in 'rejuvenating' cosmetic surgery, which Eagleton (2003) has theorised as an attempt to deny or stave off mortality.

Unlike many other forms of prejudice, ageism directed towards older people seems to be fair game. It also operates more under the radar of consciousness. It is worth noting that ageism can affect the young, who can be defined as insubstantial, inexperienced and the like, though, unlike later life, youth can be regarded as a transitory, experimental stage en route to maturity and usually experiences ageism less intensely (Bytheway, 1995; Simpson, 2015). In terms of ageism as applied to sex and intimacy, older people are stereotypically cast as prudish and beyond interest in such matters (Mahieu et al, 2014). Such thinking informs pressures towards 'compulsory non-sexuality' among older people (Simpson, 2021). Nevertheless, various, intersecting forms of differentiation (class, gender, sexuality and ethnicity) strongly influence the capacity to challenge ageism generally and the presumption of sexlessness or post-sexual status and lack of desirability in later life specifically.

It is also worth noting that ageism may be one of the factors behind the relative paucity of scholarship on an international scale, though a critical literature is beginning to emerge on later life sexuality, especially in Britain, Australasia, Europe and the United States. (See Bauer et al, 2012; Doll, 2012; Simpson et al, 2018b; Villar et al, 2014 for examples.) Also, it has been observed (in a British context) that ageism ensures older people's opportunities for sex and intimacy are 'designed out' of care environments and services, structurally and discursively, and especially in relation to residential and nursing homes (Hafford-Letchfield, 2008). The pervasive silence across society, academe and healthcare practice and in everyday interaction has reinforced older people's exclusion from the sexual/intimate imaginary. However, this exclusion is perhaps more revealing of wider social anxieties than of older individuals' own wishes, feelings, desires and practices (Simpson et al, 2018b).

The kind of anxieties just mentioned have also been described as reflecting 'ageist erotophobia'; a particular form of ageism (like that expressed in the chapter title) itself reflecting thought and practice that involves failure or refusal to imagine older people as sexual beings, and which older people themselves can subconsciously come to accept as 'natural' and inevitable (Simpson et al, 2018b). Indeed, this think-piece chapter will demonstrate how ageist erotophobia is implicated in various relational constraints on the expression of sexuality and intimacy in later life. It will then focus on major barriers, operating at three 'levels', that contribute to the desexualisation of older people. These inter-related themes concern the wider social relations of ageism evident at the macro-discursive level, which, in turn, influence thought and practice within healthcare provision (care homes) concerning the sexuality of older people at the meso- (institutional) level. I also attend to the limited scholarship that provides glimpses into how ageist erotophobia works in interpersonal relations involving significant others at the micro-level of interaction. In order to avoid homogenising later life and older people as overly constrained and compliant with wider cultural expectations, the concluding section briefly draws attention to the ways in which older people can avoid and challenge ageist erotophobia. For details of the literature search method used to help write this chapter, see note at the end of the chapter.[1]

Discursive relations and ageist erotophobia

Put simply, 'discursive' (referring to the operation of discourse) signifies ways of talking (Beasley, 2005). More specifically (working at the level of language) it refers to how narratives circulating within society and exchanged through various social mechanisms and daily interaction are imbibed by human actors (Fairclough, 2013; Foucault, 1980). Discourse is often internalised in ways that preconsciously regulate or at least strongly influence thought and practice in relationships with ourselves and others known, unknown or imagined (Foucault, 1977). While this idealist conceptualisation of constraint (referencing poststructuralist theorising) provides a premise for understanding at the level of language/ideas, it is argued that such a conceptualisation is incomplete. Such an approach tends to see discourse as free-floating, when a fuller, more convincing account would also recognise that narratives are grounded in or least imbricated with practices, structures and institutions (reflecting materialist thinking), which can function differently in different contexts (Simpson, 2015). For instance (as can be intuited in the examples later in the chapter), ageism operates differently not just in different cultures but in different forms of advertising and representation. It can also work differently in relation to labour markets and workplaces, as well as in social groups and personal lives.

Ageist erotophobia itself works discursively and indicates deep-seated anxieties about older people as sexual, erotic or intimate beings and, in some cases, can even act to constrain solo masturbation (Villar et al, 2015) or use of pornography/erotica (Simpson et al, 2017). As such, ageist erotophobia is implicated in a lack of awareness of the diverse lived experiences, realities and needs of older people. It is commonly expressed in denial, discomfort or disgust at the idea of older people as sexual beings (Simpson et al, 2018b). On this view, sexual activity among old(er) people might also be considered 'rare, astonishing and ridiculous' (Hodson and Skeen, 1994). Such thinking also seems to be implicated in the erasure of older people's sexual histories. Indeed, sexual activity is commonly seen as irrelevant to ageing identities, older people's sense of belonging and their sense of citizenship (Bauer et al, 2014a; Doll, 2012; Gott, 2004; Hafford-Letchfield, 2008; Hockey and James 1993; Villar et al, 2014).

While ageist erotophobia has been identified or referenced (perhaps more often indirectly) in empirical work (see Simpson et al, 2018b), where might we see evidence of it sanctioned in society and broader cultural phenomena? Earlier I referred to its normalisation in birthday cards for the over-forties. Moreover, an internet search yielded images of older people, and especially of older women, which *implies* that lack of attractiveness, metonymic with sexlessness, is characteristic of later life. For instance, in an estate agent advert (later banned by the Australian advertising authorities for ageism, sexism and allusion to domestic violence), a photograph of an older, fat woman with curlers, dressed in a nightgown, wearing spectacles and brandishing a shotgun, is positioned over the headline: 'Is your property manager a grumpy cow?' See the image at: https://mumbrella.com.au/grumpy-cow-ad-banned-sexist-ageist-violent-advertising-watchdog-418488.

The image is significant in various ways. The old woman featured here is presented as decidedly frumpy (fat, drab and old-fashioned) yet may simply be 'guilty' of acting in compliance with age-appropriate discourse that polices older women's appearance (Clarke et al, 2009). The woman appears like many of her age-group who may be concerned to maintain an age-appropriate feminine appearance while avoiding accusations of dressing too young (Clarke et al, 2009). It seems that some older women may be damned if they do observe wider cultural expectations concerning sexualisation and damned if they don't. In contrast to adverts representing 'the sexy oldie' (see Gott, 2004), the size of the woman depicted and her hair rollers might encourage interpretation of her not as someone trying to care for her appearance but as having let herself go: the failing individual who has given up the battle against the pathology of bodily ageing (Phillipson, 1998; Eagleton, 2003; Howarth, 2014). It seems that the old woman portrayed (perhaps the term 'old battleaxe' could be applied here) is not just unpleasant but, counter-intuitively, is threatening for wielding a shotgun. Not only does this suggest an age-inflected gynaephobia, or fear of older women and for their latent power or potential for resistance (Delahunty, 2013), it also suggests a fear of their latent sexuality, which can be denied or neutralised by mockery and trivialisation, especially in relation to the menopause and beyond (Greer, 2018).

Images used in advertising of the UK-based dating app (https://lumenapp.com/), *Lumen*, for 'silver singles' aged 50 and over, represent a marked improvement on the image just analysed. The images represent an older white man and an older black woman who are clearly represented as valid sexual beings. Indeed, such representation is typical of the images chosen to advertise the app, which present certain dimensions of difference that might appeal ethically to consumers (actual and potential) and suggest a form of inclusiveness and agency as sexual beings. The images, which attempt to resexualise, are clearly sex-positive (for some) and of particular note are the emotionally saturated, political messages that reverse the discourse and usual expectations to reclaim value as older sexual citizens who seek control over their bodies and how they could be better understood by (younger) others. The messages on the placards assert that being 'older, wiser and (emotionally) stronger' are as appealing as maintaining physical allure and imply that such qualities form part of a more holistic (and less superficial) notion of being attractive. The placard, held by the female figure asserting 'It's Our Time to Be Seen' is reminiscent of an intersectional politics of visibility that claims recognition as a sexual citizen (Plummer, 2011) on the grounds of age combined with gender and race.

However, such images are partially inclusive and could perpetuate in relation to older people rather youth-oriented, conventional notions of attractiveness and desirability in later life (Gott, 2004; Hinchliff, 2014). This is not meant as criticism of such important resources that attempt to validate older people, but we need to acknowledge that all images suggest limitations as well as possibilities. These kinds of image, or what Gott (2004) might call the 'sexy oldie', largely represent the younger-old who may be thought to look good or attractive 'for their age' (or despite it). It has also been observed that such expectations about self-care can become integral to expectations of health and successful ageing (Hinchliff and Gott, 2016). This kind of discourse sets up the possibility that those not achieving this status could be judged by others for poor life choices, failure of self-care or lack of innovation in later life. In effect, internet searches failed to produce images of non-normative older body-selves as sexual, for example, featuring older disabled people (even though disability correlates highly with age). Those who are or appear old, wrinkled, 'plainer' or fat are seldom portrayed, if at all, as sexual beings. There is, therefore, still a way to go in terms of broadening out legitimacy to include other people who may be perceived as less glamorous but who desire a sexual life. It is, though, possible that any such lack of images is related to the influences of social class and commodification processes (that rely on appeal of certain kinds of body-self) common within advertising and commerce. Indeed, although such images do not shy away from presenting people with grey hair as sexual, individuals here appear validated less as older people but, again, more in terms of how they approximate a youthful appearance (Simpson, 2015).

Erotophobia and relations within care home contexts

This section concerns how ageist erotophobia works at the meso-level of care homes for older people (as organisations). In Britain, the average age of admission to a care home is 85, and therefore such homes accommodate the oldest and frailest citizens. Older care home residents constitute nearly 500,000 people in the UK, or nearly 5 per cent of all those aged 65 or older. About two-thirds of residents are affected by some degree of dementia (ONS, Office for National Statistics, 2011). Although 5 per cent of the age cohort may seem a modest figure, half a million people is roughly equivalent to the population of the English city of Manchester or the county of Wiltshire (ONS, 2019).

Arguably, one of the starkest instances of ageist erotophobia at this organisational level appears in a French study, which concluded that staff's perception of residents as ill occludes any consideration of them as sexual beings. The logical corollary of this thinking is that if you are old and cared for, you are sick, and if you are sick you cannot be sexual (Darnaud et al, 2013). Further, in the author's own research as part of the Older People's Understandings of Sexuality (OPUS) Research Group, the workings of ageist erotophobia were visible in accounts of those who considered themselves *and* fellow residents to be post-sexual (Simpson et al, 2018b). Indeed, an older male resident in the OPUS study asserted that a state of sexlessness was related to decline, decrepitude and (assumed) closeness to death. Such views are not only suggestive of the internalisation of a wider discourse by residents/older people themselves but also of the consequences of this, which could prompt surveillance and which, in turn, has the potential to regulate and prevent displays of desire and intimacy by self and others.

In effect, that residents, relatives and care workers alike tend to speak of sexual activity as a subject that was commonly ignored provides evidence that ageist erotophobia is implicated in the panoptical silencing of sexuality and intimacy. By panoptical, I refer to how subjects internalise and comply with dominant social expectations because they feel they are under surveillance (Foucault, 1977, 1980; Simon, 2005; Simpson et al, 2016). Panopticism concerning expression of sexuality is also implicit in work by Hafford-Letchfield (2008) in Britain, Bauer et al (2012) in Australia and Villar et al (2014) in Catalonia/Spain. Indeed, the latter study concluded that a significant minority of staff and residents considered even marital heterosexual sex unacceptable in care homes accommodating older people. Nevertheless, and as will be seen in the conclusion section, various expressions of ageist erotophobia do not go without challenge in the particular contexts of care homes.

Furthermore, the view of the male care home resident expressed earlier could well reflect that opportunities for sexual/intimate self-expression are considerably more restricted than compared to older people living independently (Bauer et al, 2014a; Doll, 2012; Phillips and Marks, 2008; Villar et al, 2014; Wornell, 2014). Drawing on poststructuralist theory, Simon (2005) has illuminated how the very organisation of environments reflects and subconsciously encourages the internalisation of order and compliance with contextual/social norms. This thinking could be applied to care homes, where compulsory non-sexuality, itself the product of ageist erotophobia, is given tacit legitimisation within the organisation (Hafford-Letchfield, 2008; Simpson et al, 2016). In practical terms, this can mean a lack of double beds, double rooms or even a lack of sofa seating in communal areas where a couple could hold hands (Simpson et al, 2018b). Also, the privacy which is prerequisite for sexual autonomy can be more often compromised in such spaces (Bauer et al, 2012; Simpson et al, 2018b). Although residents' rooms are understood as private/personal, staff may feel they have a legitimate right to access these spaces for care delivery, resulting in difficulties for residents in maintaining choice and autonomy (Eyers et al, 2012). Equally, there are communal areas where privacy around sexuality and other matters might be further compromised and anyone read as sexually active may attract moral opprobrium (Villar et al, 2015; Yelland and Hosier, 2015).

In a UK context, although Government guidance regarding sexuality in care homes for older people emerged more than a decade ago (Department of Health, 2007), it was concerned more with rights to respect, recognition, equality and inclusion for lesbian-, gay-, bisexual- or trans-identified (LGBT) residents in the life of the home. Official concern with rights to sexual/intimate self-expression in care contexts seems to be of more recent vintage and appears in the form of Local Government Association (2014) guidance on safeguarding wellbeing that cautions against the desexualisation and infantilisation of adults receiving care (Local Government Association, 2014). In terms of medical practitioner-generated guidance, the Royal College of Nursing (RCN) (2011) had drawn attention to the need to address sex and sexuality in residents'/older people's (holistic and personalised) care plans and care homes' policies. The RCN resource (with case study examples of good practice) identified staff embarrassment around sexual issues, organisational cultures within homes that disregard sexuality, and religious influences as significant inhibitors to addressing sexuality (RCN, 2011). The various factors just mentioned suggest sex-negative discourse working intertwined with ageist erotophobia.

While the afore-mentioned practical resources recognise at least implicitly the effects of ageist erotophobia, despite their valiant efforts, anxieties about the sexuality of residents and older service users/ people seem to persist. Indeed, research by the OPUS Research Group has set out to develop a more practical, practitioner-friendly 'app' (as opposed to wordy, official reports/formal guidance) and staff development curriculum that aims to encourage care staff to *discuss* how they can support residents' choices concerning sexuality and intimacy. This resource was considered necessary because official and practitioner guidance is either unknown or ignored, arguably because much of it does not fit well with staff/organisational needs and realities (Simpson et al, 2018b). Failure to challenge assumptions of non-sexuality is also not helped by the current funding situation, where privatisation of care home provision has undercut investment in staff development and pay, and resulted in understaffing, casualisation and high staff turnover (Laing, 2014). The factors just mentioned can contribute to a bed-and-body model of care which militates against the kind of skilled rapport-building necessary to gain trust to initiate sensitive conversations relating to resident choices about sex, intimacy and sexual identification (Han et al, 2014).

Ageist erotophobia can also work differently in relation to non-normative forms of gender and sexuality. As intimated, older LGB&T people can face difficulties in addition to ageist erotophobia. Indeed, they risk being 'twice hidden' or doubly denied as different sexual beings given the combined effects of ageism, homophobia and heterosexual and cisgender assumptions. Commonly, LGBT individuals report underuse of end-of-life care services because of subtle forms of (indirect) discrimination. This has been attributed to lack of awareness among care staff, which can translate into failure to differentiate services for LGBT service users/residents (Stein and Almack, 2012). An approach based on 'treating them [service users] all the same', has also been identified as problematic in a survey by Simpson et al (2018a), which concluded that individual staff goodwill was not matched by the collective consciousness and good practice at the level of the institution that is pre-requisite for recognising sexual needs and normalising inclusion of LGBT individuals/residents. Indeed, Cook et al (2017) recommend that care homes develop ethically-informed education and organisational policies that enhance staff's capacity to advocate for resident autonomy in relation to choices concerning sex and more generally.

In effect, 'treating them all the same' commonly proceeds from a presupposition of heterosexuality and cisgender status and involves imposition rather than choices over and differentiation in service provision (National Council for Palliative Care and Consortium of Lesbian, Gay, Bisexual and Transgender Voluntary and Community

Organisations, 2012). A uniform service based on normative cisgender and heterosexual status has serious consequences for inclusion/ exclusion. Not only can older LGBT residents/service users face desexualisation, they risk having their difference denied, which can also mean going back into the closet, having spent a lifetime building a valid identity in the face of hostility. Even in today's less prejudiced climate in the UK, it can mean being isolated from community, friends and sexual partners (Willis et al, 2013), which can affect mental health/ self-esteem (RCN, 2011).

Ageist erotophobia and interpersonal relations: a rare footnote

While relations in care homes or other healthcare settings can involve everyday interpersonal relations, this section addresses what little has been written about how closer relationships with 'significant others' (with whom older individuals share a history) can affect older people's sexuality. Spouses/partners, relatives, and especially grown-up children, friends and same-age peers, animated by ageist erotophobia, can act as a brake on older people's sexual and relational opportunities. It has been observed that the views of grown-up children (in the context of care provision at home or in a care home) can be prioritised over the wishes of older people/residents themselves (Bauer et al, 2019). It is, though, important to emphasise that friends and relatives should not be blamed for their reactions that indicate an impulse to protect. They may need information and support to think about the many hidden influences that could animate protective responses, especially when a dementia is involved. In this respect, see a helpful review article by Wiskerke and Manthorpe (2019).

Compared with the literature relating to care homes, scholarship addressing the influences of closer personal relations appears massively under-developed if not dispersed and interstitial, commonly involving passing reference to the issue in more general concerns about sexual health. This limited scholarship, although it has focused on how professional care staff can help older service users to meet their own sexuality and intimacy needs, has little to say about how such staff can mediate sensitively the influences of family/significant others. (See, for example, Thys et al, 2019). In the UK, guidance aimed at nurses and professional carers concerning sex and intimacy and older service users only mentions the need to consider a family's views and omits any reference to how relatives can influence or constrain older people's choices (RCN, 2011).

Further, a study of heterosexually-identified 'post-menopausal' women's sexuality in Hong Kong (Ling et al, 2007) was typical in briefly discussing how medical problems (in this case related to male spouses' loss of sexual capacity, largely because of 'erectile dysfunction') represents a barrier to satisfaction by both partners and is implicated in marital conflict. Even though the study recognises the enhanced role of sex and emotions in later life relationships, this largely asociological body of work tends to be heteronormative and over-focuses on problems *intrinsic* to individuals or the couple/dyad rather than extrinsic influences such as ageism. It also risks minoritising older people engaged in more adventurous forms of sexual activity that may, for example, involve polyamory/multiple partners and non-genitally focused forms of sexual/erotic activity, which include bondage, domination and sado-masochistic power play and fantasy/fetish. As such, this more medically-oriented scholarship tends to show little awareness of the workings of discourse at the micro-level, in particular.

Furthermore, the thinking and practical guidance of Gibson (2013) stands out because it addresses the restrictions imposed by grown-up offspring on old(er) parents' sexual and emotional autonomy. In a manual designed to help healthcare professionals support older people's autonomy concerning sex and intimacy, Gibson observes how younger relatives grant permission to those of their own generation(s) yet try to impose all manner of practical and psychological obstacles to restrict their parents' or grandparents' sexuality: people who, ironically, are likely to be more sexually experienced and far less prudish than imagined. One wonders whose feelings are being (over-)protected?

Not only does such thinking indicate a sense of distaste, consonant with ageist erotophobia, it can also be mixed in with other motives in relation to older relatives who are divorced or widowed/widowered and attempting to pursue a new relationship. As Gibson has observed, motives can arise from fears about loss of inheritance and can lead to attempts to control an older relative through manipulation and even physical violence. This kind of situation is briefly alluded to in a study by Garrett (2014) as part of a raft of constraints that include lack of partner availability (especially for older women) and expectations of sexual decline in later life. Further, Gibson notes that grown-up children may also restrict cultivation of a (new) relationship and sexual autonomy, which can reduce access to the labour of older parents as providers of no-cost childcare. (See also Hafford-Letchfield, 2021.)

Finally, in this section, and suggesting a more positive line of enquiry, in an Australian context, Bauer et al (2014b) have observed some supportive responses by family members to older relatives'/parents' sexual relationships within care homes, including residents affected by a dementia. Even here, though, the authors note that such support was tinged with paternalism, especially where compromised capacity to consent was evident, but they also note the fine line between relatives' wishes to be kept informed of the older person's attachments and their ability to exercise control over the older individual.

Conclusion

This chapter has drawn attention to the ways in which ageist erotophobia, operating at societal, organisational and interpersonal levels, can restrict older people's autonomy in relation to sex and intimacy and contribute to their desexualisation. It appears that this kind of discourse largely works subconsciously and effectively to regulate what is permissible in terms of self-expression and that it is also inflected by (intersecting) differences of gender, sexuality and social class. There is a need for representation of diverse older people as sexual beings. Further, the chapter has highlighted the urgent need for more research concerning influences of significant others on *diverse* older people's sexual and intimate self-expression, as well as the need for more critical engagement with discourses of lack and to move beyond problems that are seen as intrinsic to older people. In terms of policy and practice to support older people's bodily and sexual autonomy, consideration needs to be given to care environments, opportunities for privacy and the conduct of sensitive negotiations, where appropriate, between older people, their significant others and healthcare professionals.

Although older people face considerable constraints on sexual and intimate self-expression, such constraints do not pass without challenge. Not to recognise this would be to deny older people autonomy generally and sexual agency in particular, though the epistemic and emotional resources required to challenge ageist erotophobia are not equally distributed. Indeed, I have noted elsewhere (Simpson, 2021) that they are strongly linked to intersecting forms of differentiation such as class and gender. It appears that challenge to ageist erotophobia has come largely from older people (and some younger allies who often play important roles in supporting them professionally and sometimes personally). While some challenges can be consciously political, others (though reflecting a more liberal political sensibility) are much quieter and pragmatic and visible in simple solutions to dilemmas and difficult situations that, nevertheless, thwart ageist erotophobia (Simpson et al,

2018b). As such, they enable older people/care home residents to exercise autonomy over their erotic, sexual, intimate and personal lives.

The last decade or so has seen the emergence of a more critical and often empirically-based body of work with international reach that addresses ageism in relation to sex and intimacy. (For examples, see Bauer et al, 2012; Hafford-Letchfield, 2008; Villar et al, 2014.) Such work illuminates the workings of ageism as it applies to sex and intimacy and its intersections with other aspects of identity difference, such as those related to class, race, sexuality and gender. Indeed, a study conducted by the OPUS team has identified how care home residents (and, by extension, older people generally) can express more ambivalent ways of thinking about sex and intimacy (Simpson et al, 2018b). For instance, one heterosexually identified female participant in her eighties expressed a desire for or openness to further intimate experience but with the right person, but was constrained by the lack of available men of her age/generation as well as wider social expectations of older femininity. Some older people can tell stories of continuity and where sex is transformed into intimacy. This was particularly noted where a male partner was affected by a degenerative condition and ramified in terms of relationship longevity and a deep intimate knowledge of each other. This relational longevity can be contrasted with the vigorous sex that tends to be associated with youth. Yet other study participants were proudly defiant and prepared to express their intimacy in public regardless of attempts at surveillance.

Not only can ageist erotophobia be ignored, it seems that it can also be challenged head-on through words and deeds and in ways that indicate resexualisation of older people. The diverse responses just described provide evidence that older people may express, contrary to homogenising stereotypes of non-sexuality, a spectrum of reactions from compliance with ageism, to a genuine lack of interest in sex, through to continuity of erotic practice. Also, the OPUS research has noted how sexuality can be supported by some care-givers, who provided accounts of simple environmental adjustments and practices concerning privacy (Simpson et al, 2018b). Such practical actions represent a more measured attitude towards safeguarding and enabling intimacy, determined more by the needs and reactions of residents than anxiety about the residents' sexuality (Simpson et al, 2018b).

Finally, we need to bear in mind what is at stake politically as a result of widespread denial of diverse older people's needs for sex and intimacy. Such neglect in research, policy and practice risks reinforcing infringements of equality and human rights legislation, which concern fundamental issues such as liberty, self-expression, respect for private life and freedom from discrimination. Addressing such issues, moreover, could meet criteria concerning genuinely holistic care, while helping to maintain older people's and service users' self-esteem, and thus reduce or help prevent negative mental health (RCN, 2011).

Note

[1] The search strategy involved word combinations based around 'older people, sex and social class'. The combinations were entered mainly into academic search engines: the multidisciplinary Academic Search Premier; CINAHL Complete; Medline; PSYCHInfo; Scopus; and the Web of Science. This strategy was supplemented by specific searches through my former university library and Google Scholar. The various search devices were chosen to yield disciplinary variety across health studies, social sciences, social gerontology and the humanities, and simultaneously providing focus and manageability.

References

Bauer, M., Fetherstonhaugh, D., Tarzia, L., Nay, R., Wellman, D. and Beattie. E. (2012) '"I Always Look Under the Bed for a Man". Needs and Barriers to the Expression of Sexuality in Residential Aged Care: The Views of Residents with and without Dementia', *Psychology & Sexuality*, 4(3): 296–309.

Bauer, M., Fetherstonhaugh, D., Tarzia, L., Nay, R. and Beattie, E. (2014a) 'Supporting Residents' Expression of Sexuality: The Initial Construction of a Sexuality Assessment Tool for Residential Aged Care Facilities', *BMC Geriatrics*, 14(1): 82–8.

Bauer, M., Nay, T., Fetherstonhaugh, S., Wellman, D. and Beattie. E. (2014b) '"We Need to Know What's Going On": Views of Family Members Toward the Sexual Expression of People with Dementia in Residential Aged Care', *Dementia*, 13(5): 571–85. DOI: 10.1177/1471301213479785

Bauer, M., Haesler, E., Fetherstonhaugh, D. (2019) 'Organisational Enablers and Barriers to the Recognition of Sexuality in Aged Care: A Systematic Review', *Journal of Nursing Management*, 27(4): 858–68.

Beasley, C. (2005) *Gender and Sexuality: Critical Theories, Critical Thinkers*. London: SAGE.

Biggs, S. and Daatland, S.O. (2006) 'New Ageism: Age Imperialism, Personal Experience and Ageing Policy', in Biggs, S. and Daatland, S.O. (eds) *Ageing and Diversity: Multiple Pathways and Cultural Migrations*. Bristol: Policy Press, pp 95–106.

Bytheway, W. (1995) *Ageism*. Buckingham: Open University Press.

Clarke, L.H., Griffin, M. and Maliha, K. (2009) 'Bat Wings, Bunions, and Turkey Wattles: Body Transgressions and Older Women's Strategic Clothing Choices', *Ageing & Society*, 29(5): 709–26.

Cook, C., Schouten, V., Henricksen, M. and McDonald, S. (2017) 'Ethics, Intimacy and Sexuality in Aged Care', *Journal of Advanced Nursing*, 73(12): 3017–27.

Darnaud, T., Sirvain, S., Igier, V., Taiton, M. (2013) 'A Study of Hidden Sexuality in Elderly People Living in Institutions', *Sexologies: European Journal of Sexology and Sexual Health*, 22(4): e93–9.

Delahunty, M. (2013) 'Liars, Witches and Trolls: on the Political Battlefield', *Griffith Review*, 40: 18–30.

Department of Health (2007) *Putting People First*. London: The Stationery Office.

Doll, G.A. (2012) *Sexuality and Long-term Care: Understanding and Supporting the Needs of Older Adults*. Baltimore: Health Professions Press.

Eagleton, T. (2003) *After Theory*. London: Penguin.

Eyers, I., Arber, S., Luff, R., Young, E. and Ellmers, T. (2012) 'Rhetoric and Reality of Daily Life in English Care Homes: The Role of Organised Activities', *International Journal of Ageing and Later Life*, 7(1): 53–78.

Fairclough, N. (2013) *Critical Discourse Analysis: The Critical Study of Language*. London: Routledge.

Foucault, M. (1977) *Discipline and Punish: The Birth of the Prison*. New York: Pantheon.

Foucault, M. (1980) *The History of Sexuality, Volume 1: An Introduction*. London: Vintage.

Garrett, D. (2014) 'Psychosocial Barriers to Sexual Intimacy for Older People', *British Journal of Nursing*, 23(6): 327–31.

Gibson, H.B. (2013) *The Emotional and Sexual Lives of Older People: a Manual for Professionals, Volume 7*. London: Springer.

Gott, M. (2004) *Sexuality, Sexual Health and Ageing*. London: McGraw Hill Education.

Gott, M. and Hinchliff, S. (2003) 'How Important is Sex in Later Life? The Views of Older People', *Social Science & Medicine*, 56(8): 1617–28. DOI:10.1016/S0277-9536(02)00180-6

Greer, G. (2018) *The Change: Women, Aging, and Menopause*. New York: Bloomsbury.

Hafford-Letchfield, T. (2008) 'What's Love Got to Do with It? Developing Supportive Practices for the Expression of Sexuality, Sexual Identity and the Intimacy Needs of Older People', *Journal of Care Services Management*, 2(4): 389–405.

Hafford-Letchfield, T. (2021) 'Heterosexual Sex, Love and Intimacy in Later Life: What Have Older Women Got to Say?', in Hafford-Letchfield, T., Simpson, P. and Reynolds, P. (eds) *Sex and Diversity in Later Life: Critical Perspectives*. Bristol: Policy Press.

Han, K., Trinkett, A., Storr, C., Lerner, N., Johangten, M. and Gartrell, K. (2014) 'The Associations between State Regulations, Training Length and Perceived Quality of Job Satisfaction among Certified Nursing Assistants: A Cross-sectional Secondary Data Analysis', *Journal of Nursing Studies*, 51(8): 1135–41.

Hinchliff, S. (2014) 'Sexing up the Midlife Woman: Cultural Representations of Ageing, Femininity and the Sexy Body', in Whelehan, I. and Gwynne, J. (eds) *Ageing, Popular Culture and Contemporary Feminism: Harleys and Hormones.* London: Palgrave Macmillan, pp 63–77.

Hinchliff, S. and Gott, M. (2016) 'Ageing and Sexuality in Western Societies: Changing Perspectives on Sexual Activity, Sexual Expression, and the Sexy Older Body', in Harding, R. and Peel, E. (eds) *Ageing and Sexualities: Interdisciplinary Perspectives.* Abingdon: Taylor & Francis, pp 11–31.

Hockey, J. and James, A. (1993) *Growing Up and Growing Old: Ageing and Dependency in the Life Course.* London: SAGE.

Hodson, D. and Skeen, P. (1994) 'Sexuality and Aging: The Hammerlock of Myths', *Journal of Applied Gerontology*, 13(3): 219–35.

Howarth, C. (2014) 'Encountering the Ageing Body in Modernity: Fear, Vulnerability and "Contamination"', *Journal for Cultural Research*, 18(3): 233–48.

Laing, W. (2014) *Strategic Commission of Long-Term Care for Older People. Can We Get More for Less?* London: LaingBuisson. Available at: http://www.laingbuisson.co.uk/Portals/1/Media_Packs/Fact_Sheets/LaingBuisson_White_Paper_LongTermCare.pdf [Accessed 3 December 2019].

Ling, D.C., Wong, W.C. and Ho, S.C. (2007) 'Are Post-menopausal Women "Half-a-Man"? Sexual Beliefs, Attitudes and Concerns among Midlife Chinese Women', *Journal of Sex & Marital Therapy*, 34(1): 15–29.

Local Government Association (2014) *Making Safeguarding Personal.* London: Local Government Association.

Mahieu, L., Anckaert, L. and Gastmans, C. (2014) 'Intimacy and Sexuality in Institutionalized Dementia Care: Clinical-ethical Considerations', *Health Care Analysis*, 25(1): 52–71.

National Council for Palliative Care (NCPC) and the Consortium of Lesbian, Gay, Bisexual and Transgender Voluntary and Community Organisations (CLGBTVCO) (2012) *Open to All? Meeting the Needs of Lesbian, Gay, Bisexual and Transgender People Nearing the End of Life.* London: NCPC and CLGBTVCO.

ONS (Office for National Statistics) (2011) 'Press Release: Characteristics of Older People – What Does the 2011 Census Tell Us about the Oldest Old Living in England and Wales?'. London: ONS.

ONS (Office for National Statistics) (2019) 'Population Estimates, United Kingdom, Mid-2018'. London: ONS.

Phillips, J. and Marks, G. (2008) 'Ageing Lesbians: Marginalizing Discourses and Social Exclusion in the Aged Care Industry', *Journal of Lesbian and Gay Social Services*, 20(1–2): 187–202.

Phillipson, C. (1998) 'Modernity and Identity: Theories and Perspectives in the Study of Older Adults', *Journal of Aging and Identity* 3(1): 1–24.

Plummer, K. (2011) *Intimate Citizenship: Private Decisions and Public Dialogues*. Seattle: University of Washington Press.

RCN (Royal College of Nursing) (2011) *Older People in Care Homes: Sex, Sexuality and Intimate Relationships. An RCN Discussion and Guidance Document for the Nursing Workforce*. London: RCN.

Simon, B. (2005) 'The Return of Panopticism: Supervision, Subjection and the New Surveillance', *Surveillance & Society*, 3(1): 1–20. DOI: 10.24908/ss.v3i1.3317

Simpson, P. (2015) *Middle-Aged Gay Men, Ageing and Ageism: over the Rainbow?* Basingstoke: Palgrave Macmillan.

Simpson, P. (2021) 'Older People, Sex, Intimacy and Social Class', in Hafford-Letchfield, T., Simpson, P. and Reynolds, P. (eds) *Sex and Diversity in Later Life: Critical Perspectives*. Bristol: Policy Press.

Simpson, P., Brown Wilson, C., Brown, L., Dickinson, T. and Horne, M. (2016) 'The Challenges of and Opportunities Involved in Researching Intimacy and Sexuality in Care Homes Accommodating Older People: A Feasibility Study', *Journal of Advanced Nursing*, 73(1): 127–37.

Simpson, P., Horne, M., Brown, L., Dickinson, T. and Torkington, K. (2017) 'Older Care Home Residents, Sexuality and Intimacy', *Ageing & Society*, 37(2): 243–65.

Simpson, P., Almack, K. and Walthery, P. (2018a) '"We Treat Them all the Same": the Attitudes, Knowledge and Practices of Staff Concerning Old/er Lesbian, Gay, Bisexual and Trans Residents in Care Homes', *Ageing & Society*, 38(5): 869–99.

Simpson, P., Brown Wilson, C., Brown, L., Dickinson, T. and Horne, M. (2018b) '"We've Had Our Sex Life Way Back": Older Care Home Residents, Sexuality and Intimacy', *Ageing & Society*, 38(7): 1478–1501.

Stein, G. and Almack, K. (2012) 'Care Near the End of Life: The Concerns, Needs and Experiences of LGBT Elders', in Ward, R., Rivers, I. and Sutherland, I. (eds) *Lesbian, Gay, Bisexual and Trans Ageing: Biographical Approaches for Inclusive Care and Support.* London: Jessica Kingsley, pp 114–31.

Thys, K., Mahieu, L., Cavolo, A., Hensen, C., Dierckx de Casterlé, B. and Gastmans, C. (2019) 'Nurses' Experiences and Reactions towards Intimacy and Sexuality Expressions by Nursing Home Residents: a Qualitative Study', *Journal of Clinical Nursing*, 28(5–6): 836–49.

Villar, F., Celdrán, M., Fabà, J. and Serrat, R. (2014) 'Barriers to Sexual Expression in Residential Aged Care Facilities: Comparison of Staff and Residents' Views', *Journal of Advanced Nursing*, 70(11): 2518–27.

Villar, F., Fabà, J., Serrat, R. and Celdrán, M. (2015) ' "What Happens in Their Bedrooms, Stays in Their Bedrooms": Staff and Residents' Reactions toward Male-Female Sexual Intercourse in Residential Aged Care Facilities', *The Journal of Sex Research*, 52(9): 1054–63.

Willis, P., Maegusuku-Hewett, T., Raithby, M., Miles, P., Nash, P., Baker, C. and Evans, S. (2013) *Provision of Inclusive and Anti-Discriminatory Services to Older Lesbian, Gay, Bisexual Identifying People in Residential Care Environments in Wales.* Swansea: University of Swansea.

Wiskerke, E. and Manthorpe, J. (2019) 'Intimacy between Care Home Residents with Dementia: Findings from a Review of the Literature', *Dementia*, 18(1): 94–107. DOI: 10.1177/1471301216659771

Wornell, D. (2014) *Sexuality and Dementia: Compassionate and Practical Strategies for Dealing with Unexpected or Inappropriate Behaviors.* New York: Demos Health.

Yelland, E. and Hosier, A. (2015) 'Public Attitudes toward Sexual Expression in Long-term Care: Does Context Matter?', *Journal of Applied Gerontology*, 36(8): 1016–31.

4

The aesthetic(s) of eroticism in later life

Ricardo Iacub and Feliciano Villar

Introduction

Human sexuality requires complex frames of understanding because of the multiplicity of factors influencing how it is constructed and expressed. One of these factors lies in the capacity to promote and the actual generation of sexual desire traditionally associated with the notion of sensuality.

In this chapter, we reflect on how narratives and social practices contribute to shaping understandings of later life (Iacub, 2006), taking later life not as some life-stage with fixed and 'objective' chronological boundaries but as a cultural concept, which enables classification of certain people as 'older'. In turn, such understandings have an impact on eroticism in older age. Such narratives and practices are also responsible for enabling certain cognitive, affective and behavioural responses (both explicit and implicit) concerning the acceptance or rejection of later life and older persons as subjects and objects of sexual desire.

As will be seen, estrangement appears as one of the reactions to an ageing body, including, for instance, the feeling that one's (inner self) is separate from one's own ageing body. We will review how bodily estrangement has its roots in some historic accounts, as well as how it is expressed in stories told by older people themselves. Focusing on this sense of estrangement is important in helping us understand how individuals relate to older adults and how older adults relate to their own bodies. It appears as a reason for rejection, not always explicit and socially understood, but one strongly associated with emotions like shame, embarrassment, disgust, or ridicule, which, in turn, naturalise ageist cultural interpretations and limit critical and political thinking about sexuality, eroticism and desire in later life.

However, cultural analysis of alienation from ageing embodiment shows the construction of an erotic aesthetic associated with rejection and one that coexists alongside more recent images of active, youthful, and energetic (in terms of sexual self-expression) older people. These polar opposite accounts signal contradictory and diverse narratives that, on the one hand, de-eroticise older age by associating it with ugliness, health risks or even death but, on the other hand, eroticise it by relating later life to freedom from reproduction (Héritier, 1992), lifelong enjoyment of an ageless self and the diversity of sexual desire (Iacub, 2006, 2011).

As a result, we encounter deeply historically-rooted narratives in tension with alternative emergent narratives. While traditional hegemonic frames constrain sexual desire to specific kinds of bodies, in which age-associated marks are thought to connote exclusion, within such dominant discourse there have appeared alternatives to restricted conceptions of legitimate objects of sexual desire. For instance, MILFs ('Mother I'd Like to Fuck', a label assigned to women, typically with children, who are sexually attractive), daddies, bears (both of them will be defined and discussed later in this chapter), and other kinds of unconventional sexual prototypes show how fruitful is the construction of alternatives that defy the hegemonic pattern of slim, youthful and athletic sexual selves.

Finally, we will introduce an empirical perspective to this chapter in a discussion of some studies that shed some light on how individuals understand eroticism in older age by creating categorising frames (Fillmore, 2006), which explicitly mark their relation to ageing and implicitly demarcate who or what counts as legitimate objects of desire in relation to age. We will analyse the ways in which a sample of Psychology undergraduates understood and evaluated an erotic scene featuring older people, taken from the film *Cloud 9* (Dresen, 2008), and also discuss how a sample of people aged 60 and above view their own and other people's ageing bodies and eroticism.

At root, this chapter is concerned to examine critically the factors regulating the aesthetics of eroticism in older age largely through application of psychological theorising to analysis of fragments of historic narratives and everyday discourses on eroticism and sexuality in later life. However, before discussing these issues, we will begin by clarifying the theoretical perspective which guides our interpretations.

A constructionist approach to eroticism in later life

In this chapter, we will approach eroticism in later life based on a constructionist paradigm. A constructionist (or constructivist) epistemology is one that understands knowledge not as a reflection or description of an external reality but as a construction, cultural and historically situated, that reflects socially negotiated meanings and values which are, in turn, enacted as informal rules, practices, and systems of control and power (Gergen and Gergen, 2000).

Thus, the aesthetics of eroticism regarding later life can be analysed from a critical and political perspective, understanding 'policies' as cultural devices of disciplinary action, enacted as informal means of control or formal guidelines, regulations and laws. Such control mechanisms over individuals and their bodies, in turn, generate technologies of self, of the body, and of life, understood as signs and mechanisms of power to transform thought or behaviour and our bodies to achieve feelings of happiness, purity, wisdom, perfection or immortality (Behrent, 2013). Taken together, these constitute what Foucault (1993) has termed 'biopower'.

With these considerations in mind, the aesthetics of later life give rise to certain 'age policies', by which we mean forms of social control that do not necessarily entail legal sanctions, but which are capable of regulating beliefs, behaviours, emotions and desires through a broad ordering criterion, such as age, or a more specific one, such the cultural concept of later life (Iacub, 2006). Forms of control related to age are implemented through narratives and social practices and play a key role in the provision (or not) of meaning and beauty regarding older age and their representations and external indicators, including ageing bodies. Therefore, such forms of control express what is right and can be done and what is not permitted and must be avoided concerning ageing, sexuality and sexual desire. A particularly clear example of that can be found in institutional settings such as nursing homes (Villar, 2019). Older people living in such institutions remain embedded in highly regulatory regimes (most of them implicit, but some even explicitly expressed in guidelines and norms) that define sexual behaviors 'as potentially risky, problematic or even pathological' (Villar, 2019, p 165) and restrict clearly what can (and mainly cannot) be done and expressed regarding sexuality.

Aesthetics help to organise how we interpret experiences and generate forms of knowledge relating to stimuli in our environment. They promote emotional responses and likes and dislikes, defining what is beautiful and the frontier between bad and good taste. Such models serve as everyday filters that enable us to discern between beauty and ugliness, or between what is attractive or repulsive, arousing and positive or negative emotional responses accordingly (García Sierra, 1999).

In consequence, such cultural and historically contingent aesthetic frames of reference legitimate what is desirable and who can desire who or what. They describe the sociocultural conditions that promote the narration and enjoyment of erotic pleasure, which, in turn, invoke scenes that illustrate forms of desire, courtship, fantasies and practices, and provide the rules and parameters of such experiences. Indeed, cultural sociologist Zygmunt Bauman (1999) has defined eroticism as 'the cultural processing of sex'.

From such constructionist perspectives, eroticism emerges as 'sexuality transfigured by human imagination' (Paz, 1993), which includes the many direct or indirect ways of representing sex and sexuality, capable of bringing images, affects and sensations together. Eroticism is made explicit through narratives articulating diverse ideas and body sensations oriented to activate, promote and understand an individual's sexual enjoyment and sexual objects of desire (Iacub et al, 2020).

To elaborate our argument, thinking of an aesthetic of eroticism in later life (Iacub, 2006) implies the recognition of the cognitive frames that organise human perception, sensibility and judgement regarding what is erotic and the diversity (or restriction) of eroticism throughout the lifespan. We will analyse the way these frames are expressed in stories, and stories that are susceptible to change according to time and social context.

Subsequently, we will explore some conditioning cultural factors by analysing implicit and explicit perceptions and reactions to eroticism in later life. It is important to take into account that, while implicit processes are automatically activated, beyond conscious control, there are more explicit processes indicating conscious, purposeful forms of thought and action that are potentially under individuals' control (Kawakami and Dovidio, 2001). Being able to discern the difference between implicit and explicit processes enables us to understand why cognitive dissonance (that feeling of discomfort, tension or heightened physiological arousal experienced when our cognitions, behaviours or emotions are incompatible and in conflict; Festinger, 1957; McGrath, 2017) appears and, at the same time, illuminates what can be expressed and what remains tacit in certain contexts.

Cultural analysis of age-related eroticism

Every culture and historical time has its own understanding and practices concerning sexuality and eroticism and, consequently, has developed a normative position towards their expression in later life. In this section, we will sketch briefly some key ideas on how different cultures have approached eroticism in later life, and how such approaches have evolved in historical time. In fact, we can trace the origin of our present narratives and practices in relation to eroticism in later life (which will be discussed in a subsequent section) in some of these culturally and historically situated understandings.

Regarding such cultural and historical analysis, it is useful to recall the work of philosopher and cultural historian Foucault (1993), and his concept of discourses,[1] which he conceives as forms of power that circulate in the social field, whose tactical functions are neither uniform in their effects nor entirely stable. With specific reference to eroticism, discourses serve to construct and distinguish hegemonic forms of desire, and the establishment of certain 'commonsense' conceptions about whom or what can (and cannot) be the object of desire. Discourses convey power and can be instruments to exert it, but at the same time, they can also imply criticism and, to an extent, can modify the primary meaning which they were built on.

Therefore, there is a relationship between forms of social control and narratives related to later life and their effects on the aesthetics of eroticism, which, in turn, obliges consideration of the historical and cultural variability of narratives, as well as the discontinuities and contradictions emerging across time and place. In consequence, the discourses that constitute the aesthetics of eroticism in old age encompass diverse stories across different cultures and historical periods (Iacub, 2006).

A good example of the temporal and cultural mutability of discourse exists in the form of Françoise Héritier's (1992) anthropological studies, which have shown how older women in certain societies (see later in the chapter), who have reached or even passed the menopause, have developed the ability to exercise new forms of expressions of their sexuality that they had not enjoyed earlier in life. Indeed, Héritier proposes that it is not sex, but the reproductive capacity, that underpins male domination over women. The end of reproductive capacity here is seen less as deficit than gain, as women would be released from traditional expectations of passive femininity and freer to enjoy greater autonomy and sexual pleasure. Diverse examples are also described in Lewis' research (1941, in Heritier, 1992) that concerned the Piegan people, among whom postmenopausal women (seen as 'women with male heart') take a dominant role and are conceived as sexually active and capable of practicing different ways of loving.

The kind of autonomy just referred to can account for many but not all cases. Héritier herself identified certain factors, such as wealth and status, that enabled older women to reach those powerful positions. Nevertheless, they are an excellent illustration of how certain beliefs about gender can influence policies in relation to later life and allow for an alternative and positive erotic aesthetic, at least for some older people.

From a different tradition and form of narrative, Judaism also values sexual encounters throughout the adult lifespan. One of the most remarkable founding Jewish stories refers to how the origin of Jewish people is located in sexual intercourse between two older people, Abraham and Sara. They managed to have a baby, despite Sara's infertility and postmenopausal status. However, such a miracle did not exclude sexual intercourse. Following Sara's death, Abraham received an offer to marry again, and this offer is associated with the Bible's provision that, 'it is not good that the man should be alone' (Genesis 2:18), which is materialised through companionship and sexuality.

References to the continuity of desire describe an erotic aesthetic associated with the whole life. In the Proverbs book (5:18–19), it is stated 'May your fountain be blessed, and may you rejoice in the wife of your youth. A loving doe, a graceful deer – may her breasts satisfy you always, may you ever be intoxicated with her love'. We can read the following from Ecclesiastes in a similar way (9:9): 'Enjoy life with your wife, whom you love, all the days of this meaningless life that God has given you under the sun—all your meaningless days. For this is your lot in life and in your toilsome labor under the sun'.

Furthermore, the issue of whether sex is for reproductive purposes is contested in the Talmudic texts, which are the collection of Jewish law and tradition. They express how the sexual connection is privileged even if its aim is not reproduction but a strengthening of marital bonds, as Saadia Gaón Hodara (1992) exemplifies in the sadness of the wise man who, as an older person, mourned the loss of 'the instrument for home harmony'. In a similar way, according to the Talmudic text Iggeret HaKodesh ('The Holy Letter', which dates back to the twelfth century), a man should sexually arouse his wife, and even has to make sure that she reaches orgasm before he does.

Discourses about ageing recognised by the Hebrew people are quite clear: the power and status reached by older people is indisputable, and it is related to the very value attributed to life itself, related to the number of years already lived and in an older body. Being blessed with a long life implies having more power and approaching a certain 'God-like' status. The very first biblical genealogies identify people who enjoyed extremely long lives, such as Mathusalem, and despite this fact, such texts highlight that they still were fertile (Genesis 5).

Being able to complete the whole long-promised life (Isaiah 65:20) and the eschatological views announcing the older people's return to Jerusalem (Zechariah 8:4) reflect the power and esteem of older individuals within Jewish communities (Isenberg, 1992).

Turning the focus onto Ancient Greece, stories about older age eroticism are so rich and numerous that they are difficult to summarise. However, it is safe to say that the main motif here also concerns negative aesthetics that exclude older people as both the objects and subjects of desire: considered neither desired nor desiring.

Such constructions of older age emerge from a discourse that emphasises age (and youth, of course) as the criterion regarding *eros*. Youth is enshrined as an object of desire and equated with God-like qualities such as endless time and brightness. In contrast, older age is the object of erotic rejection, showing the most mortal side of human beings (Vernant, 1986). Interestingly, thinking that involves avoiding (and even fear of) ageing and later life because it reminds us of our own mortality, is one reason advanced to account for ageism (for example, Greenberg et al, 2017; Ayalon and Tesch-Römer, 2018).

Further, polarised thinking has been identified as a primary rhetorical device in Ancient Greek thought (Lloyd, 1992), which could explain the reason why youth and old age are represented as opposites, and what was asserted for one became the contrary for the other. Thus, while *eros* is present at a young age, associated with vitality, activity, brightness, warmth or moisture, older age, in contrast, was related to opposite qualities, such as mortality, cadaverousness, passivity, darkness, dryness and cold. An illustration of such associations is shown in the Homeric anthems, which, for instance, state: 'Those who come from outside, would believe them immortal and forever released from an older age since grace has been bestowed on all of them'.

Furthermore, *Cháris* is the Greek word to define the charming grace that makes our body shine (like charisma), which in turn refers to sensuality that entices desire. When talking about later life, the emphasis is placed on the 'not to be any more', conveying a feeling of the sorrow of those who are still able to feel desire but have lost access to it because they are no longer considered sexually desirable. Consequently, human relationships involving desire are attributed to others: it is because we are not objects of desire to others that we are denied access to our own desire.

Since the nineteenth century, western views regarding older age and eroticism have been progressively influenced by medical discourse (Bourdelais, 1993), which propitiates control mechanisms based on the difference between what is considered normal and what is pathological.

Such discourse forged aesthetic ideas in which health and beauty are located in the same axis, and closely related (Cole, 1997), which has had serious consequences for the eroticism of older people.

Sexuality in later life also ramifies in terms of 'libidinal exhaustion' and the many physical and psychological risks to which it may lead. Related to the conservation of life, libido is conceived as a kind of 'non-renewable energy', which, if wasted, may lead to death. This association of death and orgasm is still present in our culture (for instance, orgasm has been called in French '*la petite morte*'; see also Levin, 2011 or Yen Chiang and Chiang, 2016). It is also the foundation, for instance, of the so-called 'death by orgasm', that is, when life ends in the very moment the person ejaculates, an idea that is also present in a rather sinister metaphor concerning the sexual fate of older people (they are supposedly risking their life when having sexual intercourse), frequently portrayed in the mass media and popular culture, despite its actual occurrence being extremely rare (Kimmel, 2000; Mondello et al, 2018).

In terms of psychological perspectives, psychoanalysis is, without doubt, the main source of references concerning sexuality and older age. Freud (1988), for instance, proposed that older people often revert to pre-genital, libido stages, becoming 'polymorphously perverse' (Ferenczi, 1966), which variously could involve committing paedophilic acts, showing excessive sexual interest or developing lesbian tendencies. According to Freud, the polymorphously perverse are even prone to jeopardising others' mental health. Particularly, this could involve 'young males who may have sexual interest only towards decrepit older women, or young females who are sexually attracted to decrepit old men', labeled by Krafft-Ebing as gerontophilia (Iacub, 2006).

Ideas and images as just described that concern danger and risk tend to depict a Romantic character or split personality, as represented in the literary figures of Dr Jekyll and Mr Hyde. The first is thought devoid of any trace of sensuality and defined by a kind of family tenderness, but, in contrast, the second is considered so perverse, excessive and pathological as to generate rejection and revulsion.

Current scenarios

At present, diverse narratives feed eroticism in older age. Some of them are made up of traditions that draw from medical or religious sources. However, regardless of the narratives, considerations of aesthetics are very much at their heart, in a complex context in which age does not appear anymore as the decisive factor determining specific attitudes and where bodies (in both structural and functional modes) are fluid and susceptible to be manipulated and controlled by multiple technologies. Also, in such a context, older people are urged to regard sexual performance as a reachable goal and prompted to strive hard to achieve it, which could exert unrealistic demands leading to self-recrimination (Sandberg, 2015; Ferrero Camoletto, 2019).

As a consequence, some traditional narratives appear today as transformed, giving way to new approaches to old ideas. Among them, one of the most remarkable is associating age-related changes with pathology and illness (Calasanti, 2005; Jones and Pugh, 2005). From this point of view, bright and smooth skin is related to youth and beauty, but also to a vague (though compelling) 'healthy image'.

Anti-ageing discourse continues to occupy a privileged place in that context, since it allows blunt expression of horror towards old age, transforming the natural signs of age into a kind of deformity acquired and accentuated as we age. Anti-ageing discourse, articulated in apparently scientific and medical terms (for example, 'rejuvenation treatments' or 'cosmetic surgeries'; see Garnham, 2013), promises a transformation that will cancel the external marks related with the passage of time, which in turn creates new markets for a vibrant (and lucrative) industry of high-tech makeup and cosmetic products and different kinds of increasingly sophisticated plastic surgeries (Calasanti, 2005). Such anti-ageing technologies make achievable the miracle of adding years without getting older, maintaining a youthful (and supposedly healthy) appearance. We could therefore argue that the aesthetic rejection of old age motivates the modification of bodies thanks to biomedical technology, behaviours oriented to control and 'discipline' our body (such as exhausting gymnastic exercises and strict diets) or by computer software that virtualises bodies (such as Photoshop).

Such anti-age discourse ignores ageing as a possibility of positive transformation in the second half of life and underscores and gives depth to what Featherstone and Hepworth (1991) have called 'the mask of ageing', a metaphor expressing the core contradiction of a youthful inner self trapped in an organically declining outer, and basically at war with an ageing body. However, despite denying ageing, ironically, such discourse also includes older bodies, but only as long as they become submissive to certain rigid aesthetic demands. That is possible because those demands no longer invoke immutable essentialities, like in traditional discourses, but refer to the fluid nature of appearance (Foucault, 2002). Bodies become pliable and ductile, and the age-related marks are no longer inevitable. Enjoying a younger, healthy body for longer is now seen as a choice available to all, since bodies are liable to transformation.

Consequently, the present body can be thought of as mobile and mutable. That is, we can alter its forms to a degree and extent that seems unimaginable for many of us. From rejuvenating treatments to sex-assignment surgeries or organ transplants, the possibilities offered by medical sciences, allied to technology, are ever-increasing. Such an array of new aesthetics or forms of body modification tend to aim at a standard model of beauty based on the resemblance to youth but built with diverse cartography of isolated pieces that the client chooses from a catalogue, pieces that are susceptible to be cut and pasted and applied on any body or face. Such rebuilt bodies and faces end up being a collection of swollen lips, tight skin, wide-open eyes and balloon-like breasts, among other 'body objects' susceptible to be transformed or replaced.

Similarly, another way of virtually representing everlasting youth and beauty is the use of sophisticated computer software, such as Photoshop or Reface, which have turned bodies into clumsy image-containers accommodated to a juvenile and erotic dream. Denials of ageing imply that: you are good-looking insofar as you keep a middle-aged (or even better, an 'ageless') external appearance; and age-related external signs are open to choice and personal control (that is, looking 'young' is available to anyone who wants to), which, taken together, indicate a way of introducing ageism though the back door, a critique frequently raised when considering academic concepts of 'positive' or 'successful' and 'active ageing'. (See, for instance, Rubinstein and de Madeiros, 2015; Martinson and Berridge, 2015.)

Such a trend coincides with (and seems to be fed by) another kind of exclusion, in which not only are characteristics associated with older age denied, but also other more traditional and ancient representations of that stage of life are labeled as 'old-fashioned'. In fact, the most de-eroticised and invisibilised expressions of older people are related to the proximity to disused, ancient and sepia-toned representations of older age (Twigg, 2013).

From another point of view, the postmodern promise of a life without the limits and constraints imposed by age-related norms and stereotypes also adds to more recent accounts of the greater pliability and variability of old age eroticism. This is a trend that Featherstone and Hepworth (1991) have called the postmodern life course, which includes a change of social positions and status related to the increasingly blurred frontiers between life stages and periods of life (Katz, 1996).

The evaporation of regulations regarding 'life stage' or 'life cycle' helps erases guidelines and expectations based on age and facilitates the emergence of an increasing demand for ageless roles and attitudes, also (and maybe particularly) within the sexual realm.

With this thinking in mind, it could be argued that today's older people are facing a new requirement to achieve what is considered a good life: to keep on leading an active sexual life, which is now deemed to be a basic ingredient to enjoy a high 'quality of life'. At least since the turn of the twenty-first century, information about sexuality in older age has spread widely in many world regions, including Latin America. In this region, Argentina has been a pioneering country, enjoying a tradition of greater openness towards sexuality and sexual diversity and being the first county in the region to recognise and regulate gay and lesbian marriage (Law for Equal Marriage, 2010) and sexual and gender identities (Law for Gender Identity, 2012). Thus, in Argentina, sexuality has become one of the structuring issues regarding older age, resulting in an increasing number of media reports, conferences and courses for older people, as well as medical advice programs and sexual education workshops. Particularly in the media, sexuality has been approached in various ways: as an object of curiosity, and even shocking; sometimes involving a more empathetic stance; and at other times being seen as integral to health and quality of life.

The variability of narratives just mentioned, in a context in which diversity is culturally appreciated, has led us to reflect on the present circumstances of the aesthetics of eroticism in later life, which could entail pressure to maintain youthful bodies, and other models of ageing that do not see age as a negative quality (such as 'bears', as defined later in this chapter) or adopt a stance indicating openness to multiple objects of sexual desire, including older body-selves. Such trends can give rise to stories and social practices that prompt a clash between social demands and the reality of older bodies but simultaneously facilitate the emergence of counter-narratives (Nelson, 2001) or alternative narratives (Iacub and Arias, 2016) about sexuality in older age that are more questioning of dominant expectations.

Emerging narratives

Some particular stories have emerged that exemplify more questioning if not resistant stances towards traditional notions of ageing sexuality. Hence, gay ageing is a good example to illustrate the broad variety of cultural criteria and multi-layered discourses used to understood non-normative ageing trajectories. On the one hand, there is much evidence detailing the many forms of discrimination against gay men (Simpson, 2015). On the other hand, we have recently witnessed the emergence of other more inclusive perspectives, showing less restrictive criteria associated with age, and some of them even associated with older (or at least not-so-young) bodies (Bimbi, 2020; Iacub, 2006). Such work represents an interesting reflection on how the current value attributed to diversity is beginning to challenge hegemonic models of ageing sexuality but, at the same time, it also contributes to further advancement of consumer society looking for alternatives of desire as a way to increase sales (Iacub, 2006).

As for aesthetic models that challenge traditional restrictions and that broaden our horizons with new sexual possibilities for older people, we can mention, for instance, the prototype of the 'bear' as a figure within gay male culture. The bear is defined as 'a masculine male, strong, protective, hairy, neat and frequently bearded (in this order). Being more or less tall, brawny, young or bald does not matter' (www. ososcuriosos.blogspot.com, 2009). Bears may embody a masculine look – jeans, plaid shirts and boots – but they can, contradictorily, be very camp. So, they represent by no means a straightforward appropriation of macho or blue-collar masculinity.

There are even alternatives or finer distinctions within this category, like the 'polar bear' (or 'daddy bear'), characterised by grey/white hair and beard, and covered by abundant white, silver-shining body hair. In most cases, they are regarded with respect not just because of their appearance but also because of their warmth and experience (El blog de Mando, 2013). Although sometimes daddies could be defined as 'sugar daddies' (which specifically implies offering financial security), the term clearly connotes chivalry and protection, that is, the use of maturity to protect or care for others who may be younger and less affluent.

Such definitions indicate how older age is no longer a sole decisive factor and can be over-shadowed by other ones, such as protection, security, warmth or experience, which redefine age and deactivate the exclusionary power of youth and athletic bodies. Of course, age could still be an aesthetic criterion in these spaces but with secondary importance. Regardless of age, such aesthetic models continue to be alternatives to hegemonic ones that position beauty outside ageing bodies.

In the last ten years or so, we have witnessed an increase of webpages showing naked older people, depicted as objects of desire. This tendency also appears clearly in pornographic films, in which the presence of older people has been more frequent. Similarly, these films, actors and actresses representing older people are not just in their forties or fifties but also include others in their seventies and beyond. Older people's bodies are not represented as younger by using young-looking older actors or young actors made up to look old with ageing makeup, and they appear without invoking youthful values. This runs counter to ageist images of older people that validate them only when they approximate or mimic youth. In such films, older people are validated as older and not as surrogate youth. Such inclusion of alternative models might be part of an increasingly diverse market of bodies in hidden spaces of desire, which pornography can recover or transfer to more open spaces (for example, in the case of bears), illustrating, again, an alternative erotic aesthetic.

Analysis of our psychological study on ageing sexuality

As mentioned earlier, we conducted studies in Buenos Aires designed to assess awareness of how hegemonic narratives define or exclude older people as objects and subjects of erotic desire. This section briefly analyses their results.

The first study was carried out in the Faculty of Psychology, University of Buenos Aires (Iacub et al, 2019). We presented 60 undergraduate Psychology students with the initial seven-minute scene of the film *Cloud 9* (Dresen, 2008) and then asked for participants' opinions. The scene shows Inge, a seamstress older than 60, who decides to bring a pair of trousers to her client, Karl, a man who is in his seventies. He is at home and tries on the trousers in front of Inge, though appears slightly bashful while doing so. After exchanging suggestive glances, they begin kissing, which leads to genital contact. After the sexual act, Karl goes to the bathroom to clean himself and returns to find that Inge is no longer there.

While viewing, participants were asked to write down words describing whatever ideas or emotions came into their minds. After viewing, they were encouraged to give full written expression to any thoughts and feelings and with use of full sentences. Finally, participants were asked as a group to discuss and analyse their thoughts.

The most frequent words were included in four categories. Such categories, from the most to the least frequent, were as follows:

- Strangeness: the most frequent terms were 'strange' and 'bizarre', included in sentences such as 'I've never seen a thing like that' or 'I never thought it could happen'. This category indicates a lack of knowledge, a contradiction to 'what is supposed to happen', a schema that is not able to account for the experience narrated in the scene.

- Outside aesthetic values: this second category includes words as 'shock' or 'reject'[ion], among others. Subsequently, they were elaborated in sentences such as 'I'm used to seeing young bodies', 'It's hard to watch it', 'Sometimes I wanted to stop looking at that' or 'It was distasteful and even disgusting'.
- Tenderness: the third category refers to the appearance of the word 'tenderness' and its derivatives, which were included in sentences such as, 'The situation seemed very tender to me', or 'What nice hands, I liked the way they looked at and caressed each other'. In these sentences, eroticism or lust seems to be absent from participant's responses.
- The value of difference: in the last category, difference and a sense of 'otherness' appear as the main reactions. The attitude seems positive, but the pronoun 'they' is clearly underlined and separate from 'we' or the common (youthful) experience. We can see this in sentences such as: 'It's nice they have found a soul mate of their age', or 'They like each other'.

All categories represent, sometimes in a crude way and other times in a more gentle or subtle way, the 'othering' of older people, suggesting an ageist exclusion from the erotic imaginary that Simpson et al (2017) have identified as 'ageist erotophobia', that is, a failure to imagine older people as sexual or legitimate sexual beings, which helps position older people's sexual expressions and relationships as abnormal and unnatural.

In the discussion, strangeness appears in two different ways: while some participants said that they did not know what happened, most of them did know but they could not imagine it. In other words, they did not have an anchor image to help them understand the scene. The absence of frames of reference concerning ageing sexuality facilitated the strangeness that was also associated with other meanings, including ugliness, pathology, or even that attraction to either character would represent a kind of incestuousness. For example, some participants tended to identify characters in the film with parental figures.

Aesthetic criteria were identifiable in relation to the appearance of the ageing bodies represented, but also from the way the scene was filmed: according to participants, everything occurred 'too quickly', the woman looked untidy, movements were clumsy, and images were 'too crude', without filters or cover-ups. Taken together, such comments suggest how in reality 'unexpected' characters and scenarios contain and both propitiate and exclude erotic desire.

Despite the fact that 'tenderness' appeared quite frequently in the ideas raised in response to the scene, in the subsequent discussion, this issue was swiftly questioned by participants, who noticed that 'tender' scenes were not the most significant ones. Some participants even interpreted the reference to tenderness as a way of making sense of loveless sex in older age, perhaps suggesting the intellectual somersaults involved in denying the obvious: the characters were having sex.

Finally, in this section, the recognition of older adults' right to be sexually active is associated with freedom and capacity for autonomous decisions about their own lives. However, in participants' discussion, such rights and freedoms seemed to be restricted to having relationships among the same age group: they could not imagine that someone representing an 'old sexuality' could be involved with a younger person and even less so that the former could be included in this terrain of desire, neither as the objects of an older person's lust nor as being capable of feeling sexual attraction for an older adult. For instance, when asked about the possibility of having sexual contact with the film's characters, responses clearly indicated denial and expressions of rejection and distancing. The few dissenting voices, showing approval and contradicting the general trend, belonged to women and particularly to women in their thirties or above. They seemed to position themselves as 'older', which may have made it easier to empathise with the protagonists of the film, be more 'open-minded' and separate themselves from mainstream opinion concerning sex and age difference.

Moreover, we conducted two further qualitative studies, which aimed to explore the subjective representation of the body among older adults. The first one was aimed at exploring subjective representations of the body among older people and involved an interview with 30 participants aged between 65 and 92 years, all of them living in Buenos Aires (Iacub, 2007). The purpose of the second qualitative study was to understand the diversity of narratives about the eroticism of older adults and explore stories expressing the ways they experience sexual pleasure and desire. This study involved 40 people (28 women and 12 men) whose ages ranged from 65 to 82.

Both studies drew conclusions clearly related to the erotic aesthetic in older age. In both studies, erotic and aesthetic issues appeared to be in tension with social requirements concerning beauty and the difficulty of fulfilling standards regarding sexual desirability. Another main theme raised in the studies was the visibility of what participants considered as aged parts of their body, managing what can be exposed and what should remain hidden. For instance, some mentioned that wearing scarves or long sleeves helped to hide wrinkled or flaccid necks and arms. Such issues seemed to be particularly significant among women, for whom ageing appearances were pivotal to their experience of ageism and to fight against social and sexual invisibility (Clarke and Griffin, 2008; Slevin, 2010). Furthermore, disabilities also appeared as a key issue, conceived as an obstacle to attain a different kind of pleasure and hindering corporal abilities enabling the erotic encounter with others and with oneself.

Ageing appears as negative aesthetic change for oneself and others. However, the interpretations of these changes are not exactly the same for oneself and others, and even in our own body, ageing seems to depend on which part is considered. Thus, certain body objects or parts are deemed 'old' (for example, wrinkled hands, face or neck, an extended or pot belly and weight accumulating around the hips), while others may still preserve youth, such as sparkling eyes or shiny fingernails, among other qualities.

The aged body parts are described as 'missing parts' and our participants expressed literally (in Spanish), 'I don't have lips (or waist or a (nice) face) any more'. In contrast, when these body parts have not experienced so many (or such deep) age-related changes or when they have been modified by physical training or aesthetic surgeries, older participants said 'My waistline is back', or 'I'm myself again'. In other words, they felt that their body returned to approximate the 'normality' of youthful standards. It is remarkable how in many of these 'recovering expressions' the verb 'to be' is far more frequent than the verb 'to have', which could indicate permanence and continuity, including such 'rejuvenated' parts as belonging to their true self, not as mere accessory possessions that one can have (or lose). The contrast between 'being' and 'having' in this context obliges consideration of aged parts of the body as alien elements, externally imposed to the self, which do not represent the person and their identity, akin to how one might talk about an illness or pain.

In a similar way, in our older participants' words, it was quite common to find references to realising, with surprise and 'all of a sudden' (for instance, when inadvertently looking in a mirror), how stunningly old their appearance is from outside the self, and the feeling of estrangement from that image of oneself. Self-continuity is expressed by integrations, including 'aesthetic arrangements' (for example, surgeries and Botox), indicating an identity recovery, although, maybe ironically, a recovery of a transformed identity.

As mentioned, aesthetic deterioration is not just noticed in oneself but is also visible in critical views of older people's looks, whether talking of older age as a generic stage or specific older persons (including their partners). Such qualifications about appearance (the external or presented self) can be even more harsh and demeaning, and range from slightly derogatory descriptions to expressions of fear or disgust. In any case, open exposure of the old body appears to be rather furtive, fearing the judgemental look of other people, which one's body worth seems to depend on. In other words, what should be the main libido-arousing instrument, the body, and its aesthetics, becomes threatening, unreliable and an inhibitor of lust and desire.

It could then be argued that fragmented bodies are shown in contexts where views of them can be controlled and organised. Body parts perceived as 'old' are commonly disguised, while those deemed as young can be exposed. Polarities concerning what is young and what is old become aesthetic erotic mediators that enable or inhibit someone else's acceptance and bodily value.

However, and particularly in studies with older participants, a certain social demand for eroticism emerges as a positive force. Study participants were able to speak of personal trajectories of sexual liberation, both showing more knowledge about sexual issues and asserting attitudes associated with the value of personal autonomy. In this vein, for instance, the joys of masturbation are talked about more openly and frankly, which contrasts with past associations with sin and shame. Similarly, some women can claim the 'right to desire' beyond traditional subjugation to men's pleasure. Besides, the value of seduction, fantasies or the recognition of alternative sensitive pleasures, among others, are highlighted, which suggest new scenarios that provide models of and possibilities for reinterpreting the role, importance and the 'when' and 'where' of eroticism.

We also noticed some gender-specific themes in both studies. In the case of women, their stories tended to be biased towards beauty requirements. For them, attaining certain standards of beauty was the key to maintaining eroticism and feeling 'sexually desirable'. Among men, the demand for eroticism was inherent in feelings about being powerful, in genital terms, which made for less rich and diverse stories (with fewer displacements, where we channel less socially acceptable wishes and desires into more acceptable ones). However, among men, what we found commonplace were stories that involved restoring and embellishing the possibility of a sexual encounter. Even, in some of them, Viagra (Sildenafil) or Cialis (Tadalafil) appeared to be associated with a kind of 'mischief', alongside concerns with male self-confidence. For instance, they humorously spoke of being concerned about the right time to 'take the magic pill', being unsure about the right functioning of the medicine, running out of 'pills', or how they have to hide 'the secret weapon' from their partner.

Finally, physical changes were also the protagonists within other stories. Surgeries, illnesses, disabilities or medication lead to challenging (if not denying) the very possibility of sexuality in older age, particularly from a point of view that views the physically frail body as de-eroticised, thus generating aversion or rejection. For instance, some participants expressed that rejection by gestures or facial grimaces, or mentioning pee stains in trousers or flabby breasts.

Conclusion

Hegemonic cultural understandings, expressed through forms of control on ageing bodies and selves, organise and shape the aesthetics of eroticism in later life. They spring from traditional narratives and metaphors, although, at the same time, hegemonic views could also compete with alternative meanings and interpretations, particularly in changing contexts, which can challenge commonplace, taken-for-granted knowledge frameworks. As we have seen, the dynamics of postmodern times need to balance the traditional view of ageing as a barrier to sexuality and desire in later life, either because older people are not able to (because of physical and body reasons) or should not (because of moral prescriptions) remain sexually active. This process occurs in the context of the new alternatives created by the construction of an ageless and fluid external look and behaviour (thanks to the continuation of middle-aged clothes and lifestyles well into later life, or the surgical and non-surgical cosmetic interventions), such as the 'Viagra revolution' (Camoletto, Wentzell and Barrett, 2017; Tiefer, 2006).

Thus, we have identified narratives expressing a positive aesthetics of eroticism in later life, whether in historical terms (for example, Judaism) or in current times (as per the emergence of sexual prototypes such as 'bears' in gay male culture). However, other aesthetics have clearly detrimental effects on older age eroticism, given the historical tradition of classic Greece or the anti-age discourses in the present.

At present, there is a hegemonic approach that fragments bodies, differentiating between visible parts and other parts that should remain hidden or be modified. At the same time, some narratives enable alternative forms of embodiment to make age differences less relevant and promote unconventional erotic preferences, which, although still marginal or local/context-bound, still indicate a broadening of sexual aesthetics in later life and the emergence of new aesthetics.

The psychological studies described in this chapter have shown different meanings according to age group but all of them seem to share a common reaction of surprise, estrangement and difficulties about including older age and its marks into the self. In effect, this encourages misinterpretations about what is known (such as younger people associating older age eroticism with the weird or bizarre) and what can be seen (as the result of older people's management of which body parts they show and hide), also generating certain dissociations in representations of self.

It appears that we do not have clear, conscious frameworks to make sense of erotic experience in older age. When erotic experience does appear, it is commonly rejected and felt as cognitively and emotionally strange or 'other'. When trying to interpret such experience, dissociation emerges as a mechanism enabling which body parts are displayed and thus can be available for sexual desire.

Hegemonic understandings of ageing and later life tend to reject certain aesthetics of eroticism, mainly promoting the unbelievable and shocking, cognitive dissonance and feelings of embarrassment, shame or disgust, as well as a fear of the unknown, since we map older age as a foreign country in which only others, but not ourselves, inhabit. At the same time, we have also seen that, in a society in which age differences are increasingly blurred, age is beginning to be included positively in some emerging accounts of eroticism, generating newer views of the ageing body, enabling the possibility of erotic pleasure, whether transforming bodies through anti-ageing technology or creating models, such as 'daddies' or 'bears', capable of accepting difference. Therefore, the aesthetic eroticism of later life requires broader and more flexible understandings, so that traditional meanings organising our sexual desires could be challenged and expanded to integrate new realities.

Note

[1] We mainly use the notions of narrative and story interchangeably, but when referring to Foucault's thought we will speak of 'discourse', to respect his theoretical position and the terms he used.

References

Ayalon, L. and Tesch-Römer, C. (2018) 'Introduction to the Section: Ageism—Concept and Origins', in Ayalon, L. and Tesch-Römer, C. (eds) *Contemporary Perspectives on Ageism: International Perspectives on Aging*. New York: Springer, pp 1–10.

Bauman, Z. (1999) 'On Postmodern Uses of Sex', in Featherstone, M. (ed.) *Love and Eroticism*. Thousand Oaks: SAGE, pp 19–34.

Behrent, M.C. (2013) 'Foucault and Technology', *History and Technology*, 29(1): 54–104.

Bimbi, B. (2020) *El Fin del Armario: Lesbianas, Gays, Bisexuales y Trans en el Siglo XXI*. Marea Editorial: Buenos Aires.

Bourdelais, P. (1993) *L'Âge de la Vieillesse. Histoire du Vieillissement de la Population*. Paris: Odile Jacob.

Calasanti, T. (2005) 'Ageism, Gravity and Gender: Experiences of Bodies on Ageing', *Generations*, 29(3): 8–12.

Camoletto, R.F., Wentzell, E. and Barrett, C. (2017) 'Challenging the "Viagrization" of Heterosexuality and Ageing', in Barrett, C. and Hinchliff, S. (eds) *Addressing the Sexual Rights of Older People*. London: Routledge, pp 145–58.

Clarke, L.H. and Griffin, M. (2008) 'Visible and Invisible Ageing: Beauty Work as a Response to Ageism', *Ageing & Society*, 28(5): 653–74.

Cole, T. (1997) *The Journey of Life: A Cultural History of Aging in America*. New York: Cambridge University Press.

Dresen, A. (2008) *Cloud 9*. Germany. Film.

El blog de mando@vzla_69 (2013) elblogdemando.blogspot.com. Blog.

Featherstone, M. (ed.) (1999) *Love and Eroticism*. Thousand Oaks (CA): SAGE.

Featherstone, M. and Hepworth, M. (1991) 'The Mask of Ageing and the Postmodern Life-course', in Featherstone, M., Hepworth, M. and Turner, B. (eds) *The Body: Social Process and Cultural Theory*. London: SAGE, pp 371–89.

Ferenczi, S. (1966) *Problemas y Métodos del Psicoanálisis*. Buenos Aires: Paidós.

Ferrero Camoletto, R. (2019) 'Questioning the Sexy Oldie: Masculinity, Age and Sexuality in the Viagra Era', in King, A., Almack, K. and Jones, R.L. (eds) *Intersections of Ageing, Gender and Sexualities*. Bristol: Policy Press, pp 219–22.

Festinger, L. (1957) *A Theory of Cognitive Dissonance*. Stanford: Stanford University Press.

Fillmore, C. (2006) *Frame Semantics. Cognitive Linguistics*. New York: Mouton de Gruyter.

Foucault, M. (1986) *Historia de la Sexualidad, Volumes I, 2, 3*. México: Fondo de Cultura Económica.

Foucault, M. (1993) *Las Redes del Poder*. Buenos Aires: Almagesto.

Foucault, M. (2002) *Vigilar y Castigar: Nacimiento de la Prisión*. Buenos Aires: Siglo. XXI Editores.

Freud, S. (1988) *Obras Completas*. Madrid: Biblioteca Nueva.

García Sierra, P. (1999) 'VII: Estética y Filosofía del Arte'. *Diccionario Filosófico*, p 649.

Garnham, B. (2013) 'Designing 'Older' rather than Denying Ageing: Problematizing Anti-ageing Discourse in Relation to Cosmetic Surgery Undertaken by Older People', *Journal of Aging Studies*, 27(1): 38–46.

Gergen, K.J. and Gergen, M.M. (2000) 'The New Aging: Self-construction and Social Values', in Schaie, K.W. (ed.) *Social Structures and Aging*. New York: Springer, pp 281–306.

Greenberg, J., Helm, P., Maxfield, M. and Schimel, J. (2017) 'How our Mortal Fate Contributes to Ageism: A Terror Management Perspective', in Nelson, T.D. (ed.) *Ageism: Stereotyping and Prejudice against Older Persons*. Massachusetts (MA): MIT Press, pp 105–32.

Héritier, F. (1992) 'El Esperma y la Sangre en torno a algunas Teorías Antiguas sobre su Génesis y Relaciones', in Nadaff, R., Tazi, N., Feher, M. (eds) *Fragmentos para una Historia del Cuerpo Humano, Volumen. 3*. Madrid: Taurus, pp 158–79.

Hodara, R. (1992) 'Tu Be' av: el Judaísmo, la Sexualidad y Woody Allen (II): una Opinión poco Ortodoxa Extracto de Internet'. Available at: http://wzo.org.il/go.asp.

Homer (2000) *La Ilíada (I)*. Madrid: Gredos.

Iacub, R. (2004) 'Erotismo y Vejez en la Cultura Greco- Latina', *Revista Brasileira de Ciencias do Envelhecimento Humano*, 2(2): 84–103.

Iacub, R. (2006) *Erótica y Vejez. Perspectivas de Occidente*. Buenos Aires: Paidós.

Iacub, R. (2007) *La Representación Subjetiva del Cuerpo en la Vejez*. Unpublished doctoral dissertation, University of Buenos Aires.

Iacub, R. (2011) *Identidad y Envejecimiento*. Buenos Aires: Paidós.

Iacub, R. (2015) 'Erotic Wisdom in Old Age', *Kairós Gerontología*, 18: 87–102.

Iacub, R. and Arias, C.J. (2016) 'La Estilización de la Vejez', in Medeiros, T. (ed.) *Repensar as Pessoas Idosas no Século XXI*. Ponta Delgada: Letras Lavadas, pp 71–92.

Iacub, R., Mansinho, M. and Machluk, L. (under development) *Analysis of Reception of Cloud 9*. Buenos Aires: University of Buenos Aires.

Iacub, R., Hidalgo-López, P., Winzeler, M.O., Bourlot, V., Gil de Muro, M.L., Paz, M., Bellas, M.L., Machluk, L., Vazquez-Jofré, R. and Boggiano, P. (2020) 'Desarticulando las Fronteras del Erotismo en la Vejez', *Research on Ageing and Social Policy*, 8(1): 1–24.

Isenberg, S (1992) 'Aging in Judaism: "Crown of Glory" and "Days of Sorrow"', in Cole, T., van Tassel, D. and Kastenbaum, R. (eds) *Handbook of Humanities and Aging*. New York: Springer, pp 147–74.

Jones, J. and Pugh, S. (2005) 'Ageing Gay Men: Lessons from the Sociology of Embodiment', *Men and Masculinities*, 7(3): 248–60.

Katz, S. (1996) *Disciplining Old Age: The Formation of Gerontological Knowledge*. Charlottesville: University of Virginia Press.

Kawakami, K. and Dovidio, J.F. (2001) 'The Reliability of Implicit Stereotyping', *Personality and Social Psychology Bulletin*, 27(2): 212–25.

Kimmel, S.E. (2000) 'Sex and Myocardial Infarction: An Epidemiological Perspective', *American Journal of Cardiology*, 86: 10F–13F.

Krafft-Ebing, R. (1999) *Psychopathia Sexualis*. Paris: Editions Payot.

Law for Gender Identity N° 26.743 (2012) Official Bulletin of the Congress of the Argentinian Nation, 24 May 2012.

Law for Equal Marriage N° 26.618 (2010) Official Bulletin of the Congress of the Argentinian Nation, 22 July 2010.

Levin, R.J. (2011) 'The Ever-continuing Life of that "Little Death" – the Human Orgasm', *Sexual and Relationship Therapy*, 26: 299–300.

Lloyd, G.E.R. (1992) *Polarity and Analogy: Two Types of Argumentation in Early Greek Thought*. Bristol: Classical Press.

Martinson, M. and Berridge, C. (2015) 'Successful Aging and its Discontents: A Systematic Review of the Social Gerontology Literature', *The Gerontologist*, 55(1): 58–69.

McGrath, A. (2017) 'Dealing with Dissonance: A Review of Cognitive Dissonance Reduction', *Social and Personality Psychology Compass*, 11(12): e12362.

Mondello, C., Ventura Spagnolo, E., Cardia, L., Ventura Spagnolo, O., Gualniera, P. and Argo, A. (2018) 'An Unusual Case of Sudden Cardiac Death during Sexual Intercourse', *Medico-Legal Journal*, 86(4): 188–92.

Nelson, H.L. (2001) *Damaged Identities, Narrative Repair*. Ithaca: Cornell University Press.

OsosCuriOsos (2009) www.ososcuriosos.blogspot.com. Blog.

Paz, O. (1993) *La Llama Doble. Amor y Erotismo*. Barcelona: Seix Barral.

Rubinstein, R.L. and de Medeiros, K. (2015) ' "Successful aging," Gerontological Theory and Neoliberalism: a Qualitative Critique', *The Gerontologist*, 55(1): 34–42.

Sandberg, L.J. (2015) 'Sex, Sexuality and Later Life', in Twigg, J. and Martin, W. (eds) *Routledge Handbook of Cultural Gerontology*. New York: Routledge, pp 218–25.

Simpson, P. (2015) *Middle-Aged Gay Men, Ageing and Ageism: Over the Rainbow?* Basingstoke: Palgrave Macmillan.

Simpson, P., Horne, M., Brown, L., Brown Wilson, C., Dickinson, T. and Torkington, K. (2017) 'Old(er) Care Home Residents and Sexual/Intimate Citizenship', *Ageing & Society*, 37(2): 243–65.

Slevin, K.F. (2010) '"If I Had Lots of Money… I'd Have a Body Makeover": Managing the Aging Body', *Social Forces*, 88(3): 1003–20.

Tiefer, L. (2006) 'The Viagra Phenomenon', *Sexualities*, 9(3): 273–94.

Twigg, J. (2013) *Fashion and Age: Dress, the Body and Later Life*. London: Bloomsbury.

Vernant, J.-P. (1986) *Cuerpo Oscuro y Cuerpo Resplandeciente. Fragmentos de una Historia del Cuerpo*. Barcelona: Taurus.

Villar, F. (2019) 'Sexual Expression and Sexual Practices in Long-term Residential Facilities for Older People', in King, A., Almack, K. and Jones, R.L. (eds) *Intersections of Ageing, Gender and Sexualities*. Bristol: Policy Press, pp 153–70.

Yen Chiang, A. and Chiang, W.Y. (2016) 'Behold, I Am Coming Soon! A Study of the Conceptualization of Sexual Orgasm in 27 Languages', *Metaphor and Symbol*, 31(3): 131–47.

5

Menopause and the 'menoboom'[1]: how older women are desexualised by culture

Clare Anderson

Introduction

> It is sometimes said that women of a certain age constitute a 'third sex', and in truth, while they are not males, they are no longer females.
>
> (De Beauvoir, 1949 [1997], p 63)

Although written 70 years ago, Simone de Beauvoir's description of women of a certain age as a 'third sex' illuminates the uneasy relationship that still exists between gender and age, visible in the continuing cultural ambivalence towards female ageing, and in particular towards the older (post-menopausal) female body as a site for the continued performance of femininity and sexuality (used here to refer explicitly to sexual interest/desire). The cultural as well as the subjective gaze continues to characterise the process of female ageing as one of loss; a journey of inevitable decline. The focus of this trajectory of decline is the menopause: the biological process that ends menstruation and thereby a woman's reproductive life, but by which the female body is both desexualised and degendered by prevailing culture. In exploring the deeply problematic relationship between menopause, sex and sexuality, I draw on selected data from a wider research study (see Anderson, 2019), gathered between 2012 and 2015: a menopause narrative published in the 'lifestyle' section of the *Daily Mail* newspaper (representative of a number of such public-private discourses at the time); and two texts from the growing sub-genre of semi-autobiographical midlife narratives. I compare these public voices with the private voices of individual accounts of a number of midlife women, using data from a series of qualitative interviews.

The self-described age theorist Margaret Gullette contends that the menopause is culturally constructed by a profusion of menopause discourses which she terms 'the menoboom' (1997, p 98). My analysis unpacks the role of the 'menoboom' in shaping the experiences of individual women; by artificially conflating menopause with decline, a normal biological process becomes a narrative of loss: of physical strength; of emotional stability; and of sexual attractiveness.

Sadie Wearing (2007, p 284) describes the 'often unexamined links' between gender, ageing and sex, and indeed, the complex reciprocal relationship between ageing and gender has historically been somewhat neglected as an area of academic enquiry. This study has, therefore, an important contribution to make to what is still an under-explored and under-examined area within the field of gender studies, but, as importantly, in the wider world. The increasing visibility of older women on the public stage means that this work also has potentially far-reaching implications for the message-makers in the public domain – for the powerful voices of the media and advertising industries and the ways in which they talk to and about the women they target.

Frida Furman argues that there is a moment when 'the aging female body comes into deep conflict with cultural representations of feminine beauty' (1997, p 5). This tension, often triggered by the 'menopause event' (see Gullette, 1997), delineates the perceptual gap between the prevailing model of normative femininity in which youth=beauty=sexual desirability, and the reality of female ageing. As a consequence, there is seemingly no accepted trajectory for accommodating ageing and femininity within the stringent cultural 'rules' which determine how women are expected to perform their ageing. Wearing discusses these contradictory attitudes in terms of the 'cultural work the aging body is expected to perform' (2007, p 278) – complex, fraught with contradiction and more problematic than ever, given the greater visibility conferred on ageing women, particularly by the media. By contrast, Kathleen Woodward's rallying cry is that the notion of the ageing female body 'entailing gender and sexuality as the continuing site of identity, need not be a contradiction in terms' (2006, p 177). I explore these tensions as they are expressed through public discourses and the 'real' voices of women's individual experience of the menopause. Inevitably, the limited scope of the study imposes limitations on the data, which aims to be representative, but which does not claim to be definitive. The data discussed here explores a snapshot in time, but, in doing so, supports a number of conclusions which could inform future research: that such attitudinal collisions will persist while the ideological, visual and linguistic repertoire of contemporary culture is unable to accommodate a notion of ageing, which permits both sexual desirability and femininity, and a notion of femininity which can meaningfully encompass the ageing female body.

Cultural context

A culture of binaries

This study can be considered in the context of a number of dominant cultural forces shaping Western European culture: the first of these is the polarisation of youth and age, which, it can be argued, is one of the most powerful influences shaping contemporary attitudes to ageing. It is embedded in the cultural infrastructure and characterises many prevailing discourses of ageing and gender. The impact of this cultural binarism is profound and means that age and ageing continue to be problematised – pathologised – in the socio-cultural narrative. Woodward writes that 'our culture's denial and distaste for ageing … is understood in terms of decline, not in terms of growth and change' (1999, p xiii). Not only that, she further argues that dominant representations of ageing are deeply embedded in the cultural sediment so that 'youth, represented by the youthful body, is good; old age, represented by the aging body, is bad' (1991, p 7). The cultural as well as the subjective gaze continues to discursively construct the process of ageing as one of loss, in a way which particularly disadvantages women: the female body is both desexualised and degendered by the age-as-decline narrative; and, as will be discussed in more detail later, the menopause – the end of female reproductive life – is a highly significant focus for such cultural binarism.

The mass-mediated female body

The dual forces of consumerism and the mass media, overwhelmingly powerful in shaping all aspects of the cultural landscape (see Featherstone, 1982; Williamson, 1978; Chaney, 1996; Scanlon, 2000), remain extremely influential in how age/ing and gender are viewed and constructed, and reflected back in the opposing mirrors of youth and age. The emergence of the body as the central focus of discourses of consumerism is particularly significant for this study; the momentum of consumer culture dictates that as the 'inner and outer body become conjoined' (Featherstone, 1982 [1991]), increasingly the (sexualised) body becomes the vehicle for, and expression of, individual self-identity (see Shilling, 2003). According to the feminist philosopher Sandra Bartky, discourses of 'body work' generated by

79

what she terms the 'fashion-beauty complex' (1990, p 40) position the female body as inherently deficient, as an object in constant need of transformation. The imposition of this discourse of deficiency on the female body, its status as 'cultural text' (Bordo, 1993) appropriated by the conglomeration of advertising, beauty/cosmetic branding and women's magazines, makes the female body the particular object for the cultural gaze with a complex role to play in the construction of ideal (i.e. youthful, sexual) femininity.

The role of ageing femininity as constructed by these powerful public voices is contested and problematic, not least in the domain of mainstream women's magazines, powerful repositories for cultural ideals of femininity (Winship, 1987; Ballaster et al, 1991; Ferguson, 1983; Twigg, 2010). The considerable body of research which explores women's magazines as ideological texts suggests that there is still a relatively limited range of feminine identities offered to women within their pages, and that the foremost of these – appearance – remains the key index of 'successful' femininity. The pervasive and influential discourses of the woman's magazine deal uneasily with ageing – or indeed other constructions – of femininity. In her analysis of *Vogue* magazine Twigg states that 'reflecting the values of the fashion world, it [sc. *Vogue*] has remained preoccupied with the youthful and transgressive; remarkably little work has been undertaken that addresses older people or the processes of ageing. Beyond 40 there is silence' (2010, p 485).

The implication for older women is that post menopause, the relationship between gender identity and sexuality is more, not less, conflicted at this point in the twenty-first century. Femininity, which is culturally required, must accommodate the ageing body, which is culturally denied. It could be argued that one of the principal challenges confronting beauty and cosmetic corporations as well as the media and advertising industries lies in the complex navigation needed to reconcile the (lucrative) needs of a growing cohort of midlife consumers with embedded attitudes towards ageing which remain, as Woodward writes, 'profoundly ambivalent, and primarily negative' (1991, p 8). At the heart of this collective unease lies the dilemma of sexuality (used in the sense of being sexually desirable/desiring), and its role as a component in the performance of ageing femininity.

Ageing, femininity and sexuality

[W]e will watch ourselves grow invisible to youth worshippers and to the male gaze.

(Heilbrun, cited in Woodward, 1999, p xiv)

Cultural discourses tend to characterise the process of ageing as one of loss. Among the general catalogue of physical losses, perhaps one of the least documented is the desexualising effect of ageing. This is distinct from the process of 'degendering' as discussed by Catherine Silver in her 2003 paper on (de)gendered identities in old age, in which she describes the post-menopausal female body as 'no longer attract[ing] the gaze of men' (2003, p 386). The distinction between 'degendering' and 'desexualising' is more than merely semantic, in that it encodes the taken-for-granted expectation that older women, while still presenting as female, are no longer evaluated or represented as objects of sexual interest. Peter Oberg writes that 'older women are rarely portrayed as sexual, and sexual desire in older women is usually a point of ridicule' (2003, p 116). Furman's (1997) study of beauty parlour culture also demonstrates that the way in which older women evaluate their bodies is in constant tension with representations of youthful, sexually desirable femininity. As Christopher Faircloth contends, in Western culture, where the male body is considered to be normative and the female body, by comparison, as 'other' (2003, p 6), an older female body that can still be sexual may be doubly 'othered'.

Elizabeth Markson, in her analysis of the ageing female body in film, writes that 'the postmenopausal body, having lost its reproductive (and by implication, sexual) charm is neither the object of the appreciative male gaze nor does it fit into contemporary cultural discourses about "ideal" female beauty' (2003, p 80). A central theme of Gullette's work is that menopause is a culturally constructed 'discursive phenomenon' (1997, p 98; see also Greer, 1991) before it is a physical/biological one; it desexualises women so that, as Silver argues, post-menopausal women are perceived to be 'useless sexual objects' (2003, p 387). Railton and Watson's (2012) analysis of Madonna characterises her as a transgressive icon of ageing femininity, polarising and challenging cultural attitudes towards the performance of ageing femininity largely because she remains sexualised. This illustrates the rigid and yet contradictory nature of the cultural 'rules' which are enshrined in the discourses of mass media publications. The requirements of ageing femininity as laid down by these powerful public voices are based primarily around the complex balances involved in maintaining an 'appropriate' appearance. Older women must contrive to disguise the signs of ageing without appearing too young, while maintaining an (appropriately) youthful appearance and remain attractive without appearing overtly sexualised. As the journalist and author Anne Karpf writes 'the more you dig, the clearer it becomes that, most of the time, a strict set of rules operates

... you can get work as a model if you're older as long as you're not too sexy' (2014).

The problematic status of the ageing female body, caught between cultural expectation and biological reality, suggests that for women, as Wearing comments, 'the achievement of a stable and coherent gendered identity over time' (2007, p 286) is a highly complex and uncertain task. Her analysis of 'the complex psychic processes that may accompany the production of gendered identities as we age' (Wearing, 2007, p 285) argues that for individuals, as well as for prevailing culture, ageing is experienced and viewed as the foremost threat to this task.

Having discussed the broader cultural context for this study, menopause discourses in both public and private domains are now examined. In her writing on midlife and the menopause, Margaret Gullette argues that 'this lifecourse decline narrative requires as its pivot a critical moment, an event. The event crudely divides all women's lives into two parts, the better Before and the worse After, with the menopause as the magic marker of decline' (1997, p 98).

The culturally constructed 'better before, worse After' division in the life course, signalled by the menopause, further embeds the opposition of youth and age by imposing an artificial evaluative watershed on individual experiences of ageing. Bound up in 'the blunt binary' (Woodward, 1999, p xvii) of youth and age are darker and more complex evaluations in which 'youth=beauty=health=sexual attractiveness' and 'old age=ugliness=decline=desexualisation' appear as largely unquestioned polar opposites. The menopause heralds the end of reproductive capability and, with it, youthfulness and the possibility of being – and being 'allowed' to be – a sexual being. The new phase, post menopause, is defined by absence: of youthfulness, attractiveness and sexual desirability.

The way in which menopause is constructed and represented in public discourse will now be discussed, using a lifestyle newspaper article and the semi-autobiographical books about midlife of two feminist writers.

Public voices: menopause, the 'menoboom' and narratives of midlife

The analysis focuses on a first-person narrative authored by the journalist Mandy Appleyard, featured in the lifestyle section of the *Daily Mail*: 'Welcome to my menopause nightmare' (2013). By way of context I consider this text alongside the well-known works of two influential feminist writers on menopause: Margaret Morganroth Gullette (1997) *Declining to Decline* and Germaine Greer (1991) *The Change*.

While Gullette argues that menopause is a cultural construct, 'a discursive phenomenon' (1997, p 98) through which prevailing culture ages women, Greer reintroduces the historical designation of menopause as the 'climacteric' (1991, p 25) a Greek term meaning 'critical period', arguing that menopause *is* a critical life event for many women but one which they need to reclaim from its appropriation by male researchers and writers. Interestingly, and linked to Greer's point, one of the 2019 election pledges by the UK Labour Party[2] argued for women to be allowed time off for menopause-related issues. Large employers with over 250 employees would be required to: 'ensure absence procedures are flexible to accommodate menopause as a long-term health condition; carry out risk assessments to consider the specific needs of menopausal women and ensure that their working environment will not make their symptoms worsen' (taken from a manifesto announcement by Dawn Butler, Shadow Women & Equalities Minister, 21 September 2019).

It could be argued that not only is this a political appropriation of menopause, but that such public discourses reinforce the cultural pathologisation of menopause by framing it discursively as an illness with 'symptoms'. Such public messages form part of the discursive landscape which produces personal narratives such as Appleyard's. Her account also sits within a growing sub-genre which could be characterised as the personal midlife narrative presented to the external gaze, a phenomenon which may be a product of the postmodern blurring of boundaries between private and public domains of life (see Featherstone and Hepworth, 1988). Appleyard's article, in common with other such accounts, suggests that the way midlife is experienced is inextricably interconnected with the phenomenon of menopause. One of Gullette's central tenets is that women are culturally conditioned by the profusion of menopause discourses, which she collectively terms the 'menoboom' (1997, p 98), to accept the cultural view which conflates midlife with menopause, creating a single narrative of decline which is fundamentally gendered and to which all bodily changes are ascribed: 'if a man breaks a bone at forty, people say 'bad luck'; if a woman does, they tut-tut "osteoporosis". The culture fits *her* bone into a decline story' (1997, p 108).

Gullette argues that cultural discourses construct female ageing as a 'lifecourse decline narrative [which] requires at its pivot a critical moment, an event' (1997, p 98) and that the power of the 'menoboom' positions the menopause as the 'critical moment' for midlife women so that they are 'aged by culture' (1997, p 99) more profoundly than by biology. Greer (1991) notes that the proliferation in menopause literature in recent decades has generated a number of (generally negative) stereotypes, often rooted in the language of the diseased/ deficient/unproductive body. By way of an illustration of this point, the Deputy Governor of the Bank of England, Ben Broadbent, recently stated that 'the economy is at a menopausal moment' (*Guardian* online, 16 May 2018). When challenged, he explained that this was an accepted term within the Bank of England lexicon to signify an economy that is declining and no longer potent. Unsurprisingly, his comment generated considerable negative commentary.

Such discourses, and the underlying ideologies they represent, contextualise the analysis of Appleyard's narration of her own menopause experience. The semiotic resources (images, composition, text and so on) used to present her experience, as well as the evaluative stance they construct, immediately position her narrative for the reader. The headline statement reads: 'Welcome to my menopause nightmare: she's wrinkling like a prune, sweating like a bull – and going to bed with a man has never been so scary! A brutally honest yet life-affirming account of the menopause' (Appleyard, 2013).

The text is prominently positioned and used in combination with an image of the author that, far from reinforcing the textual message, adds a visual dimension which seems to work in subtle opposition to it. A full-body image of Appleyard smiling confidently at the reader, wearing a tight-fitting cocktail dress and high heels, is placed directly next to a headline inviting the reader directly into her 'menopause nightmare'. As Matheson (2005) argues, direct address has the effect of positioning/aligning the reader to a particular authorial standpoint – in this case Appleyard's evaluation of her feminine identity. Even before the reader-as-audience has had an opportunity to engage with the article's content, the combination of visual and verbal semiotic resources encodes a number of ideological assumptions: menopause, positioned in Gullette's words as 'a major life event' (1997, p 98), is discursively constructed as if it were a personal catastrophe, through intensified negatively evaluative lexical choices ('hell', 'nightmare', 'scary'). By conflating physical ageing and menopause ('she's wrinkling like a prune and sweating like a bull'), all changes to the body are attributed to this single phenomenon. There is a disjunction, though, in that while Appleyard's confidently smiling image implies that this is an experience with a tangible end, the accompanying headline presents her menopause as a 'nightmare' which is still ongoing.

The language Appleyard uses to describe the changes she perceives in her body is powerfully negative and in that sense can be seen as a product of prevailing cultural menopause ideology, reproduced in many media discourses: menopause as the origin of all negative bodily changes; menopause-as-illness; menopause as the defining and dividing event in the life course: 'here I am, 53 years old, wrinkling faster than a plum in the sun, hair thinning, more life behind me than in front of me – and now a fresh hell of decline to contemplate'.

Physical signs of ageing are not only conflated with unattractiveness but also constructed as harbingers of inevitable, nightmarish decrepitude ('a fresh hell of decline'). She expresses her most profound insecurities about the changes to her body in terms of loss: of fertility, youthfulness and sexual attractiveness, evoked through the use of personification:

> My friend jokes that she's been the victim of the 'Menopause Thief': he's taken her figure, quite a bit of her hair, her sex drive, and what she describes as 'my sense of myself as a woman'. I know what she means. He's taken quite a few bits of me too. (Appleyard, 2013)

Significantly, the 'Menopause Thief' is given a male persona, perhaps illustrating Greer's argument that this essentially female physical phenomenon has historically been appropriated and 'owned' by men. Furthermore, in the course of her narrative Appleyard often draws on the language of illness in evaluating her bodily changes: 'I ran home to consult my Family Health Encyclopaedia and blanched as I read the common symptoms of menopause'.

These discourses locate menopause in the domain of disease rather than 'normal' bodily process; the conflation of 'symptoms' of menopause with 'symptoms' of ageing not only reinforces the narrative of decline but also perpetuates a wider tendency to medicalise natural bodily changes.

However, Appleyard's greatest struggle with her changing body is rooted in culturally embedded perceptions of menopause as a desexualising force. According to Greer, this is another aspect of menopause mythology, originating in the male-generated essentialist discourses, which produced the cultural equation of fertility=femininity=sexual attractiveness. In the context of the complex conjunction of sex, gender and sexuality, the effect of de Beauvoir's well-known categorisation of women of a certain age as a 'third sex' (as mentioned earlier) is both to degender as well as to desexualise (post)menopausal women. Appleyard's own experience of the intersection of ageing and sexuality is framed in powerfully negative language:

> When my menopause first started I was single and wondering whether I would ever have sex again. Even if I was lucky enough to find a needle in a haystack at this 11th hour, I questioned whether I could bear to be seen naked by a man now that I am sagging, receding and creasing. (Appleyard, 2013)

There is an implicit contrast between her current unsparing evaluations of her ageing body and sexual attractiveness and earlier phases in her life in which the unquestioned assumption is that sexual confidence is a consequence of youthfulness. The lived impact of menopause on notions of femininity is painfully present in Appleyard's account. Greer, however, decouples femininity and femaleness, stating that 'what women in the climacteric are afraid of losing is not femininity, which can always be faked and probably is fake, but femaleness' (1991, p 59).

By contrast, Appleyard's experience suggests that, for her, femininity and femaleness are intimately interconnected – she fears the loss of libido as much as she fears the bodily changes she documents. Through her 'continuing investment in the insignia of a gendered body' (Woodward, 1991, p 3), the make-up she 'slathers on ... so as not to look like a dying old crone', Appleyard sustains a feminine self which is bound up with a socially constructed notion of youthfulness and central to her sense of *female* self.

Connecting public voices and individual experience

Appleyard's narrative, and accounts from the lived experience of the midlife women I interviewed in my own study (to be discussed later), indicate that the relationship between femininity and femaleness is complex, individual and co-dependent. The dimension of identity where notions of gender and sexual attractiveness intersect is where the desexualising potential of the menopause is most keenly felt. Appleyard's experience exemplifies a common linguistic feature of midlife narratives, also reflected in the data from my study, which is to conceptualise the lifecourse in terms of a binary division into 'before' and 'after'. 'Before' describes the pre-midlife period, generally positively evaluated, and characterised in terms of (relative) youthfulness, sexual and physical attractiveness, and fertility; 'after' represents the post-midlife phase, generally negatively evaluated, viewed as the entry point into old(er) age and therefore synonymous with decline, defined by loss of libido, attractiveness and fertility. Gullette's premise is that it is the power of cultural discourses which make the menopause into an artificial and needlessly momentous division in the lifecourse. There is, however, a powerful 'after-is-better' rhetoric in literary as well as media discourses. Greer states that: 'The object of facing up squarely to the fact of the climacteric is to acquire serenity and power. If women on the youthful side of the climacteric could glimpse what this state of peaceful potency might be, the difficulties of making the transition would be less' (Greer, 1991, p 9).

Arguably, the effect of linguistic encapsulations such as 'peaceful potency' is to sanitise and homogenise the messiness and diversity of individual experience, and indeed the after-is-better discourse may even constitute as much of a stereotype as the menopause-is-hell rhetoric. The analysis of these public menopause discourses shows that the messages they embody continue to be deeply influential for the way in which women such as Appleyard, as representatives of a wider female community, construct their age identity. Gullette argues strongly for the need to override 'both the biologism and the pessimism of the menoboom' (1997, p 103) and perhaps also to counterbalance the expectation of resolution. The data from the midlife women in my own study suggests that the pessimism of the menoboom which Gullette describes is still embedded in their lived experience.

Private voices: lived experience of menopause

As explained in the introduction, I contrast my discussion of public menopause discourses with analysis of individual women's lived experience of the menopause – the private voices. The data I draw on is from a larger piece of research carried out between 2012 and 2015 (see Anderson, 2019), which examined discourses of ageing more widely, and the role of menopause discourses as part of the relationship between cultural and individual constructions of ageing. The analytical focus of this wider study was the access it gave to a rich (relatively unexplored) corpus of commentary on women's day-to-day experience of ageing, against the backdrop of frequently negative, often conflicting public discourses of ageing. I wanted to understand how these public messages are received by the women they target and used in the process of constructing age and gender identity.

The menopause is intimately bound up in women's experience of ageing, therefore I have drawn on the individual accounts of the midlife cohort of women from my earlier research study. I use their stories to critically examine Appleyard's personal-yet-public narrative, and to add a more nuanced perspective to the feminist-academic lens of Gullette and Greer. The data gathered from these individual accounts has allowed unique insights into people's innermost feelings about ageing – a deeply personal, intimately experienced phenomenon that is lived, monitored and evaluated as part of the texture of daily life – and an empirical perspective on how the complex process of constructing and expressing gender and age identity is managed in everyday life. The limited scope of my original study meant restricting my sample: my analytical focus was the impact of ageing on gender, therefore representing different age categories drove recruitment. It is important to acknowledge that as a consequence, in terms of other markers of identity, the sample is a necessarily narrow one; my participants are white, heterosexual, mostly professional (with one exception) British, middle-class women. Key intersections such as race, class, culture, sexual orientation are not explored here but undoubtedly point to opportunities for future research. For the purposes of this chapter the focus is primarily on the midlife women in my sample, experiencing their ageing at a specific point in the twenty-first century, in a specific cultural context.

Pinnacle and decline

The cultural visibility of the 'new middle age' (Featherstone and Hepworth, 1988, p 383) and the uneasy territory it occupies between the (culturally-driven) requirement for youthfulness and the imperatives of appropriate ageing makes midlife contested terrain. Among the midlife women in my study, and perhaps more widely, this makes the process of identity construction an uncertain and risky undertaking. While it could be argued that attitudes to ageing are shifting and that the cultural, linguistic and visual repertoire is becoming more flexible, it can also be argued that powerful cultural 'master narratives' (Gullette, 1997, p 8 and passim) continue to appropriate the process of ageing, and in doing so shape individual attitudes profoundly. One of these, which appears as a recurring motif in many participants' accounts, is the notion of 'pinnacle and decline', whereby the expectation of a (culturally constructed) sense of 'being in one's prime' is followed by an inevitable (culturally constructed) decline. Twigg's analysis exemplifies how this and other 'master messages' are embedded – almost taken for granted – in the narratives of magazines such as *Vogue*: 'for magazines like *Vogue*, however, aging sets in early, starting at the point at which youth begins to fade, often regarded as the late twenties' (2010, p 473).

My analysis shows that participants' individual stances appear to owe much of their construction and ideological foundation to such cultural-media appropriation of ageing. For participants in their twenties, the pinnacle is the present moment, briefly enjoyed, which already carries within it the sense of accompanying decline: "You know we must make the most of our 20s 'cos it's all downhill from there (laughs)" (female, 23).

For the midlife women in the sample, the perspective is retrospective, with the sense that the intervening period of time between the 'optimum year' and the present has been a falling away from that pinnacle, as this example reveals: "I took out a photograph of when I was probably the age that I liked myself best at … 27 … I would say that was the sort of optimum year physically" (female, 56). The language of this pinnacle moment, common to all participants who talk about it, suggests an assumption already taken for granted by the second decade, that the lifecourse is constructed around a brief peak which is at the same time a foreshadowing of the inevitability of decline ('it's all downhill from there').

The notion of pinnacle and decline is particularly powerful for the midlife participants in that it is bound up in the complex constellation of discourses around menopause as the trigger for the cultural narrative of 'better Before, worse After' discussed previously. Implicit in the idea of 'pinnacle', along with youthfulness and physical prime, is fertility and sexual subjecthood. Conversely, 'decline' is understood in terms of diminishing physical attractiveness, intimately interlinked with loss of fertility and sexuality. A 45-year-old woman says: "I'm conscious that at some point my menstrual cycle will start to change I don't know when that will be … but thinking about the menopause is quite horrific." She expands on what she means by 'horrific': "Well that means that I'm no longer … I am definitely middle-aged basically I'm no longer able to produce children … I've got this image of kind of shrivelling up and drying and you know drying up."

What this participant dreads most about the onset of menopause is the loss of fertility; the lexical group she draws on ('drying up', 'shrivelling') conveys at a literal level the drying up of bodily fluids related to fertility, and at a metaphorical level, the drying up of the forces which constitute her sense of self-identity and which drive her sexual energy. Tellingly, she still recalls how her father characterised the start of her menstrual cycle: "I remember my dad saying to me when my periods started really embarrassing 'oh you're a woman now.'" His words may continue to resonate with her because they echo wider cultural attitudes towards the menopause: if the start of menstruation symbolises transition into womanhood, then the end of reproductive life marks the transition to something less than womanhood. Her subsequent comment, "you therefore cease to become [sic] a woman" is an unconscious echo of de Beauvoir's notion of a 'third sex' (1949 [1997], p 63) and suggests that her projection of life post-menopause is more complex than merely a phase of decline. This participant is calling into question the foundations of her gendered identity, seeing herself consigned by culture and biology to the genderless, desexualised hinterland described by de Beauvoir as 'not male but no longer female' (1949 [1997], p 63).

For another midlife participant, the menopause also marks an unwelcome transition to a sort of decline: "Up until a couple of months ago, I was having regular periods and then I was having hot flushes and I said, 'am I in the menopause …?' But what I hated about it is I started to wonder, 'ooh I feel a little uncomfortable now I wonder if that's menopause'?" (female, 54). Her anxiety has a specific, slightly different point of origin: "I don't think it's loss of fertility it's I don't want to feel bad and I want to have a healthy sex life for as long as possible." She fears the loss of physical and sexual energy more than the loss of her reproductive ability. However, both women view the menopause as the harbinger of inevitable decline, a perception that can be tracked back to public menopause discourses. The dominance of such menopause commentary – the 'menoboom' (see Gullette, 1997) leads these women to view it as a physical as well as an emotional phenomenon, a profoundly significant transition marker, heralding the decline after the pinnacle, the start of a life stage defined by loss: of youthfulness; energy; fertility; sexuality; and femininity. The force and intensity of the negative language used by both women is notable and does point to the influence of the cultural problematisation of the menopause. Counter-discourses that attempt to construct post-menopause more positively (for example Greer's writing in the early 1990s, and more recently the accounts of female celebrities such as Dawn French, Emma Thompson and Cynthia Nixon (Sutton, 2018)) have seemingly yet to make an impact on how the menopause is experienced by women in their everyday lives.

Conclusion

This chapter, and the wider study from which it is drawn, has discussed the complex, often contested relationship between age, gender and sex, symbolised by the life stage 'event' of the menopause, which is still constructed by cultural discourses and individual perceptions as the signifier of the prevailing age-as-decline narrative. Within a cultural context in which 'successful' femininity equates youthfulness, beauty, sexual desirability and fertility, there is little place for the ageing female body. What is perhaps less well documented and understood is the way in which the continuing pathologisation of the menopause in mainstream media means that the cultural as well as the subjective gaze continues to conflate female ageing with loss: of fertility; of femininity; of sexual desirability; of visibility. These powerful voices desexualise and degender the ageing female body, leaving older women without a culturally approved trajectory for ageing, required to maintain a youthful, attractive appearance by the same cultural 'rules' which deny these attributes to older women.

Although attitudes to the menopause may be slowly changing in public discourse, it seems there is yet to be a real impact on individual lived experience, as evidenced by the individual accounts I have drawn on. Although this is a small-scale study, it nonetheless raises the possibility of a more generalisable conclusion: currently, it appears that the notion of an older (post-menopausal) woman who can still be sexual remains too challenging for the narrow ideological, visual and linguistic repertoire of prevailing culture. Collectively we seem unable to accommodate an idea of ageing which permits sexual desirability, and an understanding of sexual desirability which can encompass the ageing female body.

The research undertaken here has an important contribution to make, not only as a contribution to the body of research on age, gender and sexuality within the field of language and gender studies, but also in the wider business environment where women are increasingly visible, but where attitudes towards older women are still slow to shift. My wider study (Anderson, 2019) exposes the conflicted and contested nature of cultural attitudes to ageing as they are focused on the female body. My research has sought to give a voice to women themselves, to understand the impact of prevailing age ideology on the complex, day-to-day business of identity construction. Many further research directions suggest themselves, for which this study is only a starting point. Debates on ageing, menopause and sexuality need to be broadened to include other intersectionalities (race, sexuality, non-binary genders and so on), to allow a more meaningful challenge to the 'menoboom' by generating new thinking, new ways of talking which start to normalise the menopause and decouple it from its desexualising power. Such insights have potentially powerful applications in the wider domain of advertising and brand communication in raising awareness about the language used about and by older women, and in doing so, even in a small way, to start to change the conversation.

Notes

1 'Menoboom' is Gullette's term, taken from her 1997 book *Declining to Decline: Cultural Combat and the Politics of Midlife*.
2 The Labour Party is a centre-left political party in the UK, one of the three main political parties. The Labour Party lost conclusively to the Conservative Party (led by Boris Johnson) in the 2019 UK General Election.

References

Anderson, C. (2019) *Discourses of Ageing and Gender: The Impact of Public and Private Voices on the Identity of Ageing Women*. Switzerland: Palgrave Macmillan.

Appleyard, M. (2013) 'Welcome to My Menopause Nightmare', *Daily Mail*, 28 October 2013.

Ballaster, R. et al (1991) *Women's Worlds: Ideology, Femininity and the Woman's Magazine*. Basingstoke and London: Macmillan.

Bartky, S.L. (1990) *Femininity and Domination*. New York: Routledge.

Berger, J. (1972) *Ways of Seeing*. London: Penguin.

Bordo, S. (1993) *Unbearable Weight*. Los Angeles: University of California.

Chaney, D. (1996) *Lifestyles*. London and New York: Routledge.

De Beauvoir, S. (1949) *The Second Sex*. London: Vintage (Published in paperback 1997).

Faircloth, C. (ed.) (2003) *Aging Bodies: Images of Everyday Experience*. California: AltaMira Press.

Featherstone, M. (1982 [1991]) 'The Body in Consumer Culture', in Featherstone, M., Hepworth, M. and Turner, B. (eds) *The Body: Social Process and Cultural Theory*. London: SAGE.

Featherstone, M. (1988) 'The Mask of Ageing and the Postmodern Lifecourse', in Featherstone, M., Hepworth, M. and Turner, B. (eds) *The Body: Social Process and Cultural Theory*. London: SAGE.

Ferguson, M. (1983) *Forever Feminine: Women's Magazines and the Cult of Femininity*. London: Heinemann.

Furman, F. (1997) *Facing the Mirror*. London: Routledge.

Greer, G. (1991) *The Change: Women, Ageing and the Menopause*. London: Penguin.

Gullette, M. (1997) *Declining to Decline: Cultural Combat and the Politics of Midlife*. Charlottesville: University Press of Virginia.

Karpf, A. (2014) 'Older Models: The Women in Their 60s, 70s and 80s Who Are Shaking Up Fashion', *Guardian Weekend*, 22 February 2014.

Markson, E. (2003) 'The Female Aging Body Through Film', in Faircloth, C. (ed.) *Aging Bodies: Images and Everyday Experiences*. Walnut Creek: AltaMira Press.

Matheson, D. (2005) *Media Discourses: Analysing Media Texts*. Maidenhead: Open University Press (Reprinted 2010).

Oberg, P. (2003) 'Images versus Experience of the Aging Body', in Faircloth, C. (ed.) *Aging Bodies: Images and Everyday Experiences*. Walnut Creek: AltaMira Press.

Railton, D. and Watson, P. (2012) '"She's so Vein": Madonna and the Drag of Aging', in Dolan, J.M. and Tincknell, E. (eds) *Aging Femininities*. Newcastle upon Tyne: Cambridge Scholars Press.

Scanlon, J. (ed.) (2000) *The Gender and Consumer Culture Reader*. New York: New York University Press.

Shilling, C. (2003) *The Body and Social Theory* (2nd edn). London: SAGE.

Silver, C. (2003) 'Gendered Identities in Old Age: Toward (De) Gendering?', *Journal of Aging Studies*, 17(4): 379–97.

Sutton, M. (2018) '11 Celebrities Get Real About Going Through the Menopause', 3 July. www.goodhousekeeping.com

Twigg, J. (2010) 'How does *Vogue* Negotiate Age? Fashion, the Body and the Older Woman', *Fashion Theory: The Journal of Dress, Body & Culture*, 14(4): 471–90.

Wearing, S. (2007) 'Subjects of Rejuvenation: Aging in Postfeminist Culture', in Tasker, Y. and Negra, D. (eds) *Interrogating Post-Feminism*. Durham and London: Duke University Press.

Williamson, J. (1978) *Decoding Advertisements*. London: University of Glasgow.

Winship, J. (1987) *Inside Women's Magazines*. London: Random Press.

Woodward, K. (1991) *Aging and Its Discontents*. Bloomington and Indianapolis: Indiana University Press.

Woodward, K. (ed.) (1999) *Figuring Age*. Bloomington: Indiana University Press.

Woodward, K. (2006) 'Performing Age, Performing Gender', *NSWA Journal*, 18(1): 162–86.

6

Ageing, physical disability and desexualisation

Susan Gillen and Paul Reynolds

Older people experience their sexual and intimate relations as intersectional agents. Their relationships are influenced not simply by age itself, but by gender, ethnicity, sexuality, class and other identarian differences. It is not necessary to subscribe fully to the benefits of intersectionality as a theoretical paradigm to recognise the impact of difference on how older people enjoy or endure the process of ageing (for relevant summaries of intersectionality, see Hancock, 2016; Hill Collins, 2019; May, 2015; Taylor, Hines and Casey, 2011). These differences extend to the sexual and intimate constraints and limitations that constitute desexualisation. This is particularly the case with the intersection of age and physical disability, which becomes more significant as the body ages and its functionality tends to decline. While the rate and form of that decline is differentiated dependent on variables such as robust physical health, income and resources and access to healthcare, the general proposition holds. Bérubé (cited in Gallop, 2019, p 7), commenting on this convergence, sagely observes: '[that] many of us will become disabled if we live long enough is perhaps the fundamental aspect of human embodiment'. These changes are exacerbated by the shared cultural prejudices and pathologies that dominate common perceptions of older people and disability. These perceptions produce material physical and regulatory constraints alongside ideological orthodoxies and internalised discursive framings by which older people's sexual agency is diminished and subsumed beneath notions of 'healthy' and 'normal' sex and intimacy.

Both age and physical disability share common desexualising factors and impacts. Both are steeped in conventionally negative, normative characterisations of physical change across the life course, with changes measured by scientific-medical criteria with a culturally determined functional index. Bodily change or difference impacts on the capabilities and everyday experience of individuals but is considerably more pronounced and compounded by social and cultural discursive representations. They both carry equivalent prejudices, pathologies and assumptions about sex and intimacy, and communicate subordinated positions within late capitalist modern societies, where the capacity to labour and physically participate in economic activity is privileged (indicatively, Campbell and Oliver, 1996; Phillipson, 1982). While the character of pathologies of age and disability may differ, their architectures are similar, and one common feature of that architecture is that both age and disability are subject to desexualisation – older and disabled people do not want sexual intimacy, or are incapable of or have diminished sexual performance, or are not sufficiently sexually attractive to motivate it. As ageing invariably involves the development of degrees of physical impairment, the correspondence between age and disability is progressive and complementary. Older disabled people will experience ageing as a deterioration of their impaired capabilities. Both processes – ageing and disability – are reciprocally reinforcing.

For the purposes of this chapter, the focus of analysis is on physical disabilities. Intellectual disabilities will be the focus of the next chapter. Physical disability takes in disabilities that have an impact upon, or offer a challenge to, 'normal' physical functions and the capacity to operate within the boundaries of social conventions and customs, social and cultural spaces, places and representations, and the material environment (see Barnes et al, 2010; Goodley, 2016). The focus is on two intersected identities: disabled people whose intimate lives are impacted through ageing; and older people who experience physical disability as a feature of ageing (there is a lively terminological debate as to whether to talk of disabled people or people with disabilities or other such formulations. There is not space to represent it here, but the authors subscribe to social/queer/crip approaches and use 'disabled people' without accepting that this implies an individualising pathology rather than a product of social processes). Across these approaches, there is both the incidence of physical condition and disabling environment, and the way in which cultural representations and prejudices internalise the association of diminishing ability with the ageing process within older people. As such, external pathologies are absorbed and reinforced by older people themselves.

The chapter begins with a discussion of key paradigms and models of disability and how they provide an analysis of the age–disability intersection as desexualised. It will then look at some of the recent studies that have explored the desexualising impact of the intersection of age and physical disability. One general conclusion from such a review is that this area, while it may touch a majority of people by the end of their life course, is relatively under-researched and reflects a paucity of studies. It will then consider the implications and responses to the issues raised and the problems created for older people with disabilities that impact on their intimate lives.

From impairment to disability to crip: theorising disability

The concept of disability (and its development as a field of study) is complex and contested (see indicatively Goodley, 2014, 2016). How 'deficits' of ability are identified and characterised, and what it means to bring together 'disability' as both a social process and as the physical composition of individual 'deficit' (such as deficit from what?) are critical questions. The World Health Organisation (WHO) focused on function, impairment and social and environmental factors in its revised international classification (ICIDH-2):

> Functioning refers to all body functions, activities and participation as an umbrella term; similarly, disability serves as an umbrella term for impairments, activity limitations or participation restrictions. ICIDH-2 also lists environmental factors that interact with all these constructs. In this way, it provides a useful profile of individuals' functioning, disability and health in various domains. (WHO, 2001, p 1)

This illustrates a central problem in disability studies that is relevant to the intersection with older people. If a central criterion is the capacity to function in a culture normalised around 'able-bodiedness', where do individual impairments end and disabling social-cultural factors begin, and how is such differentiation operated, incorporated into and tested in both theorising and developing policy and practice? The space between the social process and practices that constitute a disabling context and the instantiation of disability as a feature of individuals, framed as 'impairments', is both different, dependent on the wide varieties of impairments, and blurred as a conceptual attribution of individual happenstance or sociocultural structure.

Impairment is used to describe physical deficits that impede what would be regarded as 'normal' physical activities (functions). Impairments can be visible or invisible, ranging from being a wheelchair user without the use of legs or with restrictive movement due to a form of arthritis, to hearing or speech impairment, or conditions like diabetes and cerebral palsy that have physical effects. This 'normal' upon which

97

'impairment' departs is based upon a naturalised notion of how the form and function of the human body and the species genus 'human' should be constituted at its 'optimal' state. Like any abstraction, this 'optimal' form is an ideal measure against which people's 'abilities' are valued (so degrees of mobility, height/weight appropriateness, dexterity). While the ideal does not resemble human experience, it persists as a measure that organises differences hierarchically rather than seeing them as particular and incommensurate.

The focus on impairment as a feature of the individual or an individual condition is dominated by a medical model and its focus on bodily function, where medical responses attempt to minimise or manage the impact of impairments, for example through the prescription of prosthesis or surgical or pharmaceutical interventions. While this clearly can improve the lives of individuals with impairments, Illich (2010) and Illich, Zola and McKnight (1992) have provoked a considerable literature on the issues of professional power and limited accountability, the objectification of 'treatment subjects' and the influences of capital and state authority on the shaping of the character, scope and limitations to medical responses.

The last 30 years of disability studies has coalesced around a far clearer emphasis on the social and cultural construction of disability (Barnes et al, 2002; Barnes et al, 2010; Charlton, 2006; Goodley, 2014, 2016; Oliver, 2009; Shakespeare, 2000, 2017). This focus centres on the impacts of a disabling society, where culture, spatial planning and architecture is built upon a modernist model of the functionally able body (Swain et al, 2013). The social model recognises the exclusionary, oppressive and discriminatory character of everyday life for disabled people. It focuses on sociocultural barriers to participation, belonging and the enjoyment of equity with 'able-bodied' people in work, leisure and home lives. It recognises these barriers are attitudinal–ideological, physical–environmental and language–communicative, and historically and culturally deeply embedded in society. Disability relates more to the social consequences of ableism as a dominant model of social, economic, political and cultural functioning than it does impairment.

The social model of disability refocuses attention upon the normalisation and naturalisation processes that both 'other' disabled people as 'lacking' and have disabled people and those who live and work with them internalise that 'othering'. Disabled people take ownership of pathologies and prejudices, self-identifying by their disability – so as to become 'the amputee', for example, as opposed to a person with an amputation. Those who work and care for them make a similar attribution sympathetically in seeking to support disabled people. This is classically illustrated in the discursive example of 'does he take sugar?', where 'able' people objectify disabled people in the process of interacting with/supporting them (see Guthrie, 1973 and Rogers and Marsden, 2013).

The medical (individual) and social models are juxtaposed as antagonistic. Jones (2001, p 377) reflects that: 'one side implies that if you are an advocate of the medical model you can't understand social impact, and the other that if you advocate the social model you must ignore physical impairment'. Reindal (2000, p 93) observes that this dichotomisation is reflected in scholarship, between non-disabled scholars who begin with the presuppositions of individual impairment and disabled scholars who recognise the validity of the social model, noting: 'individual models of disability, equating the problem of disability to impairments and individual conditions, is itself a discrimination against disabled people'. Harris, responding to Reindal and critical of the social model and its proponents, has argued:

> It seems to me that the correct approach is to say that disabilities are, as I have argued, physical or mental conditions that constitute a harm to the individual, which a rational person would wish to be without. It is also true that social exclusion, discrimination, ostracism and hostility are also conditions of life which a rational person would wish to be without. We need to concentrate on both. (Harris, 2000, p 98)

Siebers provides a nuanced assessment of the scope and limits to the social model:

> It is tempting, in fact, to see disability exclusively as the product of a bad match between social design and some human bodies, since this is so often the case. But disability may also trouble the theory of social construction. Disability scholars have begun to insist that strong constructionism either fails to account for the difficult physical realities faced by people with disabilities or presents their body in ways that are conventional, conformist, and unrecognizable to them. These include the habits of privileging performativity over corporeality, favoring pleasure to pain, and describing social success in terms of intellectual achievement, bodily adaptability, and active political participation. The disabled body seems difficult for the theory of social construction to

absorb: disability is at once its best example and a significant counterexample. (Siebers, 2001, p 740)

The desexualisation at the intersection of age and disability involves both a normalised notion of sex and intimacy that occludes difference in expressions and practices (that might not be penetrative, for example) and reinforces attendant pathologies and prejudicial representations. This is not to play down the impact of tangible physical changes that might be regarded as impairments but would note that the functional – penetrative and reproductive – model against which impairment may be measured represents only a small part of the possibilities of sexual and intimate pleasure. The 'normal' notion of what is sexual is reinforced by the reproduction of sexual products and representations – from sex toys to porn to social policies, provisions and practices in dealing with the sexual needs of older and disabled people. This implies the need for critical responses that are both personal and political, both aimed at enabling individuals in their changing circumstances and engaging in political change on a social and cultural level, as Oliver (2009) suggests. While social causation and constraint is recognised, the recognition of changed functionality can easily fall into medicalised traps that normalise hetero- (or homo-)normative sexualities and genito-centric penetrative practices as the domain of sex.

The more radical voices in disability studies are critical of the social model. There has always been a strand of disability studies that has focused on a Marxist-influenced analysis of the exploitative, oppressive and alienating way capitalism and class society structures disability (see Oliver and Barnes, 2012). Calder (2011) frames the politics of disability in the context of the Fraser-Honneth debate (2003) around the politics of recognition, arguing that while much of disability politics has coalesced around the recognition (and representation/participation) of disabled people, Fraser's notion of 'participatory parity' points to the limits of recognition and the necessity of addressing other factors, including the redistribution of power and resources. Calder directs attention towards the capabilities approach (selectively, Alexander, 2016; Clark et al, 2019; Nussbaum, 2013; Robeyns, 2017). Calder points to Anderson's analysis, drawing from a capabilities approach, which is worth quoting at length:

to be capable of functioning as an equal citizen involves not just the ability to effectively exercise specifically political rights, but also to participate in the various activities of civil society more broadly, including participation in the economy ... as a human being, as a participant in a system of cooperative production, and as a citizen of a democratic state. To be capable of functioning as a human being requires effective access to the means of sustaining one's biological existence—food, shelter, clothing, medical care—and access to the basic conditions of human agency – knowledge of one's circumstances and options, the ability to deliberate about means and ends, the psychological conditions of autonomy, including the self-confidence to think and judge for oneself, freedom of thought and movement. To be capable of functioning as an equal participant in a system of cooperative production requires effective access to the means of production, access to the education needed to develop one's talents, freedom of occupational choice, the right to make contracts and enter into cooperative agreements with others, the right to receive fair value for one's labor, and recognition by others of one's productive contributions. To be capable of functioning as a citizen requires rights to political participation, such as freedom of speech and the franchise, and also effective access to the goods and relationships of civil society. This entails freedom of association, access to public spaces such as roads, parks, and public accommodations including public transportation, the postal service, and telecommunications. This also entails the social conditions of being accepted by others, such as the ability to appear in public without shame, and not being ascribed outcast status. The freedom to form relationships in civil society also requires effective access to private spaces, since many such relationships can only function when protected from the scrutiny and intrusions of others. Homelessness—that is, having only public dwelling—is a condition of profound unfreedom. (Anderson, 1999, pp 317–18)

Shakespeare and Watson (2002) suggest the weaknesses of the 'modernist' social model – the duality of impairment and disability and the construction of disability identity – might be better superseded by a discursively constructed embodied ontology that they associate with post-structuralism. This elides with Shildrick's (2012) framing of critical disability studies, which focuses on taking difference and its subjectivities seriously, recognising that bodies constitute a discursive subject from which critical engagement can elude modernist dichotomies such as impairment/dichotomy. Shildrick recognises the impact of feminist, postcolonial and queer theory in constructing such a shift in focus, which promises a focus on disability and sexuality (and age) by its queer and embodied concept.

Crip theory has common characteristics with queer theory in: rejecting ableist normativities; rejecting foundational categories about human experience; emphasising the centrality of subjective experience and perception; encouraging transgression as a means of asserting self and rejecting the limits and constraints of the (in this case sexual, ageist and ableist) construction of bodies as natural, normal and normative (Kafer, 2013, and from a feminist crip queer approach, McRuer, 2006; McRuer and Mollow, 2012). This involves rejections of normative notions of dysfunction, illness, disability, (aesthetic) ugliness and the dichotomy of normative/non-normative wants and desires. These characteristics breed abjection, disgust and failure, which invariably produces desexualisation or labels older and disabled people's sex and intimacy as a subject of exception or perversion (Moore and Reynolds, 2016). Building on this, Abrams (2016) draws on queer phenomenology to articulate a politics that takes disability within an embodied and sensory ontology. Gallop (2019), in developing a notion of queer temporality, draws from contemporary literature a clear understanding that the disciplines used to study subjectivities – for example, gerontology in studying ageing – themselves embed naturalised and normalised life course categories that limit radical reframing. Crip/queer theory proposes revolutionary change in how being older and disabled is seen in terms of intimate lives. Gullette (2011, p 143) puts it succinctly: 'Queering the whole sexual life course … seems a more radical sexual revolution than history has known.'

The sum of these critical approaches to disability is a trajectory that shifts from a focus on deficit and a disabling society to a focus on the discursive forces that constitute the ability/disability conceptualisation and inscribe bodies with particular characterisations. This refocusing, and the problematisation of disability as something exercised upon and instantiated in people, rather than a singular property of them, provides a critical agenda for explorations of sex and intimacy in older people's lives. What crip/queer adds is a sense that the constitution of sex and intimate relations, expressed through different subjectivities, is not only constrained by social disablement – the very categorisation of sex, intimacy, age and disability provides a patina of discourses, representations and effects that continually act upon the sexual agents' sense of themselves, their bodies and their capabilities, how they are seen by others, and through social and cultural organisation. Or as

Siebers (2001, p 742) observes: 'The central issue for the politics of representation is not whether bodies are infinitely interpretable but whether certain bodies should be marked as defective and how the people who have these bodies may properly represent their interests in the public sphere'. In this case of the age–physical ability intersection, desexualisation constitutes a form by which ageing, sex and disability are constituted by defective or deficient categories and characterisations. Desexualisation impedes the capacity of sexual agents to exercise choice and experimentation beyond pathological representations of older/disabled bodies, or have positive sexual and intimate agency represented positively in the public sphere (for example, the promotion of pleasurable sex lives).

This is not simply a conceptual question, as policy is guided by judgements of cost and benefit (and attributed responsibility) in relation, for example, to changes to urban architectures and services to enable different impairments such as wheelchairs. When impairments and disability based on age is factored into discussion, there is a politics of both identity (where does disability and the politics of disabled people end if most people experience some form in the life course?), policy priorities and concepts of functioning in society. In the case of the desexualisation of older disabled people, where reproduction and stereotypical sexual experimentation can be said to be largely past, prioritisation might go to younger and work-age people with particular visible conditions, and as the population increases with age, there is little political impetus to engage. We will return to this in the conclusion.

Dimensions of the intersection: older people, physical disability and intimate lives

There is a paucity of literature and research on ageing, sex and intimacy. Priestly (2003), for example, takes a life course approach to disability that acknowledges ageing and bodily change but has little focus on sex or intimate relations. This is indicative of the field, and much of what follows covers elements of this intersectional convergence that can be developed towards a research agenda for ageing, sex, intimacy and disability.

The dimensions of the intersection are considerable. Notwithstanding that some older people age without disability (Manini, 2011), there is a heightened incidence of disability and function in a global ageing population (WHO, 2011). The United Nations (2020) estimates 46 per cent of over-sixties globally have disabilities, with risk proportionate and progressive by age, so that those in the 80–89 age bracket have the highest rate of risk (WHO, 2011). This trend includes both people 'ageing with disability' and those 'ageing into disability' (Verbrugge and Yang, 2002). Differences in life course experiences are balanced by commonalities in terms of support needs, potentially alleviating reduced autonomy and reliance on family and/or service provision, which may restrict sexual activity/interest. Those ageing with disability are not immune to the chronic diseases that contribute to disability in older people. Griffith et al (2010) includes, not exhaustively, heart and foot problems, arthritis, vision and cognitive impairment, chronic respiratory and cardiovascular disease, with co-morbidities also a common problem globally and increasing with age (also, Barnett et al, 2012). WHO (2020) highlights how chronic diseases were linked to approximately 46 per cent of the global burden of disease in 2011, and this is expected to increase to 57 per cent by 2020.

The burden and convergence of chronic disease and disability in later life impacts on older people's sexual health and wellbeing. The English Longitudinal Study on Ageing (ELSA) highlighted a link between increasing age and a decrease in sexual activity; it noted how poor health was associated with lower levels of sexual activity and higher rates of sexual dysfunction, such as problems with becoming sexually aroused, achieving orgasm (mainly for women) and erectile function difficulties (Lee et al, 2016). Similarly, Erens et al (2019) emphasised the negative impact of poor health/disability on sexual activity. Integrating the Third British National Survey of Sex, Attitudes and Lifestyles (Natsal-3, 2010–12) with their own research, they concluded that more than one in four men and one in six women see themselves as having a health condition/disability that impacts on their sexuality, yet only a minority sought professional health. A focus on people over 60 found that alongside physical changes associated with ageing, such as erectile dysfunction and vaginal dryness, chronic diseases such as cardiovascular, diabetes, cancers and chronic respiratory diseases, along with some medications, impacted negatively on both sexual capacity and desire (Merghati-Khoei et al, 2016). The reasons for this varied, but included: mood and energy; a lack of self-confidence, esteem and self-concept; a fear/consciousness of physical appearance; extant and reinforced culturally hegemonic representations encouraging stereotypical beliefs about ageing and illness and the stigmatisation of older age sexual activity; the impacts of chronic diseases and physiological changes impacting on sexual function/activity; and psychological and interpersonal factors. These highlight not only physical factors but the power of sociocultural discourses (Træen et al, 2017).

These desexualising trends run counter to the recognition of sex and sexuality as 'a central aspect of being human throughout life' (WHO, 2006), with its expression a basic human right for all people (Kessel, 2001) regardless of age or disability (WHO, 2006). Sexual agency and expression are regarded as central to human health and wellbeing over the life course and may serve to reduce some of the physical consequences associated with ageing, and their enhancement might mitigate disabling factors (DeLameter, 2012; Hillman, 2012; Brody, 2010; DeLameter and Moorman, 2007).

The significance of sexual agency for older people and those with physical disabilities is under-researched but nevertheless supported by the growing body of literature in these – separate – fields (for example, Bahner, 2019 for an overview of the literature related to 'disability and sexuality'). Research on the lived experiences of disability and sexuality is still 'thin on the ground' (Shakespeare and Richardson, 2018, p 82), often framed in terms of capacity, technique, fertility and abuse (indicatively, Sellwood et al, 2017), and with too little reference to sexual feelings and emotions (one exception is Liddiard, 2013). Santos and Santos (2017, p 2), for example, focus on 'how intimacy remains domesticized within the constraining grid of expectations, roles and norms that outlaws (at least culturally) nonnormative sexual practices and subjects'. They explore the experience of disabled women feeling desexualised as 'misfits' through dominant discourses of heteronormativity, focused on genito-centric penetration, alongside infantilising and dehumanising ableist discourse, in a way that inevitably fails to recognise the difference of disabled women's bodies and their ways of gaining sexual pleasure and satisfaction.

This is a consequence of scholarship focused on the conventional areas of gender, class, race and sexuality to the exclusion of disability and age (Meekosha and Shuttleworth, 2009), notwithstanding the declarations of critical sexuality studies and the sociology of sexualities stressing the significance of intersectionality (Gamson and Moon, 2004).

There are few studies that look at the intersections of 'age and disability' and touch on intimacy (Denninger, 2020; McGrath et al, 2016). What research has taken place has been criticised for: essentialising the categories of 'age' or 'disability' (McGrath and Lynch, 2013); giving primacy over disability in an attempt to give a voice to those with disabilities, resulting in the neglect of other intersections (Goethals et al, 2015); producing binary data which results from a 'with or without' disability focus (Goethals et al, 2015); or where disability (or age) has been the main focus with another intersection 'added', rather than focusing on a mutually interdependent or interactive circumstance (Yuval and Davis cited in Goethals et al, 2015). Larsson and Jönson (2018) note, for example, that older people have been excluded from disability activism, research and policies, or programmes that benefit the younger disabled. They argue that the tendency to use stereotyped age norms that divide the life courses into stages results in older disabled people being seen simply as 'older', resulting in a 'loss' of the significance of the identity intersections. This invariably has an impact in respect of considering sex and intimacy.

There are some factors that can be drawn from research focused on the intersections of 'ageing and sexuality' and of 'disability and sexuality', which emphasise the desexualisation of older people and people with disabilities through the themes of taboo, appropriate policy and service provision and inequalities.

The taboo of older age sex is not dissimilar to that of people with disabilities, often categorised as asexual or deviant. Gott (2005) highlights two broad and prejudicial representations of later life that dominate contemporary views of later life sexuality – the 'asexual old age' and the 'sexy oldie'. Other representations draw attention to the dangerous predatory nature of the 'prowling cougar' (Hillman, 2012) and the 'dirty old man' (Walz, 2002), or highlight the combination of sex and old age as 'being a joke' (Bytheway et al, 2007). Media-reinforced stereotypes of beautiful people having amazing sex perpetuate normative conceptions that communicate anxiety, and encourage the marginalisation and exclusion of non-normative bodies such as physically disabled people (Shildrick, 2007). The UK Department of Work and Pensions (DWP) reported public perceptions that people with mobility impairments being sexual was regarded as 'repulsive' (Grewal et al, 2002). Liddiard (2018, p 2) asserts that most disabled people are portrayed as asexual, lacking capability, capacity and desire for sex, where their sexual agency and selfhood are 'stripped away through stereotypes of eternal innocence and passivity'. Alternatively, like the representations of older people as 'asexual and cougars/dirty old men', she argues that people with disabilities can be 'cast as objects of fetish: exploited and abused – the vulnerable subjects of devotees' on the one hand or 'hypersexual and in need of containment'. She argues that for disabled people, sex does not fit with the dominant constructions of disabled people as vulnerable and childlike. This reinforces and replicates historical tendencies to infantilise and dehumanise both people with disabilities and older people, resulting in their desexualisation.

These conceptions of older/disabled people lead to risk-averseness in service provision (Bahner, 2019). Tepper (2000, p 285) observes that 'Sexuality as a source of pleasure and as an expression of love …

[is] not readily recognized for populations that have been traditionally marginalized in society'. This is demonstrated where people with disabilities live in a care home setting and can be subject to a 'desexualising silence', where sexuality is ignored, brushed aside and seen as 'non-essential', combined with poor/lack of training or lack of relevant policies, which compounds the issue (Bahner, 2019, p 4). Sexual and intimate behaviours other than those considered acceptable (e.g. touching, stroking), raised the greatest concerns among staff and were sometimes activity discouraged (Archibald, 1998; Nagarathnam and Gayagay, 2002). This is compounded by stereotypical views held by health professionals of older people as asexual, where the subject of older people and sex is largely taboo (Gott et al, 2004, cited in Benbow and Beeston, 2012) resulting in care home staff 'regard[ing] this as an activity that should be controlled and curtailed' (Haijar and Kamel, 2003, cited in Bauer et al, 2007, p 67).

The link between service provision and policy is highlighted by Bahner's (2019) empirical study of four countries – Sweden, England, Australia and the Netherlands – in which she develops her 'abstract notion of sexual citizenship' with the intention of making it 'practically relevant' for disabled people, service providers and policy makers (Bahner, 2019, p i). She observed a variability in policy approaches to support disabled people in expressing their sexuality, where the focus in England on issues related to vulnerability or abuse leads to issues of sex and sexuality being essentially absent (Bahner, 2019, p 98). Nor has the disability movement focused specifically on advocating sexual rights for disabled people, and although there is the provision of information and awareness raising (Bahner, 2019, p 214). Their attention has focused on other policy priorities, such as responses to austerity measures and changes in welfare provision and their effects on, for example, independent living and the volume and forms of support. This supports what a desexualised culture itself reinforces – that sex is less important than other aspects of life and citizenship (Bahner, 2019, p 98; Graby et al, 2019). For Bahner (2019, p 214), independent living is 'a foundational prerequisite for sexual citizenship'.

While Bahner (2019) does not look specifically at the intersections of 'age, disability and sexuality' per se, she applies the principle of intersectionality as an overarching framework for her analysis to consider social inequality and its relationship to power, relationality, social context, complexity and social justice. This builds on the theme of the space for sexual agency being connected to wider social, economic and cultural inequalities. Larsson and Jönson (2018) advocate the use of an equal rights framework, where older people with disabilities and care needs should have equal participation, support and representation as those without such needs. Policy then would focus on how older people who age into disability should be able to live life like others who are older, e.g. have relationships, study, travel. Older people in need of long-term support are made victims of institutional ageism through the prioritisation of younger ages, justified because the 'process of ageing' is likened to impairments – and thus normalised, i.e. something people need to adjust to rather than have mitigated (Larsson and Jönson, 2018). This disparity is then internalised, so while young people with disabilities regard themselves as prevented from participation in activities by a disabling society, older people are more likely to see themselves as coping with the inevitable consequence of ageing with impairments. This normalisation highlights how 'shrinking possibilities are consequences of the normal ageing process' (Larsson and Jönson, 2018, p 380). Rather than promoting the sexual agency of older people with disabilities, policy has been predicated on the naturalised presumption that the ageing process changes people's needs, particularly in a care environment, and so inhibits choice (Harnett and Jönson, 2017, cited in Larson and Jönson, 2018).

While drawing parallels from the research into both 'ageing and sex' and 'physical disabilities and sex' adds to our knowledge and understanding, it does not illustrate the intersections between 'age, disability' and 'sex and intimate relations'. One exception is Shakespeare and Richardson's (2018) follow-up study to Shakespeare et al (1996), *The Sexual Politics of Disability*. In questioning 'what had changed' for the original participants, Shakespeare and Richardson highlighted that despite a reduction in barriers to expressing sex and sexuality in relation to, for example, toilet facilities and transport and internet-based opportunities to meet sexual partners, social attitudes were still negative and characterised by desexualising representations. Returning to participants two decades later focused attention on 'ageing and identity' for those growing old with disabilities. Notwithstanding the potential for greater health complications, participants noted a less stigmatising attitude to their increased needs in later life, with one participant highlighting how disability was not as prominent as it had been when they were younger:

> There's an equalising process in ageing, I feel less different probably, because everyone is getting older, and this hypothetical ideal that society says we are meant to live up to is less likely for anyone as we get older ... because the

premium is on youth. So, in a way that equalising measure is reassuring, really. I'm more like everyone else, a creaky guy. (Daniel cited in Shakespeare and Richardson, 2018, p 84)

Or they were more able to 'deal with ageing' due to their experiences of living with health conditions:

I also think, ironically, whatever comes with age … it is that, we've got experience of managing that, for different reasons, so I certainly won't stop having sex, because I already know how to manage those things. Whereas it might be a shock to a non-disabled person, suddenly realising that their back is not as good as it was. (Jenny cited in Shakespeare and Richardson, 2018, p 84)

A clear negative that emerged, however, was greater co-morbidities and health complications, which links to wider evidence of how disabled people age earlier than non-disabled people:

It's like all of us as you get older as a disabled person you develop all these other medical conditions, comorbidity, so for instance I'm now diabetic so, you know, and I have a machine at night that I have to plug into, and stuff like that. I think the one thing I've struggled with is my hearing because I'm now profoundly deaf on this side, and you know, I love the chat, I love people around talking, so I do struggle with it. (Dafydd cited in Shakespeare and Richardson, 2018, p 85)

This suggests a need to understand sexuality as a dynamic, persisting yet changing aspect of life – including later life. In a desexualising context, some disabled people struggled with maintaining intimacy against isolation and loneliness (Shakespeare, 2006).

Age, disability and desexualisation: critical responses

People with disabilities want to be able to function: to live with their disability, to come to know their body, to accept what it can do, and to keep doing what they can for as long as they can. They do not want to feel dominated by the people on whom they depend for help, and they want to be able to imagine themselves in the world without feeling ashamed. (Siebers, 2001, p 750)

This sketch of the intersection of age, disability and sex/intimacy enables provisional conclusions to be drawn at the conceptual/ theoretical, policy and personal levels. The theme throughout is that desexualisation is pervasive and reinforcing across all three nodal points of intersection and in the intersection of age/disability/sex itself. This desexualisation is culturally embedded and reproduced and ingrained with social structures and institutions.

At the conceptual level, the shift from the binary of impairment-disability to a more phenomenologically based and embodied analysis that takes in the insights of crip/queer would seem to open up a theoretical framing for the age/disability/sex intersection. At the same time, the more concrete Marxist-influenced approaches encourage that frame to be embedded in the material social processes that impress upon bodies as well as bodies as a subjective focus. The capabilities approach, beyond the politics of recognition and redistribution, sets the basis for a politics that engages both within a concrete criterion that formulates around enabling capabilities and ameliorating their absence. Again, these can be turned towards the particularity of the age/disability/sex intersection.

At a policy level, research suggests that rethinking the training of professionals engaged in care and support and reconceiving aspects of the care environment could assist in enabling older disabled people to enjoy sexual agency. Yet at the same time, the little research that is covered suggests that the prevalence and embeddedness of desexualisation is such that incremental policy change may have limited and slow impact. What may be needed, as suggested conceptually, is more of a revolutionary approach to reconceiving the nature of care, support and enabling as features of social policy, where sexual welfare, wellbeing and agency are prioritised to a far greater degree.

At a personal level, disability, sexual and gerontological scholars, political activists and movements should grasp the common necessity of recognising that this intersection, conceived as intimately personal, is nevertheless political. Sexual agency, as Marcuse (1987) has argued, is connected to political agency in encouraging free-thinking, critical inquiry and radical resistance to inequalities, injustices and forms of oppression. If agents – including ageing, disabled agents – cannot exercise choice in their desires, and experiment with bodily pleasures, then the prospects of broader political change are diminished. The personal and sexual impetus is a key feature of the drive for political change, and sexual agency is a somewhat neglected but critically important area of the lives of older people who are disabled, and people for whom ageing brings disability.

References

Abrams, T. (2016) 'Disability, *Queer Phenomenology*, and the Politics of Personhood', *Interalia*, 11a. Available at: https://interalia.queerstudies.pl/wp-content/uploads/11A_2016/abrams.pdf.

Alexander, J. (2016) *Capabilities and Social Justice: The Political Philosophy of Amartya Sen and Martha Nussbaum*. London: Routledge.

Anderson, E.S. (1999) 'What is the Point of Equality?', *Ethics*, 109(2): 287–337.

Archibald, C. (1998) 'Sexuality, Dementia and Residential Care: Managers' Report and Response', *Health and Social Care in the Community*, 6: 95–101.

Bahner, J. (2019) *Sexual Citizenship and Disability: Understanding Sexual Support in Policy, Practice and Theory*. London, Routledge.

Barnes, C. and Mercer, G. (2010) *Exploring Disability: A Sociological Introduction* (2nd edn). Cambridge: Polity Press.

Barnes, C., Oliver, M. and Barton, L. (eds) (2002) *Disability Studies Today*. Cambridge: Polity Press.

Barnett, K., Mercer, S.W., Norbury, M., Watt, G., Wyke, S. and Guthrie, B. (2012) 'Epidemiology of Multimorbidity and Implications for Health Care, Research, and Medical Education: A Cross-Sectional Study', *Lancet*, 380: 37–43.

Bauer, M., McAuliffe, L. and Nay, R. (2007) 'Sexuality, Health Care and the Older Person: An Overview of the Literature', *International Journal of Older People Nursing*, 2: 63–8.

Benbow, S.M. and Beeston, D. (2012) 'Review: Sexuality, Aging and Dementia', *International Psychogeriatrics*, 24(7): 1026–33.

Brody, S. (2010) 'The Relative Health Benefits of Different Sexual Activities', *Journal of Sexual Medicine*, 7: 1336–61.

Bytheway, B., Ward, R., Holland, C. and Peace, S. (2007) *Too Old: Older People's Accounts of Discrimination, Exclusion and Rejection: A Report from the Research on Age Discrimination Project (RoAD) to Help the Aged*. Milton Keynes: The Open University.

Calder, G. (2011) 'Disability and Misrecognition', in Thompson, S. and Yar, M. (eds) *The Politics of Misrecognition*. Aldershot: Ashgate, pp 105–24.

Campbell, J. and Oliver, M. (1996) *The Politics of Disability*. London: Routledge.

Charlton, J.I. (2006) 'The Dimensions of Disability Oppression: An Overview', in Davis, L. (ed.) *The Disability Studies Reader* (2nd edn). London: Routledge, pp 217–27.

Clark, D.A., Biggeri, M. and Frediani, A.A. (eds) (2019) *The Capability Approach, Empowerment and Participation: Concepts, Methods and Applications*. London: Palgrave Macmillan.

Davis, L. (ed.) (2006) *The Disability Studies Reader* (2nd edn). London: Routledge.

DeLamater, J. (2012) 'Sexual Expression in Later Life: A Review and Synthesis', *Journal of Sex Research*, 49: 125–41.

DeLamater, J. and Moorman, S. (2007) 'Sexual Behavior in Later Life', *Journal of Aging and Health*, 19(6): 921–45.

Denninger, T. (2020) 'Behinderung und Alter – Betrachtungen aus einer intersektionalen Perspektive [Disability and Age-Observations from an Intersectional Perspective]', *Zeitschrift Gerontologie und Geriatrie*, 53(3): 211–15.

Erens, B., Mitchell, K.R., Gibson, L., Datta, J., Lewis, R., Field, N. and Wellings, K. (2019) 'Health Status, Sexual Activity and Satisfaction Among Older People in Britain: A Mixed Methods Study', *PLoS ONE*, 14(3): e0213835. DOI: 10.1371/journal.pone.0213835

Fraser N. and Honneth A. (2003) *Redistribution or Recognition? A Political Philosophical Exchange*. London: Verso.

Gallop, J. (2019) *Sexuality, Disability and Aging: Queer Temporalities of the Phallus*. Durham: Duke University Press.

Gamson, J. and Moon, D. (2004) 'The Sociology of Sexualities: Queer and Beyond', *Annual Review of Sociology*, 30: 47–64.

Goethals, T., de Shauwer, E. and van Hove, G. (2015) 'Weaving Intersectionality into Disability Studies Research: Inclusion, Reflexivity and Anti-Essentialism', *Journal of Diversity and Gender Studies*, 2(1–2): 7594.

Goodley, D. (2014) *Dis/ability Studies: Theorising Disablism and Ableism*. London: Routledge.

Goodley, D. (2016) *Disability Studies: An Interdisciplinary Introduction* (2nd edn). London: SAGE.

Gott, M. (2005) *Sexuality, Sexual Health and Ageing*. Maidenhead, UK: Oxford University Press.

Graby, S. and Homayoun, R. (2019) 'The Crisis of Local Authority Funding and its Implications for Independent Living for Disabled People in the United Kingdom', *Disability and Society*, 34(2): 320–5.

Grewal, I., Joy, S., Swales, K., Woodfield, K. (2002) 'Disabled for Life?': Attitudes Towards, and Experiences of, Disability in Britain, Research Report no. 173. Leeds: Department for Work and Pensions, Corporate Document Services.

Griffiths, L., Raina, P., Wu, H., Zhu, B. and Stathokostas, L. (2010) 'Population Attributable Risk for Functional Disability Associated with Chronic Conditions in Canadian Older Adults', Age and Ageing, 39(6): 738–45.

Gullette, M. (2011) Agewise: Fighting the New Ageism in America. Chicago: Chicago University Press.

Guthrie, D. (ed.) (1973) Does He Take Sugar in His Tea: How to Relate to Disabled People. London: National Fund for Research into Crippling Diseases.

Hafford-Letchfield, T., Reynolds, P. and Simpson, P. (2020) Sex and Diversity in Later Life. Bristol: Policy Press.

Hancock, A.-M. (2016) Intersectionality: An Intellectual History. Oxford: Oxford University Press.

Harris, J. (2000) 'Is There a Coherent Social Conception of Disability?' Journal of Medical Ethics, 26: 95–100.

Hill Collins, P. (2019) Intersectionality as Critical Social Theory. Durham: Duke University Press.

Hillman, J. (2012) Sexuality and Aging: Clinical Perspectives. Springer: New York.

Illich, I. (2010) Limits to Medicine: Medical Nemesis – The Expropriation of Health (enlarged edn). London: Marion Boyars.

Illich I., Zola, I. and McKnight, J. (1992) Disabling Professions. New York: Marion Boyars.

Jones, R.B. (2001) 'Impairment, Disability and Handicap—Old Fashioned Concepts?', Journal of Medical Ethics, 27: 377–9.

Kafer, A. (2013) Feminist, Queer Crip. Bloomington: Indiana University Press.

Kessel, B. (2001) 'Sexuality in the Older Person', Age and Ageing, 30: 121–4.

Larsson, A.T. and Jönson, H. (2018) 'Ageism and the Rights of Older People', in Ayalon, L. and Tesch-Romer, C. (eds) Contemporary Perspectives on Ageism. Cham: Springer, pp 369–82.

Lee, D.M., Nazroo, J., O'Connor, D.B., Blake, M. and Pendleton, N. (2016) 'Sexual Health and Well-being Among Older Men and Women in England: Findings from the English Longitudinal Study of Ageing', Archives of Sexual Behavior, 45(1): 133–44.

Liddiard, K. (2013) 'The Work of Disabled Identities in Intimate Relationships', Disability and Society, 29(1): 115–28.

Liddiard, K. (2018) *The Intimate Lives of Disabled People*. London, Routledge.

Manini, T. (2011) 'Development of Physical Disability in Older Adults', *Current Aging Science*, 4(3): 184–91.

Marcuse, H. (1987) *Eros and Civilisation: A Philosophical Inquiry into Freud*. London: Routledge.

May, V.M. (2015) *Pursuing intersectionality: Unsettling Dominant Imaginaries*. London: Routledge.

McGrath, C., Rudman, D.L., Polgar, J., Spafford, M. and Trentham, B. (2016) 'Negotiating "Positive" Aging in the Presence of Age-Related Vision Loss (ARVL): The Shaping and Perpetuation of Disability', *Journal of Aging Studies*, 39: 1–10.

McGrath, M. and Lynch, E. (2013) 'Occupational Therapists' Perspectives on Addressing Sexual Concerns of Older Adults in the Context of Rehabilitation', *Disability and Rehabilitation*, 36(8): 651–7.

McRuer, R. (2006) *Crip Theory: Cultural Signs of Queerness and Disability*. New York: New York University Press.

McRuer, R. and Mollow, A. (eds) (2012) *Sex and Disability*. Durham: Duke University Press.

Meekosha, N. and Shuttleworth, R. (2009) 'What's So 'Critical' About Critical Disability Studies?', *Australian Journal of Human Rights*, 15(1): 47–75.

Merghati-Khoei, E., Pirak, A., Yazdkhasti, M. and Rezasoltani, P. (2016) 'Sexuality and Elderly with Chronic Diseases: A Review of the Existing Literature', *Journal of Research in Medical Sciences*, 21(1): 136.

Moore, A. and Reynolds, P. (2016) 'Against the Ugliness of Age: Towards an Erotics of the Aging Sexual Body', *Interalia*, 11a. Available at: https://interalia.queerstudies.pl/wp-content/uploads/11A_2016/moore_reynolds.pdf.

Nagarathnam, N. and Gayagay, G. (2002) 'Hypersexuality in Nursing Home Facilities: A Descriptive Study', *Archives in Gerontology and Geriatrics*, 36(3): 195–203.

Nussbaum, M. (2013) *Creating Capabilities: The Human Development Approach*. Cambridge, MA: Harvard University Press.

Oliver, M. (2009) *Understanding Disability: From Theory to Practice* (2nd revised edn). London: Palgrave.

Oliver, M. and Barnes, C. (2012) *The New Politics of Disablement* (2nd edn). London: Palgrave Macmillan.

Phillipson, C. (1982) *Capitalism and the Construction of Old Age*. Basingstoke: Macmillan.

Priestly, M. (2003) *Disability: A Life Course Approach*. Cambridge: Polity Press.

Reindal, S.M. (2000) 'Disability, Gene Therapy and Eugenics – A Challenge to John Harris', *Journal of Medical Ethics*, 26: 89–94.

Robeyns, I. (2017) *Wellbeing, Freedom and Social Justice: The Capabilities Approach Re-examined*. London: Open Book Publishers.

Rogers, Y. and Marsden, G. (2013) 'Does He Take Sugar?: Beyond the Rhetoric of Compassion', *Interactions*, 20(4): 49–57.

Santos, A.C. and Santos, A.L. (2017) 'Yes, We Fuck! Challenging the Misfit Sexual Body Through Disabled Women's Narratives', *Sexualities*, 21(3): 1–16.

Sellwood, D., Raghavendra, P. and Jewell, P. (2017) 'Sexuality and Intimacy for People with Congenital Physical and Communication Disabilities: Barriers and Facilitators: A Systematic Review', *Sexuality and Disability*, 35: 227–44.

Shakespeare, T. (2000) 'Disabled Sexuality: Towards Rights and Recognition', *Sexuality and Disability*, 18(3): 159–66.

Shakespeare, T. (2006) *Disability Rights and Wrongs*. London: Routledge.

Shakespeare, T. (2017) *Disability (The Basics)*. London: Routledge.

Shakespeare, T. and Watson, N. (2002) 'The Social Model of Disability: An Outdated Ideology?', *Research in Social Science and Disability*, 2: 9–28.

Shakespeare, T. and Richardson, S. (2018) 'The Sexual Politics of Disability, Twenty Years On', *Scandinavian Journal of Disability Research*, 20(1): 82–91.

Shakespeare, T., Davies, D. and Gillespie-Sells, K. (1996) *The Sexual Politics of Disability*. London: Cassell.

Shildrick, M. (2007) 'Contested Pleasures: The Sociopolitical Economy of Disability and Sexuality', *Sexuality Research and Social Policy*, 4(1): 53–66.

Shildrick, M. (2012) 'Critical Disability Studies: Rethinking the Conventions for the Age of Postmodernity', in Watson, N. (ed.) *Routledge Handbook of Disability Studies*. London: Routledge, pp 30–41.

Siebers, T. (2001) 'Disability in Theory: From Social Constructionism to the New Realism of the Body', *American Literary History*, 13(4): 737–54.

Swain, J., French, S., Barnes, C. and Thomas, C. (2013) *Disabling Barriers - Enabling Environments* (3rd edn). London: SAGE.

Taylor, Y., Hines, S. and Casey, M.E. (eds) (2011) *Theorising Intersectionality and Sexuality*. London: Palgrave Macmillan.

Tepper, M.S. (2000) 'Sexuality and Disability: The Missing Discourse of Pleasure', *Sexuality and Disability*, 18(4): 283–90.

Træen, B., Hald, G.M., Graham, C.A., Enzlin, P., Janssen, E., Kvalem, I.L., Carvalheira, A. and Štulhofer, A. (2017) 'Sexuality in Older Adults (65+)—An Overview of the Literature, Part 1: Sexual Function and its Difficulties', *International Journal of Sexual Health*, 29(1): 1–10.

United Nations (2020) *Ageing and Disability* [online]. Available at: https://www.un.org/development/desa/disabilities/disability-and-ageing.html [Accessed 23 June 2020].

Verbrugge, L.M. and Yang, L. (2002) 'Aging with Disability and Disability with Aging', *Research Journal of Disability Policy Studies*, 12(4): 253–67.

Walz, T.H. (2002) *Biomedicine and Sexual Difference*. London: Routledge.

WHO (2001) *International Classification of Functioning, Disability and Health – 2*. Geneva: WHO.

WHO (2006) *Sexual and Productive Health* (working definitions). Available at: http://www.who.int/reproductivehealth/topics/sexual_health/sh_definitions/en/ [Accessed 28 June 2016].

WHO (2011) *World Report on Disability* [online]. Available at: https://www.who.int/disabilities/world_report/2011/report.pdf [Accessed 15 June 2020].

WHO (2020) *Nutrition: The Global Burden of Chronic Disease* [online]. Available at: https://www.who.int/nutrition/topics/2_background/en/ [Accessed 15 June 2020].

7

Ageing, intellectual disability and desexualisation

Susan Gillen and Paul Reynolds

Much of the conceptual architecture of the chapter on physical disability (Chapter 6) is relevant to this chapter on intellectual disabilities: intersectional subjectivities; the impairment/disability dichotomy; the social construction of disability; the heteronormative and genito-centric conception of sexual intimacy; the radicalism of crip/queer theorising; and the necessity of critical deconstructions of normative and normalising discourses that produce desexualising impacts upon disabled people. Similarly, there are important issues to explore at policy and interpersonal levels. The intersection of age and intellectual disability is composed by both the impact of ageing on forms of intellectual capacity – typically conditions such as Alzheimer's and other types of dementia – and people who have intellectual disabilities, for whom ageing might exacerbate or provide added complications – such as people with Trisomy 21 (colloquially Down's syndrome). Or put simply, intellectually disabled people growing old and older people growing into intellectual disability. Yet it would be a mistake to simply extend or map the conceptual framings and analysis of physical disabilities onto intellectual disabilities. There are important differences as well as similarities at the intersections of intellectual disabilities with sex and intimacy in later life.

Intellectual (as physical) disability and ageing both bring into question how human difference is categorised and understood according to conceptions of what is bodily or customarily normal. The notion of 'normal' dominates conventional understandings of ageing, disability and sex and intimacy, and is the discursive basis for the desexualisation of those people bearing these features. It is precisely the development of crip/queer critiques (and in this chapter, a neurodiverse equivalent), that has problematised and deconstructed these qualities and characteristics: dissembling reproduction; genito-centric and penetrative heteronormativities from sex and intimacy; dissembling ableism and the constitution of hierarchies of ability from disability; and dissembling life course developmental staging from age. This involves recognising that categories of distinctions are degrees of difference and not deficit, and the norm should not be morally and culturally privileged but recognised as a statistical measurement of population or an ideological construct that reflects power-knowledge relations and their deployment as orthodoxies to maintain a status quo (indicatively, Foucault, 1980, 2002). Such a position sees exceptions as so plural and diverse as to invert norm-exception assumptions, where constructs of normal are often the exception or minority (conforming to ideals of heterosexual, able-bodiedness and youthfulness – the discussion is well referenced in both the previous chapter and the discussion to come). What is clear, for all the nuanced differences that subvert the 'normal', is that normality remains strong as an ideological foundation for understanding social order and position. Older, intellectually (and physically) disabled sexual agents are subjected to and their subjectivities constituted within desexualising discourses.

This chapter will explore how desexualisation is constructed for people at the intersection of ageing and intellectual disabilities. Intellectual disabilities may require very different opportunities for enabling to physical disabilities, even where desexualising discourses and constraints are similar. It will begin by reviewing the conceptual and theoretical terrain, where the concept of neurodiversity and the critique of the normalising power of neurotypical stereotypes and constructions have become a central focus alongside the broader term of intellectual disability (see Harris, 2006, for an overview). It will then capture key desexualising strands within the intersection of intellectual disability and sex and intimacy in later life. As with physical disability, this intersectional identity remains very much under-researched, in part a consequence of the very desexualising discourses that require research to clarify pathologies and prejudices, recognise issues and problems and make meaningful policy and practice, as well as political responses.

Neurodiversity: problems of definition and boundary-marking

The prejudices and pathologies surrounding intellectual disability are often far more elusive than those of physical disabilities. The dominant critical concept in contemporary explorations of issues of intellectual capacities and constraints to function effectively and exercise agency in society is neurodiversity (or neuro-diversity – for a brief history of the concept, see Arnold, 2017). Neurodiversity (literally 'brain different' or 'neurological pluralism') focuses on diverse developmental, learning, sociability, disposition and performance registers that involves neurocognitive functioning.

Neurodiversity is operant on, and in part constituted by, a number of medically defined conditions: Attention Deficit Hyperactivity Disorder (ADHD); Attention Deficit Disorder (ADD); Autistic Spectrum conditions, Asperger's syndrome and Persuasive Developmental Disorder – Not Otherwise Specified (PDD-NOS); Dyslexia; Dyspraxia; Dyscalculia; Dysgraphia; Tourette Syndrome; anxiety disorder; Obsessive-Compulsive Disorder (OCD); bipolarity; schizophrenia; anti-social personality disorders and forms of psychopathia (Hendricks, 2010). What they have in common is that they are not neurotypical – ostensibly a state of common conformity with 'normal' functional parameters within society – though Muskie has caustically defined it from a neurodiverse position: 'Neurotypical syndrome is a neurobiological disorder characterized by preoccupation with social concerns, delusions of superiority, and obsession with conformity' (cited in Blume, 1998).

Many of these conditions are issues of brain function that involve difficulties in processing, storing and communicating sensory information, though it can also involve having exceptional functional qualities, such as memory recall with autistic people. It also involves inconsistency in how neurodiverse people negotiate different tasks, for example someone with Asperger's may be a brilliant mathematician who has considerable difficulties with basic functions such as making a meal. Neurodiversity is a very broad signifier for a wide diversity of different medically defined (and subjectively experienced) conditions (and contested, see Chapman, 2019). While the concept is useful in bringing together such conditions in an analytical construct, it should not be assumed that the experience of these conditions, or the needs of people with these conditions, are similar or even equivalent. Further, many (but not all) of these conditions are degenerative with ageing and variable in their impact across the life course. Neurodiversity is genuinely diverse. Intellectual disability as a construct and signifier is more so.

These conditions, as with physical disability, are conceived within a medical paradigm. Medicalisation maintains a focus on biological roots – brain chemistry, dysfunction or difference – that fit into an equivalent notion with bodily impairment. This individualist focus is centred upon the diagnosis and care/support needs of the different intellectual disabled people. As with the impairment/disability dichotomy, the medical paradigm is invariably subject to criticism from sociocultural perspectives.

A first problem is that the medical paradigm might exclude issues that impede intellectual capacities and judgement, or do not fit pathologies of brain function or chemistry. On the other hand, a wider, inclusive conceptualisation that embraces a diverse range of subjectivities and captures all impediments to intellectual capability is so porous as to be difficult for medicalised approaches to contain and utilise. The borderlines between intellectual disabilities that have some medical rationale and broader conditions of social anxiety, for example 'feeling sad', against a clinical depression or having mental states that are traumatised or exhausted, destabilises the meaning of intellectual disability. For those using a critical approach, this destabilising quality underpins a critical approach to the category of intellectual ability/disability. The medical paradigm does not work well with unstable categories.

The concept 'intellectual disability' itself is subject to question, as the terminology often shifts between different framings: intellectual, mental, learning and emotional. One form of intellectual disability is specific learning difficulties, which impact on the processing of communication of knowledge, but not necessarily the capacity of make judgements and exercise agency. This is quite distinct from a neurological condition that directly impedes agency and judgement. A further complication is that intellectual disability has a loose intersectional association with intelligence quotient (IQ). Some people with low IQ may have been sufferers of intellectual disabilities, but this overlap has no definite relationship. These complexities present difficulties at to where lines between 'ability/capacity' and 'disability/incapacity' are drawn. Not only is the labelling of intellectual disability (the choice of terminology here) not clearly bounded, but it is not easily distinguished as to its causes and impacts on the agent. While Trisomy 21 might be clearly discernible, conditions like Alzheimer's are both progressive and phasic, and so are not consistent in symptoms and impacts until advanced stages. Further, anxiety and depression can be used to cover a general sadness or 'low' disposition or a clinical inability to be functional within the world they inhabit. When considering 'intellectual' disabilities (with the inverted commas deliberate), it is necessary to see interconnections between intellect, emotional states and mental wellbeing. Using a broad category in sociocultural analyses is subject to criticism from two directions. A broad terminology may represent affinities and similarities but has the danger of obscuring particularities and specificities. Equally, a conceptualisation that encapsulates such diversity does raise issues of equivalence and disparity in how the concept is conceived and subjectivities represented, particularly when applied to issues of law, regulation or custom and convention. Yet it is necessary to have a language that attempts to conceptualise a particular plane of prejudice, pathology and discrimination.

Emotional and mental states can be as traumatising as intellectual disabilities, and so relevant to considering factors that influence desexualisation in later life. Indeed, desexualising discourses may well cause or exacerbate crises of intellectual capacity/ability as much as desexualisation may be a consequence of their condition.

Neurodiverse perspectives have affinities with the crip/queer/ poststructuralist approaches to disability, recognising sociocultural factors and the production of subjectivities that construct the neurotypical as a discursive construct, culturally hegemonic and materially instantiated in everyday products, systems and architectures (for example forms of lighting or sound production or photographic effects that have neurological effects). They recognise that the articulation of intellectual deficits and deficiencies – particularly within a medicalised model – is not simply descriptive diagnoses, but a means of exercising power and imposing norms and 'normal' parameters that reinforce the structure and functions of contemporary society. The 'fact' of debilitating intellectual conditions is experienced through a 'norm-deviance' discursive structure, which underpins a pathological and disabling environment that both produces intellectual disability and makes intellectually disabled people unable to function within its parameters.

The diversity implicit in neurodiversity means the typology and the identification of common constraints or adjustments for deficit – functional or sociocultural – and policy and practice responses are very difficult. Neurodiverse experience can be markedly different, hence the expression 'neurominorities' to describe the range of different neurodiverse subjectivities. Neurodiverse conditions can also be shared, so someone with OCD may also have anxiety and dyslexia, and these accumulations might be self-reinforcing. This only becomes more critical at the intersections of age and sexuality. Ageing itself involves a biological process that can, to varying degrees, create, augment or accentuate intellectual, emotional and mental distress, deficit and dysfunction, co-produced and compounded by sociocultural processes and representations. These factors frame older people by their 'acknowledged' conditions or 'labels', thus internalising (within the agent) and normalising conditions of inequality, prejudice and pathology. In matters of anxiety conditions, for example, there is a spectrum of causal factors, from brain-chemistry to socially and culturally contextualised conditions. These become clear when particular intersections show demonstrable prevalences, such as women's anxieties to patriarchal norms and depressions among black or mixed ethnicity in European states.

All of these considerations underline a complexity to discussing 'intellectual' disability as an intersection, particularly when intersected with age, sex and intimate relations. In this context, pathologies, prejudices and discrimination in respect of older people's sexual and intimate wants, needs-fulfilment, pleasure and belonging can be, by degrees, causal, consequential and reinforcing.

For the purposes of this discussion, rather than align with any boundary setting, there is a broad concurrence with the radical crip/ queer/neurodiverse approach to conceiving intellectual disability, for all its nuanced complexities. Of critical importance in understanding this framing is a significant difference with physical disability. Most physical disabilities can be subject to some measurement of extent, of progressive, stable or recessive trajectories and of medical, therapeutic and prosthetic responses and support services, even if there is some considerable debate around the measures applied and their measurements. Intellectual disabilities range from those that can be to some extent measurable by medical criteria, to those where measurement is far more complex. The extent to which a condition is recognised to be measurable is significant because measurement implies that a condition is medically treatable and the treatment tends towards maintaining degrees of functionality against adverse symptoms as opposed to questioning causes and addressing broader questions of quality of life.

Intellectually disabled older people, whether older intellectually disabled or intellectually disabled through advancing age, have particular desexualising challenges to their sexual and intimate lives. These desexualising discourses are both specific to some intellectual disabilities, but also more generic in their perniciousness. Three sets of desexualising problems are discernible for older people who are described as having an intellectual disability, recognising that not all the relevant research will be focused on the same intersectional constituencies, and some of those who are intellectually disabled may have diminished sexual desires and needs.

First, there is an implicit problem of capacity to consent and exercise agency, as something that involves intellectual cognitive capacity. Second, the desexualising cultural contexts to particular forms of intellectual disability suggest that their having particular intellectual disabilities is a rationale in itself for labelling a sexual agent as non-sexual or desexualised. They are neither subjects of desire nor sexual agents because they are intellectually disabled. Finally, there is the extent to which older people with intellectual disabilities are desexualised by the character of the support they receive from private, state or voluntary agencies in coping with their disability.

Consent and capacity

A crucial element of being a sexual agent is the capacity to exercise valid consent. Valid consent involves three dimensions: that the agent is informed; that they have the capacity to process information and make autonomous decisions; and that they are free from coercion (for a longer review of sexual consent see Chapter 2). Some intellectual disabilities clearly impact on capacities to absorb information, process it and make decisions from it, though in the case of others, such as the early stages of dementia, the sexual agent may well 'phase' in or out of having capacity rather than the experience being easily linear or progressive. There is, however, a general problem of law and regulation in respect of intellectual disability, which can be illustrated by the UK case, where two significant pieces of legislation would seem to contradict in the guidance they give.

Sections 74 to 76 of the 2003 Sexual Offences Act provide a definition of consent and factor in considering the veracity of a consent decision. Section 74 states 'a person consents if he agrees by choice and has the freedom and capacity to make that choice' (the male pronoun is a regrettable feature of legislative writing). Section 75 identifies evidential presumptions about consent that identify conditions by which it is invalidated: violence or threat of violence; unlawful detention; unconsciousness; the capacity to communicate (contextualised in physical disability); and substance intoxication ('causing or enabling ... to be stupified or overpowered'). Section 76 additionally refers to deception and impersonation. This raises questions as to how free choice is recognised and whether neurodiversity renders some people unable to make or express free choices to a legal standard some or all of the time, and how that is recognised. Contributory to this is the impact of medications as intoxicants and the reliability of communicative abilities when deemed vulnerable to undue influence, and what constitutes 'undue'. This constitutes a significant issue of case-by-case judgement aligned to a recognition of where common issues might arise.

Sections 30 to 37 of the 2003 Act specifically address offences 'against persons with a mental disorder impeding choice' and inducements to such people. The legislation is framed under the assumption that the person with a 'mental disorder' is the passive recipient and not the initiator, which is itself problematic. Section 30 discusses the offence against a person with 'mental disorder' in the terms of inability to refuse if: '(a) he lacks the capacity to choose whether to agree to the touching (whether because he lacks sufficient understanding of the nature or reasonably foreseeable consequences of what is being done, or for any other reason), or (b) he is unable to communicate such a choice to A'. Section 31 clarifies that it is an offence when: 'A knows or could reasonably be expected to know that B has a mental disorder and that because of it or for a reason related to it B is likely to be unable to refuse.' Sections 32 to 37 deal with someone with mental disorder being present, watching/looking (including images) and subject to inducements/threats/deception when an activity that is sexual ('obtaining sexual gratification') is taking place.

There is no distinct definition of mental disorder offered or specific reference to what mental disorder might be. The source of such a definition came two years later with the 2005 Mental Capacity Act. Section 2 sketches the meaning of a lack of mental capacity:

> (1) .... a person lacks capacity ... if at the material time he is unable to make a decision for himself ... because of an impairment of, or a disturbance in the functioning of, the mind or brain.
> (2) It does not matter whether the impairment or disturbance is permanent or temporary.
> (3) A lack of capacity cannot be established merely by reference to—
> (a) a person's age or appearance, or
> (b) a condition of his, or an aspect of his behaviour, which might lead others to make unjustified assumptions about his capacity.
> (4) ....any question whether a person lacks capacity ... must be decided on the balance of probabilities.

The breadth and limitations of the description, the recognition of variability, and the clear inference about the necessity of case specificity in measuring balance of probabilities underpin the difficulty of judgements of sexual agency. The basis of the contradiction between the 2003 and 2005 Acts is that the 2003 Act is focused on protection, and the 2005 Act on enabling those with mental capacity. Its principles are (section 1):

(2) A person must be assumed to have capacity unless it is established that he lacks capacity.

(3) A person is not to be treated as unable to make a decision unless all practicable steps to help him to do so have been taken without success.

(4) A person is not to be treated as unable to make a decision merely because he makes an unwise decision.

(5) An act done, or decision made, under this Act for or on behalf of a person who lacks capacity must be done, or made, in his best interests.

(6) Before the act is done, or the decision is made, regard must be had to whether the purpose for which it is needed can be as effectively achieved in a way that is less restrictive of the person's rights and freedom of action.

One problematic assumption is that someone deemed not of a mental disorder is the initiator of a sexual proposition. This discounts sexual relations between intellectually disabled people or their initiating sexual relations. This both deprives intellectually disabled people of a notion of having some agency – as opposed to passivity – in initiating and developing intimacy and sexual relations, and labels such expressions risk-laden and dangerous. Another problem is that sex and intimacy can only be enjoyed by those who meet a threshold of competence, notwithstanding the clear problems of judging that threshold and the impact on those who are deemed to have questionable competence. While it is important that people not competent to consent are not exploited, should we assume they have no sexual needs and desires? The problem is exacerbated when applied to older people who have enjoyed and exercised agency in such relationships and now find them restricted, sometimes without the capacity to fully understand these restrictions. The only element of the 2005 Act that mentions sex is Section 27(1) (b), which simply states that: 'Nothing in this Act permits a decision on ... consenting to have sexual relations'. This limits a decision being made for someone with intellectual disabilities (and so rules out surrogate or assisted decisions and agency) but says nothing about intellectually disabled people who desire sex but are not deemed of legal capacity.

The 2003 Act seeks to provide protection against sexual abuse and non-consenting sex by establishing a standard by which meaningful consent is understood. The 2005 Act tends to focus on enabling or facilitating intellectually disabled people to engage in everyday living, while dealing with questions of when withholding of liberty is necessary and family/guardian/power of attorney and state jurisdiction are applicable. There is a tension between the aims of enabling and protecting intellectually disabled people, and that tension is situated within a desexualising cultural context where such people are regarded as non-sexual, which orients everyday care, support and attitudes against enabling. Under such a context, sexual or intimate relations limited to 'harmless' but limited expressions of affection are 'acceptable'. A degree of sexual expression, such as masturbation, might be regarded as tolerable if done in private. Anything further is a risk that must be limited or curtailed. Given issues such as penetrative sex giving rise to pregnancy, or the passing on of forms of sexually transmitted disease infection that vary from damaging sexual organs to life threatening if not diagnosed, or violence and exploitation, there is a clear necessity for protection. The problem arises when that protection becomes a policy and practice that involves inhibiting sex and intimacy as a practice as opposed to more nuanced responses to risk, measuring the specific risks of different sexual and intimate practices and the contexts and degrees of compromise present by which the sexual agent is rendered vulnerable.

Here, the instability and porousness of the line between mental 'disorder' and mental 'order' either leads to a protectionism that is problematically restrictive or creates a confusion that is anathema to rule, law or norm making. It also creates significant difficulties for those people occupying the support roles as family, legal representative or giving care/support, who may themselves find sex a difficult area of discussion.

Intellectual disability, ageing and sex and intimacy: the terrain

As with physical disabilities, the intersection of age and intellectual disabilities shows an upward trend in prevalence (WHO, 2011). The number of people ageing with intellectual disabilities has increased significantly with better healthcare, as has the number of people ageing *into* intellectual disabilities, such as developing dementia. In western countries the prevalence of diagnosed intellectual disability is approximately 2.5 per cent (Starr, 2019). Those with mild intellectual disabilities have a life expectancy congruent with the population in general, though those reaching old age with intellectual disabilities can expect a greater burden of illness than people without intellectual disabilities (Hermans and Evenhuis, 2014; Janicki et al, 2005). For the most part, they are affected by dementia to the same degree as other adults in the general population (Janicki and Dalton, 2000). After age 60 about 5 per cent of adults with intellectual disabilities will be affected by some form of dementia (with the percentage increasing with age) (National Task Group, 2012). Adults with Down's syndrome have a significantly increased risk of dementia in later life: after age 60, 50–70 per cent of adults with Down's syndrome will develop some form of dementia (National Task Group, 2012).

How someone with intellectual disabilities is identified or self-identifies can be very different dependent on whether they are ageing with an intellectual disability or ageing into intellectual disabilities. People ageing within service provision are more likely to identify as or with intellectual disability (Bigby, 2004, p 244). Conversely, older people with dementia may seem themselves as primarily older or be identified as such.

Research into the intersections of ageing, intellectual disabilities and sexuality is very limited (for indicative overviews see Bauer et al, 2007; Benbow and Beeston, 2012). Some parallels can be drawn to physical disabilities. There are similar myths and stereotypes of asexuality or hypersexuality common to both, although for people with intellectual disabilities there is the added tension of people being seen to be childlike and in need of protection (Wilkinson et al, 2015). This is compounded with difficulties with self-efficacy and poor communication. Nevertheless, intellectually disabled people have the same sexuality and intimacy needs as others (Rushbrooke et al, 2014), and the onset of an intellectual disability such as dementia does not erase sexuality, although sexual expression and behaviour may change (Bouman, 2007).

Despite advocacy for responding to intellectually disabled people's intimate and sexual needs as closely to 'normal' as possible (Nirje, 1972), the experience is different. While there has been an increase in support, its focus has been on such things as living conditions, entertainment and employment, with sex and intimacy largely neglected (Bauer et al, 2009a, Gilmore and Chambers, 2010). There is arguably a 'silencing of sexuality', despite the established principles of individualisation and person-centred care for people with dementia in care homes (NIHR, 2018). Simpson et al (2015, p 251) characterise this approach as 'premised on a bed-and-body principle' that sees care of older people based on the physical and social needs of an 'asexual' person.

Both older people ageing into intellectual disabilities and those who age with intellectual disabilities are exponentially more likely to live in a care setting in later life. In Scotland, approximately 70 per cent of people between 16 and 34 lived with a family carer, yet by the age of 54+ this had reduced to 16 per cent, with the remainder living in a variety of care settings (SCLD, 2016, cited in Todd, 2020). In the UK, approximately 40 per cent of people living with dementia are in residential care or nursing homes (Alzheimer's Research UK, 2018). In both forms of older intellectually disabled people, the character of care is more important than the care setting when sexual and intimate expression is considered. Bahner (2019) points out that many people with intellectual disabilities live in residential facilities that are organised in such a way as to discourage sexual expressions and deny privacy or support for such intimacies. This is compounded with a lack of training and specific systems for delivering such care, which leaves only a desexualising silence. A consequence of this is that when people with intellectual disabilities express a desire to be sexually intimate, they often feel controlled by others, or appear to be controlled by others, in their experiences of sexual and intimate relations. A systematic review of the literature (in the period 2006–16) that explored the sexual experiences of people with intellectual disabilities from their perspective identified a recurring tension between promoting self-determination and sexual agency and the need to protect from exploitation and abuse. Older people with intellectual disabilities wanted sexual intimacy but the care environment – policies, staff and family members – could be inhibiting rather than facilitating its expression (Brown and McCann, 2018; see also Rushbrook et al, 2014). Similarly, a meta-synthesis of 16 qualitative studies involving 271 participants across Europe, USA, China and Australia highlighted the tension between 'control' and 'desire' (Black and Kammes, 2019).

Ćwirynkało et al (2017) examined how professionals working with adults with intellectual disabilities view sexuality and intimate relationships in a range of care settings in Poland. They found that despite staff having positive views of sexuality and intimate relationships of people with intellectual disabilities, and despite viewing people with intellectual disabilities as 'normal' and with the same rights as others, they also subscribed to wider societal views of the problematic nature of sexual intimacy involving intellectually disabled people, with a significant focus on issues of hypersexuality or on perceptions of their clients as being vulnerable and infantilised. They established that barriers to people with intellectual disabilities experiencing a 'normal' sex life included the environment itself, a lack of policy guidelines, and negative attitudes held by families.

Such normalisation and internalisation of desexualising negative and stereotypical attitudes towards people with intellectual disabilities reinforced barriers to self-expression and encouraged a retreat from intimacy and sexuality. The close association of intellectual disability with sheltering or protection serves to disempower, overprotect and desexualise. Tarzia et al (2012) reported that staff dealing with people with dementia in residential aged care facilities were often taxed by a notion of duty of care that seemed incompatible with sexual agency, particularly when the capacity to consent is questionable (see also Archibald, 1998; Bauer et al, 2009b). Conversely, Gilmore and Chambers (2010, p 22) found that positive attitudes of support by staff 'have the potential to influence opportunities for normalised life experiences in the area of sexuality'. Kramers-Olen (2016) has concluded there was a need for health and care professionals to support autonomy through person-centred approaches with a focus on support, not risk management.

Haeusermann (2018), although not focused specifically on sexuality, explored how Germany's first 'dementia village' operated as an environment that 'negotiates rivalling discourses of intimacy, professionalisation and medicalisation'. The aim of setting up this village was to allow residents to live an 'ordinary life', post dementia diagnosis, with a person-centred – rather than condition focused – approach. Haeusermann suggests the original ideals and values of the dementia village shifted to 'medicalised surveillance and discourses of professionalization that impact on the daily workings of the facility' that sees a shift from the 'ideal' to one of accountability and control (Haeusermann, 2018, p 908). Despite workers being attracted to the village by the 'idealised vision' of such a village community, they have to work within structures of regulation, hierarchy and control. What Haeusermann refers to as 'professional intimacy' highlights the tension care as person-centred and care as professional (and medicalised) support.

Conclusion

This chapter only begins to identify the conceptual problems, contexts and issues of desexualisation that are present for older people who experience forms of neurodiversity/intellectual disability. It underscores a relative absence of focus in research, and a complexity as to identifying intellectual disability and its impacts on sex and intimacy in later life. Undoubtedly, some intellectual disabilities and some broader conditions of anxiety and depression that are attendant to that appellation may have effects that discourage an agent from seeking or enjoying sexual intimacy. What is equally clear is that intellectually disabled people are limited from expressing their sexual and intimate needs and gaining satisfaction.

As with the chapter on physical disability, there are important conceptual, theoretical, policy and personal dimensions to reconceiving people with intellectual disabilities as sexual agents. Again, a crip/queer/neurodiversity approach that sees agents as embodied subjects and takes a phenomenological account of their subjectivities is an important and still underdeveloped way of looking at both sexual agents and desexualised subjects. It is through such a radical reframing that neglected areas such as sexual agency are brought into view and addressed, and sex and intimacy become recognised as equally important with other issues of wellbeing. At the same time, a Marxist–influenced sociocultural analysis underlines the cultural and material constraints to creating the space of careful, secure and enabled sexual agency. Such a possibility might be facilitated by individual care and support at the margins, but for substantive change to hegemonic desexualising discourses, the material disposition of resources and the allocation of time and space in care/support would have to change. Here, the notion of capability is of critical importance, both in taking an enabling approach to sexual agents with intellectual disabilities and in taking some account of how those with lesser capacities can be facilitated to enjoy sexual intimacy, however mediated and limited. For older people with intellectual disabilities, these considerations are particularly critical in extending the recognition of people's capabilities in the onset of intellectual disability, or recognising degrees of intellectual disability with an enabling perspective across the life course.

At a policy level, the training of care/support professionals and workers remains critical, but so does some reconceptualisation of how older people with intellectual disabilities are supported in care institutional and familial contexts so as to counter desexualising stereotypes. This is not simply a question of incremental change, as the layers of desexualising discourses that operate upon age, sex and intellectual disability are substantial. While incremental changes in policy and practice within private, statutory and voluntary sectors will have impacts at the margins, what is necessary is a more revolutionary articulation that recognises the different sexual and intimate needs and desires of older intellectually disabled people and attempts to be facilitative of their sexual choices and experimentation. In their wide-ranging discussion of the barriers to people with intellectual disabilities, distinguishing men, women and LGBTIQ, Wilson et al (2019) identify the range of desexualising cultural discourses and impediments outlined here and identify structures that give opportunities for relationships to be formed, education delivered and knowledge shared, and provide a case study of peer support as one way in which relationships can be facilitated.

At a personal level, as with physical disability, the personal and subjective choices, experience and restrictions that older people with intellectual disabilities live within are invariably political even if intensely intimate. Marcuse's (1987) connection of personal struggles with political action for change is again relevant, both in respect of older people with intellectual disabilities and those who work with and support them. Abbott (2013) provides one example of how gay men with intellectual disabilities can mobilise their own stories in illustrating the possibilities of productive intimate lives. There is no doubt that intellectual disabilities among older people present challenges to enabling their agency and avoiding vulnerabilities and forms of self- or other harm or exploitation. Nevertheless, falling back on assumptions of desexualisation, and the denial of their sexual agency, however complex and difficult the issues raised, leaves them without a significant element of wellbeing.

References

Abbott, D. (2013) 'Nudge, Nudge, Wink, Wink: Love, Sex and Gay Men with Intellectual Disabilities – A Helping Hand or a Human Right?', *Journal of Intellectual Disability Research*, 57(11): 1079–87.

Alzheimer's Research UK (2018) *Dementia statistics hub* [online]. Available at: https://www.dementiastatistics.org/statistics/care-services/ [Accessed 25 July 2020].

Archibald, C. (1998) 'Sexuality, Dementia and Residential Care: Managers' Report and Response', *Health and Social Care in the Community*, 6: 95–101.

Arnold, L. (2017) 'A Brief History of "Neurodiversity" as a Concept and Perhaps a Movement', *Autonomy, the Critical Journal of Interdisciplinary Autism Studies*, 1(5). Available at: http://www.larry-arnold.net/Autonomy/index.php/autonomy/article/view/ AR23/html.

Bahner, J. (2019) *Sexual Citizenship and Disability: Understanding Sexual Support in Policy, Practice and Theory*. London, Routledge.

Bauer, M., McAuliffe, L. and Nay, R. (2007) 'Sexuality, Health Care and the Older Person: An Overview of the Literature', *International Journal of Older People Nursing*, 2: 63–8.

Bauer, M., McAuliffe, L. and Nay, R. (2009a) 'Sexuality and the Reluctant Health Professional', in Nay, R. and Garratt, S. (eds) *Caring for Older People: Issues and Innovations in Care*. London: Churchill Livingstone.

Bauer, M., Nay, R. and McAuliffe, L. (2009b) 'Catering to Love, Sex and Intimacy in Residential Aged Care: What Information is Provided to Consumers?', *Sex Disability*, 27: 3–9.

Benbow, S.M. and Beeston, D. (2012) 'Review: Sexuality, Aging and Dementia', *International Psychogeriatrics*, 24(7): 1026–33.

Bigby, C. (2004) *Ageing with a Lifelong Disability: A Guide to Practice, Program and Policy Issues for Human Services Professionals.* London: Jessica Kingsley.

Black, R.S. and Kammes, R.R. (2019) 'Restrictions, Power, Companionship, and Intimacy: A Metasynthesis of People with Intellectual Disability Speaking About Sex and Relationships', *Intellectual and Developmental Disabilities*, 57(3): 212–33.

Blume, H. (1998) 'Neurodiversity: on the Neurological Underpinning of Geekdom', *The Atlantic*, September 1998. Available at: https://www.theatlantic.com/magazine/archive/1998/09/neurodiversity/305909/ [Accessed 10 July 2020].

Bouman, W.P. (2007) 'Sexuality and Dementia', *Geriatric Medicine*, 37(5): 3–41.

Brown, M. and McCann, E. (2018) 'Sexuality Issues and the Voices of Adults with Intellectual Disabilities: A Systematic Review of the Literature', *Research in Developmental Disabilities*, 74: 124–38.

Chapman, R. (2019) 'Neurodiversity Theory and its Discontents: Autism, Schizophrenia and the Social Model of Disability', in Tekin, S. and Bluhm, R. (eds) *The Bloomsbury Companion to the Philosophy of Psychiatry.* London: Bloomsbury, pp 371–90.

Ćwirynkało, K., Byra, S. and Żyt, A. (2017) 'Sexuality of Adults with Intellectual Disabilities as Described by Support Staff Workers', *Hrvatska Revija Za Rehabilitacijska Istraživanja*, 53: 77–87.

Foucault, M. (1980) *Power/Knowledge: Selected Interviews and Writings 1972-1977.* New York: Pantheon Books.

Foucault, M. (2002) *The Archaeology of Knowledge.* London: Routledge.

Gilmore, L. and Chambers, B. (2010) 'Intellectual Disability and Sexuality: Attitudes of Disability Support Staff and Leisure Industry Employees', *Journal of Intellectual & Developmental Disability*, 35(1): 22–8.

Haeusermann, T. (2018) 'Professionalised Intimacy: How Dementia Care Workers Navigate Between Domestic Intimacy and Institutional Detachment', *Sociology of Health & Illness*, 40(5): 907–23.

Harris, J.C. (2006) *Intellectual Disability: Understanding its Development, Causes, Classification, Evaluation and Treatment.* Oxford: Oxford University Press.

Hendricks, S. (2010) *The Adolescent and Adult Neuro-Diversity Handbook*. London: Jessica Kingsley.

Hermans, H. and Evenhuis, H. (2014) 'Multimorbidity in Older Adults with Intellectual Disabilities', *Research in Developmental Disabilities*, 35: 776–83.

Janicki, M.P. and Dalton, A.J. (2000) 'Prevalence of Dementia and Impact on Intellectual Disability Service', *Mental Retardation*, 38: 276–88.

Janicki, M.P., Dalton, A.J., McCallion, P., Baxley, D.D. and Zendell, A. (2005) 'Group Home Care for Adults with Intellectual Disabilities and Alzheimer's Disease', *Dementia*, 4: 361–85.

Kramers-Olen, A. (2016) 'Sexuality, Intellectual Disability, and Human Rights Legislation', *South African Journal of Psychology*, 46(4): 504–16.

Marcuse, H. (1987) *Eros and Civilisation: A Philosophical Inquiry into Freud*. London: Routledge.

National Institute for Health Research (2018) 'Person-Centred Care Improves Quality of Life for Care Home Residents with Dementia' [online]. Available at: https://evidence.nihr.ac.uk/alert/person-centred-care-improves-quality-of-life-for-care-home-residents-with-dementia/ [Accessed 25 July 2020].

National Task Group on Intellectual Disabilities and Dementia Practice (2012) '"My Thinker's Not Working": A National Strategy for Enabling Adults with Intellectual Disabilities Affected by Dementia to Remain in Their Community and Receive Quality Supports'. Available at: www.aadmd.org/ntg/thinker [Accessed 20 July 2020].

Nirje, B. (1972) 'The Right to Self-Determination', in Wolfensberger, W. (ed.) *Normalization: The Principle of Normalization*. Toronto: National Institute on Mental Retardation, pp 176–200.

Rushbrooke, E., Murray, C. and Townsend, S. (2014) 'The Experiences of Intimate Relationships by People with Intellectual Disabilities: A Qualitative Study', *Journal of Applied Research in Intellectual Disabilities*, 27: 531–41.

Simpson, P., Horne, M., Brown, L., Wilson, C.B., Dickinson, T. and Torkington, K. (2015) 'Old(er) Care Home Residents and Sexual/Intimate Citizenship', *Ageing & Society*. Available on CJO 2015DOI:10.1017/S0144686X15001105

Starr, J.M. (2019) 'Older Adults with Intellectual Disability: The National Institute for Health and Care Excellence (NICE) Guidelines', *Age and Ageing*, 48(1): 14–15.

Tarzia, L., Fetherstonhaugh, D. and Bauer, M. (2012) 'Dementia, Sexuality and Consent in Residential Aged Care Facilities', *Journal of Medical Ethics*, 38: 609–13.

Todd, S., Bernal, J., Shearn, J., Worth, R., Jones, E., Lowe, K., Madden, P., Barr, W., Forrester Jones, R., Jarvis, P., Kroll, T., McCarron, M., Read, S. and Hunt, K. (2020) 'Last Months of Life of People with Intellectual Disabilities: A UK Population-Based Study of Death and Dying in Intellectual Disability Community Services', *Journal of Applied Research in Intellectual Disabilities*. DOI:10.1111/jar.12744

WHO (2011) *World Report on Disability* [online]. Available at: https://www.who.int/disabilities/world_report/2011/report.pdf [Accessed 15 June 2020].

Wilkinson, V.J., Theodore, K., and Raczka, R. (2015) 'As Normal as Possible': Sexual Identity Development in People with Intellectual Disabilities Transitioning to Adulthood', *Sexuality & Disability*, 33(2): 93–105.

Wilson, N.J., Frawley, P., Schaafsma, S., O'Shea, A., Kahonde, C., Thompson, V., McKenzie, J. and Charnock, D. (2019) 'Issues in Sexuality and Relationships', in Matson, J.L. (ed) *Handbook of Intellectual Disabilities: Integrating Theory, Research and Practice*. Cham, Switzerland: Springer Nature, pp 989–1010.

8

Dancing in- or out-of-step?
Sexual and intimate relationships among heterosexual couples living with Alzheimer's disease

Linn J. Sandberg

Introduction

Although old age is still desexualised in many ways, there have increasingly been signs of more positive attitudes to sexuality in later life over the last two decades. Sexuality is increasingly positioned as significant to overall positive and healthy ageing (Gott, 2005; Sandberg, 2015). However, older people with illnesses and disabilities are still positioned as asexual, as pointed out in several other chapters of this volume. This is particularly true of the large group of older people living with dementia. Fifty million people worldwide are currently living with dementia, and this number is estimated to triple by 2050 (WHO, 2019).

Discourses on the sexuality of people with dementia are highly contradictory. On the one hand, pervasive discourses of dementia as a 'loss of self' also degender and desexualise people with dementia (Sandberg, 2018). Also, the degendering and desexualisation of people with dementia contributes further to the erosion of subjectivity in older people with dementia. On the other hand, there are discourses of sexuality and dementia as excessive, problematic and undesirable. These discourses are commonly reflected in the medical scientific literature, where sexuality among people with dementia is almost exclusively discussed in pathologising terms such as 'hypersexuality' or 'inappropriate sexual behaviours' (Sandberg et al, 2020). But the tendency to deem sexuality among people with dementia problematic is also reflected in the literature on nursing, which suggests that care staff tend to experience discomfort with, and try to suppress or redirect, sexual expressions among residents with dementia (Villar et al, 2015; Dupuis et al, 2012). Interestingly, intimacies such as kissing, sexual language and touching are sometimes considered challenging behaviour (Villar et al, 2019).

As Foucault (1990 [1976]) argues, sexuality is assumed to be at the core what it means to be a subject in western culture. Still, while sexuality is understood as desirable in normative subjects, it is, as suggested by Shildrick (2009, p 117), 'viewed as deviant, degraded or simply not acknowledged in the non-normative subject'. Both desexualisation and the construction of sexuality in dementia as problematic and excessive thus positions people with dementia as 'Other', outside the realms of ideal modernist subjectivity.

Clearly, the existing narrow discursive constructs of sexuality as either non-existing or as a problem to be 'handled' does not 'enable a consideration of the complexity of feelings people living with dementia might have regarding their intimate relationships', as Youell and colleagues (2016, p 949) succinctly put it. The aim of this chapter is thus to explore how persons with Alzheimer's disease and partners of persons with Alzheimer's disease make sense of sexuality. The chapter's discussion is based on findings from a qualitative interview study with 19 participants who were all in heterosexual coupled relationships. All interviewees with Alzheimer's disease lived at home with their spouses. Consequently the chapter does not discuss experiences of sexuality among singles with dementia, same-sex relationships, or the particular challenges to couple's sexual relationships that arise in care settings (for research on this see, for example, Bauer et al, 2013; Simpson et al, 2018; Roelofs et al, 2019; Villar et al, 2015).

What is 'dementia'?

Growing old does not always imply becoming ill with dementia, but the World Health Organization (WHO) states that 'dementia is one of the major causes of disability and dependency among older people worldwide' and that the risk of developing dementia is increasing with progressing age (WHO, 2019). Dementia is not an illness in itself but an umbrella term for a range of cognitive illnesses that affects memory, thinking and one's capacity to perform everyday tasks. Alzheimer's disease is the most common form of dementia.

Moreover, the biomedical definitions of dementia as deterioration in cognitive function are also closely intertwined with cultural discourses of dementia as 'loss of self', 'tragedy' and the most dreaded aspect of old age (McParland et al, 2017; Herskovits, 1995; Hillman and Latimer,

2017). Cultural constructions of 'the demented' focus solely on the medical condition and overlook the person and social identities behind the illness. In recent decades, these stigmatising discourses have been increasingly challenged by discourses of 'living well with dementia', which emphasise the continuing personhood and capacities of people with dementia and seek to normalise the condition. However, as argued by McParland et al (2017), 'the tragedy discourse' and 'the living well discourse' only provide highly dichotomised views of dementia, and fail to account for the complex experiences of living with the illness. As suggested by Hulko (2009), experiences of dementia are very much dependent on social location, such as ethnicity, 'race', class, gender and sexuality. Experiences of the sexual and intimate relationship when living with Alzheimer's disease should thus not only be understood in relation to pathology but just as much to the social discourses on dementia and how these intersect with social location, including one's sexual and relationship biography in the past (Baikie, 2002). This chapter will, in particular, focus on the intersections of gender and sexuality in heterosexual couples living with Alzheimer's disease, since the impact of gender is often overlooked in dementia research in general and especially with regards to sexuality (cf. Hayes et al, 2009).

"The sex therapist has arrived": the study and its participants

There are few qualitative studies on experiences of sexuality and intimacy when living with dementia, and most existing studies only include interviews with partners and not with the persons with dementia themselves (for exceptions see, for example, Wright, 1993; Harris, 2009). In this study, both people with Alzheimer's disease and their partners were included, based on the premise that people with dementia experiences ought to be heard on the matter of sexuality and that their narratives are valid accounts (Wilkinson, 2002). Participants were recruited from memory clinics, support groups and a dementia day centre, in different cities in Sweden. Recruitment turned out to be difficult and time-consuming, and this could reflect how sexuality and dementia is a sensitive topic, which few people were comfortable discussing with a researcher, and in particular if they knew their spouse was also going to be interviewed. However, those who participated often said they did so because sexuality and intimacy were topics they had missed discussing in support groups, at the memory clinic or in other contexts after the diagnosis. One couple interviewed, Anna and Anders, joked about me as the "sex-therapist", but there was some truth to this joke, in particular for the wife Anna who really wanted them to resume their former sexual intimacy, which had ended after the dementia diagnosis. Although I did not see it as my role, as a qualitative researcher, to support couples who faced difficulties in their relationships, I reflected a great deal on how participating in the study impacted on participants and their interactions in the relationships. While for most it was evidently a relief to voice feelings of frustration or loss, for some it was very emotional and painful to articulate their experiences, and I have felt a great responsibility when representing these narratives.

In total, 19 persons participated in the study – 7 of these were diagnosed with Alzheimer's disease and 12 were partners of a person with Alzheimer's disease. Participants were heterosexual, married and aged from 55 to 87. Seven interviewees were wives living with a husband with Alzheimer's disease and five were husbands living with a wife with Alzheimer's disease. Two women and five men with an Alzheimer diagnosis were interviewed. Elisabeth (all names are pseudonyms), one of the interviewees, got her diagnosis changed to mild memory impairment after the interview. She remained in the study, however, as it was her reaction to and experience of the dementia diagnosis that was of interest, not the symptoms of the illness per se.

Most interviewees were still living together with their spouse in a shared home. Only three of the interviewees had a partner with Alzheimer's disease living in a nursing home at the time of the interview. The couples had been in the relationship on average 40–50 years, and all but four interviewees had raised children together with their partner. Participants represented a mix of middle-class and working-class backgrounds. All were white and born in the Nordic countries.

All interviewees were interviewed individually in order for them to express experiences that could be potentially sensitive to share in the presence of the partner, such as infidelity, abuse or other hardships in the relationship. Interviews were semi-structured, lasted in general from 60 to 120 minutes, and were with a few exceptions one-time events. Interviews focused broadly on the themes 'pre-diagnosis sexual and relationship biographies', 'understandings of sexuality and intimacy' and 'experiences of the sexual and intimate relationship after diagnosis'. This allowed interviewees to speak of what they themselves found relevant around their relationships and sexuality in the past, define their own understandings of sexuality and intimacy (including its relevance) and discuss how the sexual and intimate relationship had unfolded over the course of dementia, as a process.

The interviews were analysed following Braun's and Clarke's (2006) guidelines for qualitative thematic analysis. The material was analysed as one set of data, interviews of partners with and without dementia were thus coded together, but, in cases where both partners in the couple were interviewed, themes and patterns were compared and contrasted between partners to have an understanding of joint and separate meaning-making in couples. Responsibility, reciprocity and recognition were three significant themes emerging from the analysis, and the following discussion will revolve around these themes.

Writing up this project has been a difficult task. I am an experienced qualitative researcher, who has conducted interview studies on topics such as sexuality and violence, which are often considered sensitive and demanding. Still, I found the analysis and writing on the interviews in this study challenging in ways that I had not anticipated. What I found particularly difficult was how to represent the great complexity in the narratives I encountered, without falling into the pitfalls of either 'tragedy' or 'living well discourse', as discussed earlier. The partners without dementia sometimes expressed so much grief, and, as a feminist researcher, I felt great affinities with the female spouses who expressed how they struggled with care and responsibilities in their everyday life. I had just had my first child as the study commenced and was pregnant with my second child as the study progressed. These experiences were points of recognition between me and some of the female spouses, which shaped the interview interactions: "You are a mother, you know what it is like to give care" (cf. Oakley, 1981). At the same time, I was also set on representing the voices of people with dementia, and did not want these to become overshadowed by the narratives of spouses without dementia. This chapter is formed out of these tensions, and I wish to lay them open for readers to reflect on as I next turn to the findings of the study.

Gendered responsibility and the impact on sexual selves

Almost as soon as the interview started, the tears rose in Christina's eyes. She was then in her sixties and her husband Carl had been diagnosed with Alzheimer's disease only a few months before we met. They had been "very happy" and had a "great marriage" she said. But dementia had changed this: "In a way I feel that we don't have a marriage the way we used to. […] I'm responsible for everything. Everything" (Christina). The overwhelming feeling of being "responsible for everything" impacted significantly on Christina's and several other female interviewees' experiences of the relationship. That they no longer shared everyday chores such as cooking and cleaning made Christina feel like she had "lost" him as a husband: "He doesn't feel like my husband anymore [...] more like a child". This in turn, made her reject him, both sexually and emotionally. Similarly, the 55-year-old Anna described how the sexual relationship with her husband had ceased after his diagnosis. They still hugged and kissed, but she had a hard time initiating sex since the overwhelming responsibilities in everyday life made her feel more like a "mother of a baby" and less as the desirable woman and the sexual subject she used to be: "I don't feel like a woman. When is there space for me to feel like a woman? Similarly to when you're the mother of a baby you have no time to feel like a woman at all. You're a mother all the time, breast-feeding, doing things all the time." To Anna, being responsible and caring, as a mother of a baby or a wife of a husband with Alzheimer's disease, was an experience of feeling degendered and thus also desexualised.

These experiences of how responsibility, ranging from financial issues to everyday household chores and providing constant reminders, impacted negatively on companionship, wellbeing and led to a decrease in sexual desire and affection, resonate with findings from several other quantitative and qualitative studies (Nogueira et al, 2017; Ballard et al, 1997; Simonelli et al, 2008; Davies et al, 2010; Dourado et al, 2010; Tsatali and Tsolaki, 2014). But, although both male and female partners in this study described how they were currently responsible for most things in their coupled relationships, there were notable gender differences in terms of how responsibilities impacted on the sexual relationship. The female spouses described in detail how increasing responsibilities not only caused tiredness and stress, but fundamentally changed the roles and identities of the partners in the couple. Such changes effectively impacted on sexual desire and how the women perceived themselves and their partners as sexual beings. None of the men interviewed pointed to care responsibilities in the past or the present as impacting on their sexual selves and desire.

How are these gendered experiences of responsibility and sexuality to be understood? First of all, it is worth considering the relationship biographies of the couples over the life course (Baikie, 2002). Most interviewees pointed to 'ups and downs' in their marriages. Some couples had gone through some significant hardships, such as the loss of a child and major illnesses and disabilities in the family. Still, almost all described their relationship as happy overall and said that the sexual relationship had been satisfying over the years. But, the extent to which men and women described gender inequalities in their relationships differed considerably. The women talked of how they earlier in life had been responsible for children and household chores while their husbands had been absent and worked a lot, a division they described in negative terms. The men also talked of gender divisions in their relationships, but they described these less negatively, as voluntary and functional divisions. Women thus had more first-hand and negative experiences of care-burden and household responsibilities from the past, which may have impacted on how they related to responsibilities when living with a spouse with Alzheimer's disease.

Moreover, the female partners seemed to engage in emotional labour and identity management to a greater extent than the male partners (cf. Calasanti and King, 2007). For example, women described how they tried to sustain their husband's self-esteem as well as their respectable outward appearance when living with dementia. This involved activities such as putting money in a husband's wallet to make it still possible for him to pay, letting him cut up the steak like he used to, or in other ways facilitating in order for him to participate and maintain self-esteem and masculinity. "I try to uphold him […] I want him to be respected still", as the interviewee Ellinor asserted when talking about how her husband was viewed in the nursing home where he now lived. This greater emotional investment in care that the women took on is likely to have caused more stress and exhaustion and impacted more on sexual desire. All told, the gendered inequalities in the past and the present that female partners accounted for seemed to exhaust them to a greater extent than the male partners with ill wives and to impact more on desire (see also Hayes et al, 2009).

In most cases, responsibility and its impact on the sexual relationship was felt to be increased by partners, though 80-year-old Elisabeth, who had herself recently been diagnosed with Alzheimer's disease, also raised the issue of care responsibility for her husband as a major concern. Their intimacy and her sexual desire and attraction for him were long gone: "It's more like work than a marriage. I run things and make things work at home as long as possible." Although she occasionally experienced sexual desire on her own, she reported that this just underscored her sadness. This sexual desire reminded her of what was lost to her, as a woman with dementia in her eighties grappling with the loss of control her own illness caused, while simultaneously caring for her husband.

"Dancing out of step": loss of reciprocity

> Christina: 'So it's not only to do with responsibility. I could have taken on that responsibility if I felt I had that bit of him that I need from him.'

Partners' experiences of increasing responsibility and its negative impact on the sexual relationship was closely intertwined with experiences of loss of reciprocity and companionship in the relationship, which is seen in Christina's words on missing "that bit of him" (also Hayes et al, 2009; Davies et al, 2010). However, experiences of loss of reciprocity were also gendered. The female partners emphasised how declining intellectual and emotional reciprocity impacted negatively on sexual intimacy. The male partners instead described the loss of sexual reciprocity in that partners no longer responded sexually like they used to.

Anna, for example, described eloquently how her sexual relationship with her husband, Anders, was disrupted by the loss of intellectual reciprocity. They had become a couple in their forties and sex had been a very important bond in their relationship over the years. Their sexual intimacy had been explorative and was not limited to penetrative intercourse. Conversations played an important role in their sexual relationship. But when Anders was diagnosed with Alzheimer's disease in his late fifties the conversations faded, and she thereafter no longer experienced him as the same person: "Anders isn't the person I fell in love with, simply. [...] One of the things I fell for completely was his brain, his intellect. And suddenly there's another person in front of me, who I can no longer encounter intellectually." As Anna was initially attracted to her husband's intellect and their conversations, and Alzheimer's disease as a cognitive illness affects thinking and language, she thus perceived him as less desirable. The 75-year-old Ellinor voiced similar experiences, and compared her husband to a child because of his declining intellect:

> 'It's not the same person. This is not an intellectual person, on the same level as me. I feel discomfort. You could compare to young children, you're taking on this protecting or parenting role, and that creates a barrier. You're not having sex with a three-year-old. You don't want him to touch you like that. It may sound coarse but I can't find a better way to put my feelings.' (Ellinor)

The lack of companionship and emotional and intellectual reciprocity was something that both male and female partners of persons with Alzheimer's disease voiced as impacting negatively on the relationship. Also, Ellinor's description of the relationship as more of a parent–child relationship than that of equal lovers figured in several interviews in this study, as well as in previous research (Hayes et al, 2009; Davies et al,

2010; Baikie, 2002). Yet, the male partners did not experience the loss of emotional and intellectual reciprocity as troubling to sexual intimacy. The 60-year-old Fredrik, whose wife had had an Alzheimer's diagnosis for four years, described the sexual relationship as a continuous source of comfort and pleasure – even as mutual support, exchange and connection was lost in other respects:

> 'It felt like I'd lost this woman who used to stand by my side, who helped me in decision-making, who comforted me when I was sad. I had already lost that woman. But my wife as my lover remained for longer. I had lost her on an intellectual level. But in a way I felt that our love life was like an oasis in the desert. Something that remained still, as a solace in this terrible disease that holds so much grief. A grief so deep you could drown in it.' (Fredrik)

Eventually, however, Fredrik's wife became increasingly disinterested in sexual activities and no longer responded the way she used to, and it is this loss of sexual reciprocity that became a problem in their relationship. "When I was touching her vagina she felt nothing. She did not respond with pleasure or sighs or, 'Oh, that feels good'. It's like the signals from her vagina didn't make it to the brain. Or, like she didn't feel anything" (Fredrik). Suddenly, the sexual interplay they had developed over many years, of knowing each other's bodies and how to satisfy each other, was disrupted. In a similar vein, the 65-year-old Bosse experienced how his wife, as her Alzheimer's disease progressed, no longer read the sexual signals like before, and that she touched him in ways he did not recognise. Bosse and his wife met when they were young, and he described them as a "jigsaw puzzle where the pieces fitted". They had also been very sexually compatible: "We could immediately see what the other wanted and there was no need for explanations, it was all very smooth." But, in the words of Bosse: "Suddenly we're dancing out of step". This description of a disrupted sexual interplay can be understood as if Alzheimer's disease challenged previous sexual scripts built on mutual pleasures of giving and taking. According to Bosse, even sexual intimacy in a broader sense, such as kissing and 'spooning', became different. While kissing before was about French kissing, Bosse now experienced their kisses as "children's kisses", with hard lips, and as such desexualised.

Bosse's experience of a sexual interaction with a wife who is becoming increasingly child-like and desexualised is quite similar to the experience of female partners. But, the metaphor of the desexualised child is also used about female wives to describe them as innocent and thus in need of protection: "It's like being with a 13-year-old girl who doesn't know what it's about, you just can't [do it], it would probably just scare her. I get no joy from that" (Fredrik). Fredrik in this quotation portrayed his wife as child-like in the sense of being in a vulnerable position. She can no longer understand (and consent) to sex, and could as such be harmed (Benbow and Beeston, 2012; Sandberg et al, 2020). For Fredrik, it was thus the lack of possibilities for consent that was undesirable, rather than the 'child-likeness' of the wife per se.

So, although loss of reciprocity was experienced by both male and female spouses, again there was a notable gender divide. These findings seem to reflect a wider gendered socialisation concerning sex, where women's sexualities are socially and culturally shaped in relation to love and emotional connection to a greater extent than men's. But the findings also resonate with the research by Hayes and colleagues (2009), who argue that women's expressions of greater discomfort with sex with a husband with Alzheimer's disease reflect how 'the identity of husbands receiving care was tarnished more by the illness' (Hayes et al, 2009, p 55). This argument applies also to the study discussed in this chapter. The female partners' attraction for their husbands were linked to the husbands' intellect, autonomy, agency and that they were 'respected', characteristics which they perceived challenged by dementia. Overall, this reflects how sexuality is bound up with asymmetrical gender relations. If men are intelligible and desirable through their intellect, as 'brains', and characteristics associated with masculinity such as independence and agency, dementia becomes a greater disruption to men's desirability compared to women's.

"She doesn't understand me": disrupted and maintained recognition

For some partners, experiences of loss of reciprocity were intertwined with experiences of a loss of recognition of the person with Alzheimer's disease: "He is not the same person"; "There's a distance between us"; "Now she's just so far away." Several partners used words of distance, difference and departing to describe their ill spouses. Very similar to the studies by Hayes et al (2009) and Youell et al (2016), where the spouses with dementia were described as having a 'new self' or as an 'absent presence', the partners found that their husbands and wives with dementia were difficult to recognise and thus represented someone who they were reluctant or unwilling to have sex with.

The feeling of no longer recognising one's partner extended also to physical encounters. Christina described it as a lack of presence even in a physical sense in how her partner touched her: "The last times we've had [sex], I've felt he's not here. I feel it in his hands immediately if he's here or not." Both the interviewees Anna and Bosse talked of being intimate as meeting a partner for the first time. They had to learn to read a person's body language, but with the significant difference that this was someone they had known for a long time:

> 'It's like meeting someone for the first time, [usually] that's exciting cause you don't know the other person at all. But being together [sexually] with a person that you've lived with for that many years and still it feels like you're doing it for the first time, that's not exciting. You thought we knew each other completely and suddenly you don't.' (Bosse)

For Bosse, not recognising his wife and having to get to know her anew was off-putting. Anna was more ambivalent. She expressed that she wanted to reignite the former sexual intimacy with her husband but first she had to figure out *who* he was now and where their relationship was going.

In stark contrast, the interviewees with Alzheimer's disease did not see themselves as different. And if there were problems in their sexual relationships, they were less prone to understand dementia as the cause of the problems. They too spoke of recognition but instead they pointed to the need to be recognised as persons still and to have one's impairments recognised. For some, sexuality and intimacy was a way to be continuously supported and recognised.

Carl, who was diagnosed with Alzheimer's disease only a few months prior to the interview, clearly expressed how he felt misunderstood by his wife. Their sexual intimacy ended quite abruptly as he received his diagnosis. Carl said that the illness had led to a lot of frustration and loss of self-esteem. Also, he became very tired and "empty", and "this emptiness affects not least the sex life". But what Carl perceived as a major cause of their sexual problems was anger and conflict between him and his wife:

> 'I think a lot had to do with us being so angry with each other; we've been very angry like we've never been before in our lives. I felt that she didn't understand that I've got an illness which does this and that. And I got really angry,

and she got really angry [...] and it was this aggression of course that destroyed the sexual desire.' (Carl)

Rather than experiencing himself as a different person, Carl understood his partner's lack of recognition of the disabling consequences of Alzheimer's disease as a reason for the disruption to their sexual relationship.

However, while Carl did not feel recognised, there were also examples of interviewees with Alzheimer's disease who felt supported and validated as persons despite dementia. In these cases, a continued sexual and intimate relationship was sometimes also understood as sustaining recognition. Henning, aged 79, described his wife as a great support, someone who stood by his side through thick and thin. They were also still mutually attracted and had penetrative intercourse regularly. When asked how he felt about their continued desire for each other, he said: "That's a great thing. Cause it's really important, this intimacy. There's some kind of recognition coming from that." In Henning's case, his life narrative centred to a great extent around masculine accomplishments such as sports achievements, sexual assertion and professional achievements. While he regretted no longer being able to work after becoming ill, continued sexual activity seemed to support his identity as a man.

Frida, an 86-year-old interviewee, also described a continued positive intimate relationship four years after her diagnosis. She and her husband, Folke, no longer engaged in penetrative intercourse because of her husband's loss of erectile function and other age-related changes, but they both spoke of continued physical intimacy, of lying close and cuddling. Living with Alzheimer's disease sometimes made her angry and frustrated, but the continued intimacy was then a source of support and recognition to her: "My husband has always been a great support, he's been able to see things in a different light. And if we just lay close together, holding each other and talk, that suffices for me." The couple had had earlier experiences of physical disability, which seemed highly significant to their intimate relationship today when living with a cognitive illness. Frida was immobile for several years in midlife and was then dependent on her husband for help and support in everyday life. For a period, she was using a wheelchair and then often found that people talked over her head, "but then my husband was amazing [and responded], 'You could talk to her yourself, she can speak'". Also, as a result of her physical disability they had had to explore other sexual practices. These earlier experiences of disability and having to re-navigate and re-negotiate the intimate relationship seemed to influence experiences of life with Alzheimer's disease. There was a continuity between Frida's experiences of recognition when living with a physical disability and feeling validated in her present life with Alzheimer's disease, which seemed to enable a continued positive intimate relationship.

Conclusion

The aim of this chapter has been to bring out the multi-faceted experiences of sexuality among people with dementia and their partners, to go beyond narrow discourses of either desexualisation or 'excessive', 'problematic' sexuality in dementia. Until recently, quantitative studies have been the main source of knowledge and focused on two topics: sexual activity and sexual satisfaction (Nogueira et al, 2017; Ballard et al, 1997; Simonelli et al, 2008; Dourado et al, 2010; Tsatali and Tsolaki, 2014). These studies point to a decrease in sexual activity and more sexual dissatisfaction, in particular for partners of a person with dementia. Still, when turning to the qualitative accounts discussed in this chapter, sexuality was not only about 'how much intercourse' and 'how good/bad' sex was. Instead, experiences of sexual relationships were much entangled with the relationship in a wider sense and the changes that dementia brought about. The three themes discussed – experiences of overwhelming *responsibility*, loss of *reciprocity*, and of disrupted or maintained *recognition* – reflected both more general experiences of the relationships and experiences that related specifically to the sexual relationship.

Evidently, experiences of the sexual relationship when living with Alzheimer's disease cannot be reduced to discourses of 'tragedy' or 'living well' (McParland et al, 2017). Burdening responsibility, loss of reciprocity, feelings of no longer recognising one's spouse or not being recognised, were experiences that caused loss of desire and problems in some sexual relationships. Remaining sexual desire could also be associated with grief for both the person with Alzheimer's disease and their partner, as the interviewee Fredrik remarked: "[Sexual desire] doesn't make me happy, it just reminds me of what I have lost." Still, there were also positive aspects. For some, being close, either through sex or touch in a wider sense, sustained the relationship and provided comfort and recognition (also Davies et al, 2010; Baikie, 2002).

As stated in the introduction to this chapter, people with dementia are very rarely involved in studies on sexual and intimate relationships. Interviewing both the person with dementia and the spouse was of significant value, however, not least because it pointed to the different perspectives of both spouses. This was most evident in couples where the sexual and intimate relationship became a problem after the onset of dementia. In these cases, the partners experienced their wives and husbands with dementia as different/not the same and child-like. In contrast, participants with dementia themselves pointed to the disabling consequences of dementia and on the need for having this recognised. This suggests that partners were more influenced by negative cultural discourses of dementia that either infantilised the person with dementia or suggested a 'loss of self'. Those directly affected by Alzheimer's disease themselves were more invested in rights discourses and how being continuously recognised and affirmed was positive for the sexual and intimate relationship.

A particular focus of this study has been on how gender matters to experiences of sexuality and intimacy in heterosexual couples. The female interviewees articulated to a greater extent than men how everyday caring responsibilities impact on sexual desire (Simonelli et al, 2008; Davies et al, 2012). Resonating with findings from previous research, such as that of Hayes and colleagues (2009), loss of emotional and intellectual reciprocity in the relationship disrupted female spouses' attraction for their husbands with Alzheimer's disease and their desire for sex. Male partners, in contrast, spoke of experiencing loss of reciprocity in terms of the sexual exchange – that the wives with dementia no longer mutually interacted in sexual and intimate situations. Taking a feminist approach, which is rarely done in dementia studies, the chapter argues that gendered inequalities in the past and present could explain the different experiences (Bartlett et al, 2018; Calasanti, 2010). The women attested to much greater involvement in care, also earlier in the life course. They also spoke more of wishing to sustain the self-esteem and identities of their husbands. Thus, men and women were not only socialised differently with regards to sexuality, the unequal positions of men and women in terms of labour and care also influenced experiences of sexuality. Asymmetrical gender relations were also reflected in how the husbands with dementia were perceived as less desirable by their wives as the illness decreased their independence and their intellectual ability. In couples where the wife was affected by Alzheimer's, sexual intimacy ceased to a greater extent because she did not respond sexually or could no longer clearly express consent. These findings are particularly surprising as the context of the study was Sweden, a country with pervasive discourses of gender equality and which is ranked high on gender equality by the UN and the World Economic Forum.

However, it was not only gender that influenced experiences of the sexual relationship. Other social positionings, such as interviewees' age and earlier experiences of illness and disability, also mattered. Among the participants there was a great diversity in terms of age and generational belonging, and this influenced both how they perceived the dementia diagnosis and how they related to sexuality. The interviewees under 65, living with so-called 'early onset dementia', experienced Alzheimer's disease as a greater disruption to their everyday lives and to their sexual relationships, not least because they had been more sexually active before the onset of the illness. The older interviewees, in contrast, spoke more of sexuality as changing from embodied ageing. They also seemed to experience Alzheimer's disease as an illness among others and more as 'senility', a natural part of ageing (for more discussion on this see Sandberg, 2020).

The continued joy in intimate touch expressed by Frida and Folke also suggests that negotiations of sexuality and ability earlier in the life course may actually allow for a more positive relationship in later life when living with dementia. Folke described how they first met 67 years ago in a way which very much underlines their enduring love: "There was social dancing at the open-air dance pavilion and three or four girls were standing over there. One of them has a yellow coat. And our eyes met. And that was it." The way Folke continued to see Frida as very much the same despite her illness, as still the girl with the yellow raincoat, points to the possibilities for a positive and empowered sexuality for couples living with Alzheimer's disease, a sexuality that needs to be explored further in research and practice.

References

Baikie, E. (2002) 'The Impact of Dementia on Marital Relationships', *Sexual and Relationship Therapy*, 17(3): 289–99.

Ballard, C.G., Solis, M., Gahir, M., Cullen, P., George, S., Oyebode, F., and Wilcock, G. (1997) 'Sexual Relationships in Married Dementia Sufferers', *International Journal of Geriatric Psychiatry*, 12(4): 447–51.

Bartlett, R., Gjernes, T., Lotherington, A.T., and Obstefelder, A. (2018) 'Gender, Citizenship and Dementia Care: A Scoping Review of Studies to Inform Policy and Future Research', *Health & Social Care in the Community*, 26(1): 14–26.

Bauer, M., Fetherstonhaugh, D., Tarzia, L., Nay, R., Wellman, D., and Beattie, E. (2013) ' "I Always Look Under the Bed for a Man": Needs and Barriers to the Expression of Sexuality in Residential Aged Care: The Views of Residents with and without Dementia', *Psychology & Sexuality*, 4(3): 296–309.

Benbow, S.M. and Beeston, D. (2012) 'Sexuality, Aging, and Dementia', *International Psychogeriatrics*, 24(7): 1026–33.

Braun, V. and Clarke, V. (2006) 'Using Thematic Analysis in Psychology', *Qualitative Research in Psychology*, 3(2): 77–101.

Calasanti, T. (2010) 'Gender Relations and Applied Research on Aging', *The Gerontologist*, 50(6): 720–34.

Calasanti, T. and King, N. (2007) 'Taking "Women's Work" "Like A Man": Husbands' Experiences Of Care Work', *The Gerontologist*, 47(4): 516–27.

Davies, H.D., Newkirk, L.A., Pitts, C.B., Coughlin, C.A., Sridhar, S.B., Zeiss, L.M. and Zeiss, A.M. (2010) 'The Impact of Dementia and Mild Memory Impairment (MMI) on Intimacy and Sexuality in Spousal Relationships', *International Psychogeriatrics*, 22(4): 618–28.

Davies, H.D., Sridhar, S.B., Newkirk, L.A., Beaudreau, S.A. and O'Hara, R. (2012) 'Gender Differences in Sexual Behaviors of AD Patients and their Relationship to Spousal Caregiver Well-Being', *Aging & Mental Health*, 16(1): 89–101.

Dourado, M., Finamore, C., Barroso, M.F., Santos, R. and Laks, J. (2010) 'Sexual Satisfaction in Dementia: Perspectives of Patients and Spouses', *Sexuality and Disability*, 28(3): 195–203.

Dupuis, S., Wiersma, E. and Loiselle, L. (2012) 'Pathologizing Behavior: Meanings of Behaviors in Dementia Care', *Journal of Aging Studies*, 26(2): 162–73.

Foucault, M. (1990[1976]) *The History of Sexuality, Volume 1: The Will to Knowledge*. Harmondsworth: Penguin.

Gott, M. (2005) *Sexuality, Sexual Health and Ageing*. Maidenhead, UK: Open University Press.

Harris, P.B. (2009) 'Intimacy, sexuality, and Early-Stage Dementia: The Changing Marital Relationship', *Alzheimer's Care Today*, 10(2): 63–77.

Hayes, J., Boylstein, C. and Zimmerman, M.K. (2009) 'Living and Loving with Dementia: Negotiating Spousal and Caregiver Identity Through Narrative', *Journal of Aging Studies*, 23(1): 48–59.

Herskovits, E. (1995) 'Struggling Over Subjectivity: Debates About the "Self" and Alzheimer's Disease', *Medical Anthropology Quarterly*, 9(2): 146–64.

Hillman, A. and Latimer, J. (2017) 'Cultural Representations of Dementia', *PLOS Medicine*, 14(3): e1002274. DOI: 10.1371/journal. pmed.1002274

Hulko, W. (2009) 'From "Not A Big Deal" To "Hellish": Experiences of Older People with Dementia', *Journal of Aging Studies*, 23(3): 131–44.

McParland, P., Kelly, F. and Innes, A. (2017) 'Dichotomising Dementia: Is There Another Way?', *Sociology of Health & Illness*, 39(2): 258–69.

Nogueira, M.M.L., Neto, J.P.S., Sousa, M.F.B., Santos, R.L., Lacerda, I.B., Baptista, M.A.T. and Dourado, M.C.N. (2017) 'Perception of Change in Sexual Activity in Alzheimer's Disease: Views of People with Dementia and their Spouse-Caregivers', *International Psychogeriatrics*, 29(2): 185–93.

Oakley, A. (1981) 'Interviewing Women: A Contradiction in Terms', in Roberts, H. (ed.) *Doing Feminist Research* (1st edn). London: Routledge, pp 30–61.

Roelofs, T.S., Luijkx, K.G. and Embregts, P.J. (2019) 'Love, Intimacy and Sexuality in Residential Dementia Care: A Spousal Perspective', *Dementia*, 18(3): 936–50.

Sandberg, L.J. (2015) 'Sex and Sexualities', in Twigg, J. and Martin, W. (eds) *Routledge Handbook of Cultural Gerontology*. London: Routledge, pp 218–25.

Sandberg, L.J. (2018) 'Dementia and the Gender Trouble? Theorising Dementia, Gendered Subjectivity and Embodiment', *Journal of Aging Studies*, 45(June): 25–31.

Sandberg, L.J. (2020) 'Too Late for Love? Sexuality and Intimacy in Heterosexual Couples Living with an Alzheimer's Disease Diagnosis', *Sexual and Relationship Therapy*. DOI: 10.1080/14681994.2020.1750587

Sandberg, L.J., Bertilsdotter Rosqvist, H. and Grigorovich, A. (2020) 'Regulating, Fostering and Preserving: The Production of Sexual Normates through Cognitive Ableism and Cognitive Othering', *Culture, Health and Sexuality*. DOI:10.1080/13691058.2020.1787519

Shildrick, M. (2009) *Dangerous Discourses of Disability, Subjectivity and Sexuality*. London: Palgrave Macmillan.

Simonelli, C., Tripodi, F., Rossi, R., Fabrizi, A., Lembo, D., Cosmi, V. and Pierleoni, L. (2008) 'The Influence of Caregiver Burden on Sexual Intimacy and Marital Satisfaction in Couples with an Alzheimer Spouse', *International Journal of Clinical Practice*, 62(1): 47–52.

Simpson, P., Brown Wilson, C., Brown, L., Dickinson, T. and Horne, M. (2018) '"We've Had Our Sex Life Way Back": Older Care Home Residents, Sexuality and Intimacy', *Ageing & Society*, 38(7): 1478–1501.

Tsatali, M. and Tsolaki, M. (2014) 'Sexual Function in Normal Elders, MCI and Patients with Mild Dementia', *Sexuality and Disability*, 32(2): 205–19.

Villar, F., Fabà, J., Serrat, R. and Celdrán, M. (2015) 'What Happens in Their Bedrooms Stays in Their Bedrooms: Staff and Residents' Reactions Toward Male–Female Sexual Intercourse in Residential Aged Care Facilities', *The Journal of Sex Research*, 52(9): 1054–63.

Villar, F., Celdrán, M., Serrat, R., Fabà, J., Genover, M. and Martínez, T. (2019) 'Sexual Situations in Spanish Long-Term Care Facilities: Which Ones Cause the Most Discomfort to Staff?', *Sexuality Research and Social Policy*, 16(4): 446–54.

Wilkinson H. (2002) 'Including People with Dementia in Research: Methods and Motivations', in Wilkinson, H. (ed.) *The Perspectives of People with Dementia: Research Methods and Motivations*. London: Jessica Kingsley, pp 9–24.

WHO (2019) 'Dementia', World Health Organization Fact Sheet, 19 September 2019. Available at: https:// www.who.int/news-room/ fact-sheets/detail/dementia [Accessed 7 April 2020].

Wright, L.K. (1993) *Alzheimer's Disease and Marriage: An Intimate Account*. Newbury Park, CA: SAGE.

Youell, J., Callaghan, J.E. and Buchanan, K. (2016) '"I Don't Know if you Want to Know This": Carers' Understandings of Intimacy in Long-Term Relationships When One Partner Has Dementia', *Ageing & Society*, 36(5): 946–67.

9

Older people living in long-term care: no place for old sex?

Feliciano Villar and Josep Fabà

Sexual needs and rights do not disappear just because older people live in long-term care facilities (for convenience, henceforth L-TCF). For instance, Bauer et al (2013) showed that most residents see themselves as sexual beings. In addition, most staff working in L-TCFs commonly report diverse sexual situations involving residents (Villar et al, 2019a). Despite the reported continuation of sexuality, the prevalence of sexual behaviours among older people living in L-TCFs is likely to be lower than for their counterparts living independently in their own homes. Probably for some older people living in L-TCFs, sex does not hold (or not any more) an important place in their life, and they simply do not miss it at all (Villar at al, 2014a). Unquestionably, individuals have the right not to be sexually active in later life, which should be equally supported as the right to continue with sexual relations. However, research in this field has also identified specific barriers that discourage or even prevent older people living in L-TCFs from expressing openly their sexual needs and maintaining their rights to a sexual/erotic life.

In this chapter, we discuss such barriers, paying special attention to the difficulties faced by specific social groups, such as people living with dementia (PLWD) and those identifying as lesbian, gay, bisexual or trans (for convenience, henceforth we will use the abbreviation LGBT). The chapter will also consider further research in this field of knowledge that could help improve sexual expression and help secure the sexual rights of older people living in L-TCFs.

Barriers to sexual expression in L-TCFs

Studies have found L-TCFs are not particularly sex-friendly places to live in, regardless of the country in question (see, for instance, Mahieu and Gastmans, 2012, in Belgium; Bauer et al, 2013, in Australia; Villar et al, 2014a, in Spain; or Simpson et al, 2018b, in England). The reasons given are diverse and interrelated. Some of them are concerned with resident demographics, in light of the high prevalence of chronic conditions (including cognitive impairment), dependency (including some difficulties related to mobility, communication) and polypharmacy (for instance, sleeping pills or anxiolytics) that could potentially impair sexual desire and the ability to engage in sexual activities. However, as well as health-related issues, other barriers may impede even these forms of sexual expression. We will therefore differentiate three kinds of barriers: some related to social attitudes toward sexuality in older age; some to the organisational culture and models of care prevalent in L-TCFs; and some to staff attitudes influencing practices and relations with older people living in L-TCFs.

Social attitudes toward sexuality in older age

Societal values and beliefs regarding sexuality, and particularly sexophobic attitudes regarding sex in later life, have an impact (and could be a barrier) for maintaining sexual activity in later life. According to Simpson et al (2017), such ageist erotophobic discourse can be even more pronounced in care homes, whose residents are perceived as basically postsexual, which can lead to infantilisation and denial of sexual rights.

In many cases, older generations have received scarce information and education concerning sexual issues (Bouman et al, 2006). Many older people have grown up in a context where sex, and particularly non-reproductive sexual behaviour, was considered dirty or sinful, and inappropriate in later life (Gewirtz-Meydan et al, 2018). Such negative views of sexuality could particularly constrain the sexuality of women, traditionally associated with virtue, who were not expected to take the initiative and who, in later life, have been stereotyped as frigid and non-sexual (Syme and Cohn, 2016). The internalisation of such social scripts in older generations could account for Lindau et al's (2007) results, which showed that women, far more frequently than men, tended to report that sex in older age is 'not important at all' and to mention lack of interest as a motive for sexual inactivity. Such attitudes, however, are susceptible to change according to generation, culture, gender or education (Villar et al, 2019b). For instance, white, highly-educated women of the baby-boomer generation, who were protagonists of the feminist movement and the sexual revolution of the 70s and beyond, may have different, more liberal, attitudes towards sex than their older, less educated counterparts (Syme and Cohn, 2016).

Therefore, it comes as no surprise that some generational beliefs, particularly deeply entrenched among the oldest old, might act as a barrier to sexuality, and that such effects are particularly intense in the closed setting of an L-TCF, where residents share time, space and activities. In this context, peers' real or anticipated negative reactions towards sex might act as a form of social control that denies the expression of sexuality among residents or may cause it to remain hidden. For instance, in a study by Villar et al (2015a), residents were much more prone than professionals to express negative emotions (among them, unpleasantness or shame) and judge adversely if prompted to imagine a sexual situation occurring in an L-TCF.

As the 'baby-boomer' generation ages, such attitudes could improve, since its members tend to be more open and liberal than previous generations regarding sexuality (Rowntree and Zufferey, 2015) and sexual issues are expected to become more central. Accordingly, some studies show that they express concerns about the capacity of aged care institutions to recognise their expectations about sexuality (Jönson and Jönson, 2015).

Discourses shaping sexuality in later life not only influence older people's attitudes, but also those of their relatives. For instance, residents' families/grown-up children could find it difficult to accept that their father or their mother is sexually active. Such denial, or even rejection, could be particularly strong if they are widows or widowers, and for those who live in L-TCF (Gilmer et al, 2010), thus becoming a major barrier that might influence staff to discourage (or at least not to support) sexual relationships within the institution, fearing relatives' reactions (Simpson et al, 2018b).

Conceptions of care and organisational culture

Cultures of care (Fine, 2015) involve a set of shared values, beliefs, expectations and practices about what is supposed to be 'good care' and which define both the responsibilities of staff and the position of older people in a care relationship.

Indeed, it has been observed that 'the biomedical culture of care' has been the traditional (and dominant) conception (Ostaszkiewicz et al, 2018). In this model, the professional is conceived as a care dispenser, an expert who decides on the type and extent of care needed by residents. Sometimes functioning in a paternalistic way, the professional bias can veer towards controlling behaviour rather than supporting residents' autonomous choices, placing a premium on efficiency as the fundamental criterion for quality care. Such a perspective tends to over-emphasise protection of patients or residents (sometimes even from themselves), which can marginalise the importance of autonomy over everyday decisions and care practices (Morgan, 2009).

Within this model of care, residents' sexual expressions can be treated as behavioural problems to be eliminated or else simply ignored, acting as if residents had no sexual interests. Thus, most L-TCFs do not have formal policy guidelines to help staff facilitate residents' choices in relation to sexual expressions. They commonly lack suitably trained staff and the facilities to support sexual practices (Shuttleworth et al, 2010), such as double beds or sexual materials (magazines or videos with sexual content, sex toys, and so on).

In more recent years, however, we are beginning to witness a more open recognition of sexuality and intimacy needs, to which L-TCFs should be responsive (Rowntree and Zufferey, 2015), but often discourse is still framed in the medical model outlined earlier, where staff identify and decide how to meet physical needs. Rowntree and Zufferey (2015), adopting a more inclusive psychosocial model of care, have argued that older people's sexuality should not just be viewed as a need but also as a right on which residents should decide.

L-TCF culture of care is important because it has an impact on staff and resident attitudes concerning sexuality, factors that, as we have already discussed, constrain or facilitate sexual self-expression. So, when staff members perceive their institution as restrictive, they will less likely feel comfortable about residents' sexuality and thus will be more prone to resort to controlling rather than enabling sexual expressions (Roach, 2004).

The culture of care is also reflected in the organisation of work and the distribution and design of L-TCFs. Thus, many care homes underline the standardisation of staff duties and residents' activities, which facilitates the smooth running of the institution regardless of its impact on expression of residents' sexuality and intimacy needs. Commonly, residents are submitted to schedules that they have not decided and spend many hours in common spaces and in company (but not necessarily interacting) with other residents. Similarly, facilities are designed like hospitals, prioritising control and quick access to residents' rooms over the maintenance of their privacy (Morgan, 2009).

In this context, maintaining sexual relationships is very difficult. In fact, lack of privacy represents the most frequent barrier mentioned by professionals and residents of long-term institutions for older people (Villar et al, 2014a). In a context where, as already argued, establishing a partnered sexual relationship is extremely difficult, masturbation might be a readily available form of sexual release and a way of compensating for and channeling residents' sexual needs. However, the lack of private spaces also leaves little room for masturbation without worry of being interrupted (Villar et al, 2016).

Professional attitudes

Broader social attitudes towards sexuality in older age and the dominant culture of care within the L-TCF are likely to have an impact on the professional stance towards sexual rights and the sexual expression of older people living in L-TCFs. Such a stance is particularly important, since staff reactions and practices regarding residents' sexuality may act as the primary barrier or facilitator (Villar et al, 2014a). Such attitudes are framed, as Trish Hafford-Letchfield discusses in Chapter 11 of this volume, in a culture of care in which the topic of sexuality and intimacy remains invisible and is considered a taboo.

Some studies have found that, when asked, many care staff express an attitude of respect concerning residents' sexual expression, whether in heterosexual relationships (Villar et al, 2015a) or involving masturbation (Villar et al, 2016), an attitude that often prevents interference in such expressions. Despite this apparently supportive approach, negative attitudes are also commonplace and take different forms. In some cases, even while recognising that some residents have legitimate sexual needs, some professionals do not believe that such needs should be promoted within the institution, and view them as a threat that can potentially complicate their work and lead to problematic situations (see, for instance, Villar et al, 2019a).

Other studies have found that staff could adopt a condescending or paternalistic stance (Bauer et al, 2016). Thus, they sometimes view sexual expressions, and particularly partnered heterosexual sexual expressions, in a romanticised way, as 'cute' or 'amusing'. However, such infantilising attitudes are less likely to occur when demonstrations of sexual desire and arousal are explicit (Ehrenfeld et al, 1999).

Joking, mocking or gossiping with workmates are also frequent reactions of staff. They are not always an overt rejection of residents' sexual expression, since sometimes they could be a way to reduce discomfort or embarrassment prompted by the situation (Bauer et al, 2016). However, such reactions could mean a lack of respect, discouraging residents to rely on staff as a source of help and advice on sexual issues.

Although overtly negative reactions to residents' sexual expressions, such as reprimands, are not general staff practice, supportive reactions, such as attempts to help or give advice, are also uncommon. In contrast, most respondents (and particularly, most assistant carers) try to avoid the problem or transfer the decision to their supervisor, which suggests that care staff, and particularly those in charge of caring in everyday activities, such as assistant carers, may lack awareness of their key role in supporting and helping to secure residents' rights (Gilmer et al, 2010). In addition, the wide diversity in staff reactions underlines the lack of a clear policy towards sexuality and intimacy (Celdrán et al, 2018), which leads to different ways of responding to sexual issues (according, for instance, to gender, religiosity, culture of origin or other factors), thus contributing to uncertainty among professionals and residents.

Sexuality in residential aged care facilities among older people living with dementia

Sexuality does not necessarily diminish with the onset or progression of a dementia (Benbow and Beeston, 2012). According to Lindau et al (2018), among PLWD, 9 per cent of women and 39 per cent of men thought about sex once a week or more, and 37 per cent of women and 74 per cent of men considered sex to be at least a somewhat important part of their life. Additionally, 46 per cent of men and 18 per cent of women with a dementia were sexually active. These percentages were higher among partnered PLWD, rising to 59 per cent and 51 per cent respectively. These statistics do challenge the notion that older people, and particularly PLWD, are sexless or non-sexual.

In spite of this, dementia may modify the way sexuality is experienced and/or expressed. PLWD can experience difficulties when it comes to expressing feelings of love, identifying their loved ones or sequencing sexual activity (Benner-Carson et al, 2015), while their partners can report losses in emotional intimacy, communication and marital cohesion, as well as feelings of stress, isolation and detachment (Quinn et al, 2015). Concerns about the appropriateness of continuing sexual activity with a person who may not totally understand what he or she is doing may lead some caregivers to discourage their partners' sexual behaviours, replacing sexual intercourse with other physically intimate activities such as caressing, fondling, holding hands, hugging and kissing (Davies et al, 2012; Pinho and Pereira, 2019).

Difficulties associated with sexual expressions of PLWD are exacerbated if they live in L-TCFs. For instance, staff's unsupportive attitudes and reactions become more frequent or intensified when sexual situations involve PLWD. Such reactions have been attributed to a tendency to assume that sexual expression is integral to dementia and linked to symptoms such as disinhibition (Makimoto et al, 2015).

In these situations, staff may choose to minimise risks and preclude any sexual expression among PLWD as a way of protecting them, which has been called the 'extreme cautionary stance' (Villar et al, 2014b). Staff's worries are particularly intense when, in partnered sexual situations, just one member of the couple has dementia, which could reflect concerns about consent and the perception that sexual relations could be coercive and therefore abusive (Villar et al, 2018a).

In this regard, a tension exists between two opposite poles: on the one hand, professionals must protect residents' right to freely engage in sexual activities, which is seen as inherently human; and, on the other hand, they must safeguard more vulnerable residents with cognitive impairment against committing, or becoming victims of, non-consensual sex and sexual harassment (Wilkins, 2015; Thys et al, 2019). While L-TCFs should enable PLWD to deploy the right to express their sexual desires to maintain agency, because sexuality is a fundamental component of quality of life and wellbeing, dementia could compromise decision-making capabilities, including those necessary to express themselves. Indeed, there seems to be an increasing awareness that the ethical dilemmas raised by the sexual expressions of PLWD should be addressed on a case-by-case basis (Tarzia et al, 2012; Thys et al, 2019).

Deciding when sexual activity should be encouraged or discouraged may involve evaluating individuals' capacity to consent, although it is not clear how such evaluation should be carried out. By implication, under this approach, it is assumed that living with a dementia does not automatically equate to incompetence in any kind of decision-making (Mahieu and Gastmans, 2012). Several authors have proposed different indicators that PLWD should reunite to consider that they are capable of consent, such as being in an early stage of dementia according to standardised psychometric instruments; understanding the nature of the relationship and the risks involving the activity (Lichtenberg and Strzepek, 1990); and having basic sexual knowledge, being able to differentiate between appropriate and inappropriate places and moments for sexual activity, or having the ability to express a personal choice (Vancouver Coastal Health Authority, 2009).

Nonetheless, some authors have been critical about these standards, since, by paying too much attention to knowledge and cognitive capacity they may become unreachable for some PLWD, and they could become a shortcut for professionals who work in L-TCFs to prohibit most types of sexual expression (Victor and Guidry-Grimes, 2019). Furthermore, Tarzia et al (2012) have argued that some of the standards imply that, in order to allow sexual activity to occur, PLWD have to prove themselves capable, when it should be the other way around, that is, professionals should prove that the individual is incapable before prohibiting sexual activity. In sum, as regards safeguarding, it has been counter-argued that, while it may be reasonable to apply rigid criteria to establish the capacity to make medical or legal decisions, adults without cognitive deterioration often make decisions about their sexual life in a barely logical/reasoned way. Such individuals are not required to search for all manner of information nor asked to balance the pros and cons and possible risks and long-term implications (Lindsay, 2010).

In response to these challenges, Mahieu et al (2014) have formulated an alternative framework for ethical decision-making. They recommend that when involved in decisions about residents' sexual expression, professionals should consider: first, the 'decentred self', which means that we cannot completely understand and possess ourselves, so decisions should not be based exclusively on the previous interests or the lifestyle of the PLWD, because dementia changes thought and action. Second, we exist through a body that acquires a tacit knowledge about how to engage with the world that may not necessarily be fully erased by cognitive decline, so our physical actions do not need to be the result of cognitive processes. Our body is always a body at risk, which makes us vulnerable, and there is no such thing as a risk-free life. Thus, PLWD cannot be protected from all harm, but efforts must be made to protect them from unreasonable harm. Third, dementia may strip objects and places of their meaning, making it more difficult for PLWD to use them as generally expected. For instance, individuals may struggle to differentiate between public and private spaces. Fourth, humans are connected to others, and such connections entail the ethical responsibility of mutual care and protection. Accordingly, 'mutual assent, not necessarily in the guise of informed consent, is without question a necessary condition for physical intimacy' (Mahieu et al, 2017, p 64).

The presence of challenging or inappropriate sexual behaviours (ISB) may further complicate responses to the sexual expressions of PLWD. Defined as physical or verbal acts of an explicit or perceived sexual nature that are not acceptable in the social context where they occur (Johnson et al, 2006), ISB should be considered one of the many behavioural disturbances associated with dementia, and include sexually explicit comments, trying to touch or grab other people's breasts or genitals, or undressing or masturbating in public (Black et al, 2005).

ISB are considered problematic by professionals working in L-TCFs, who may see them as threatening both to their own wellbeing and to the wellbeing of the other residents, and difficult to discourage, which increases the likelihood of restrictive and intrusive forms of 'treatment' (often involving pharmacology), instead of exploring non-pharmacological interventions (Thys et al, 2019). Nevertheless, since pharmacological treatments can occasion negative side effects, it is commonly accepted that ISB should be first treated using a non-pharmacological approach (Black et al, 2005; Tucker, 2010), especially when their evaluation suggests that they may have a psychosocial aetiology, and when there is no risk of harm. When treating ISB, the ultimate goal should not be to eradicate any interest in sexual activity but to modify how this interest is expressed, turning ISB into appropriate sexual expressions that can lead to their satisfaction. Providing the reader with strategies that will help achieve such a goal in every single scenario is utterly impossible, given the lack of literature on this topic and, most importantly, the fact that each ISB must be addressed in a unique way. But, let's take, as examples, the cases of a person who masturbates in common spaces, and of an individual who offers money to different staff members in exchange for sex. In these situations, it should be noticed that masturbating, or longing for shared sexual activity, is not inappropriate in itself. What turns these sexual expressions into ISB is the space where masturbation is taking place, and that having sex with a resident falls far beyond the duties that staff members shall fulfill. Perhaps the easiest solution in these situations might be interrupting masturbation each time that it occurs and deterring the resident from trying to engage in sexual relationships, but that would only lead to unfulfilled sexual need. Instead, moving the first resident to his/her room, where masturbating can no longer be deemed as inappropriate, or providing the second one with a space where he/she can be sexually active with his/her life partner (which might have ceased happening after institutionalisation), could be more sensitive options. In Chapter 11 of this volume, Hafford-Letchfield discusses some useful principles on how institutions and their staff should manage sexuality in PLWD who live in residential settings.

LGBT older adults and residential aged care facilities

Some aspects of ageing affect all of us (for instance, adapting to retirement, overcoming health problems, or facing dependency), but when compared to their heterosexual counterparts, older LGBT-identifying individuals can face different challenges in terms of support structures following bereavement, and experience a higher rate of health problems, combined with greater reluctance to seek healthcare when needed and a lower availability of informal support, which, taken together, can lead to a greater dependence in later life on formal care services, such as L-TCFs (MetLife, 2010; Brennan-Ing et al, 2014). Nevertheless, such institutions often seem ill-equipped to recognise and meet the specific characteristics and needs of those identifying as LGBT (Willis et al, 2016). Indeed, moving into a nursing home is commonly cited as a major concern of older and younger LGBT individuals.

One of the commonest fears identified by previous research is being rejected or neglected by healthcare providers. For example, in a report of the US National Senior Citizens Law Center (NSCLC, 2011), only 22 per cent of the LGBT older adults that were surveyed considered that LGBT older adults could be open about their sexual orientation and/or their gender identity with the staff working in nursing homes, assisted living facilities or other L-TCFs. Concerns about being neglected, abused, or verbally or physically harassed were also common among LGBT people aged 45 and over (AARP, 2018), and instances of mistreatment have been reported in L-TCFs. These have included verbal or physical harassment by staff, staff refusal to accept medical power of attorney, restriction of visitors, staff refusal to use preferred name or pronoun when addressing transgender persons, and failure to provide proper medical care because of sexual orientation or gender identity (NSCLC, 2011). Furthermore, a significant number of LGBT older adults perceive that most L-TCFs lack anti-discrimination policies about sexual orientation (Johnson et al, 2005).

Other commonly articulated fears relate to the attitudes of other residents. Not being accepted or respected, being isolated, or even being mistreated or ostracised by roommates or other residents, can also be counted among them (Johnson et al, 2005; Stein et al, 2010; NSCLC, 2011). Many older LGBT people grew up in (and continue to experience) sociocultural contexts where homophobic and transphobic attitudes were widespread. Actually, such negative attitudes remain a reality in L-TCFs, as fellow residents seem to constitute the main source of verbal and physical harassment (NSCLC, 2011). Further, residents' reactions towards sexually active LGBT-identified peers seems far more negative than the reactions of staff (Villar et al, 2015b), which, again, could impede sexual expression and undergird discriminatory practice.

Anticipating discrimination in an L-TCF can also lead to fear of being open about one's sexuality with staff and residents. Some LGBT older residents may find it threatening to express their identity and feel safer keeping it hidden. Indeed, this may involve 're-closeting' after many years of being 'out' and struggling to validate their difference. It is also ironic that, suddenly, people who are now denied a sexuality are gifted with a heterosexual (and cisgender) past. Gay and lesbian couples may now feel pressure to 'turn into' brothers and sisters, respectively, or close friends (Stein et al, 2010; Furlotte et al, 2016; Putney et al, 2018). This enforced self-protective strategy of denial may not be an option for some transgender persons, as they can be 'outed', for instance, during physical care. Some residents may feel obliged to take additional steps, like cutting bonds with their family of choice and LGBT cultures/communities to avoid being 'outed' by external visitors (Putney et al, 2018). Nevertheless, attempts to actively conceal sexual or gender identification come with costs and especially to mental health (Gardner et al, 2014).

In light of the kind of fears just outlined, L-TCF staff attitudes are crucial, given that staff provide direct care for residents and are involved in the making and implementing of policy decisions. Their co-operation is essential in supporting sexual and gender diversity in L-TCFs and in identifying, challenging and, hopefully, eradicating any discriminatory practices that emerge. Professionals should consider that, apart from overt discrimination, covert discrimination can occur in subtler ways, such as disparagement, stigmatisation or heterosexist presumptions (Villar et al, 2019c). For instance, many L-TCF staff seem to equate good care for LGBT residents with treating them just like their heterosexual peers, ignoring their unique healthcare needs and distinctive characteristics. As well-meant as they might be, this means that sexual orientation may not be considered a relevant variable when it comes to providing formal assistance (Dorsen and van Devanter, 2016; Simpson et al, 2018a). Similarly, although staff apparently hold positive attitudes toward LGBT individuals, most of them recognise that this collective could be a potential source of problems to deal with, and the existence of a gap between what they consider to be good practice and the ordinary practice in their care homes (Villar et al, 2018b). In this regard, it should be noted that some studies suggest that younger, female and non-religious staff may be more tolerant of sexual and gender diversity (Simpson et al, 2018a).

Finally, in this section, although some individuals would prefer LGBT-only long-term care services, most would prefer to live in LGBT-inclusive facilities (that might function as communities within a wider community), where LGBT-phobic attitudes and discrimination would be subject to censure and LGBT residents could feel safe without being excluded from their broader community (Riveria et al, 2011; Putney et al, 2018). Non-heterosexual older people currently living in LGBT-friendly L-TCFs often affirm that they chose to move there so as to live with other residents who also identify themselves as LGBT and because they expected to feel not only tolerated, but seen as part of the residential community (Matthews et al, 2016).

Conclusion

This chapter has shown how the expression of sexual and intimacy needs and the enactment of sexual rights are limited in L–TCFs and, that when apparent, such forms of self-expression can be subject to monitoring by staff who perceive them in problematic, if not pathological, terms. Indeed, studies in this field of knowledge have amply shown how staff attitudes are key to implementation of sexual, erotic and bodily rights of older people living in L–TCFs. Evidence highlights the importance of taking into account the diversity of staff, but also particularly the broad diversity of residents, whose gender, age, religiosity, sexual orientation or cognitive status, just to name a few factors, define particular needs and require specific responses.

Professionals who work in L–TCFs should proactively work to create an environment where it is ensured that sexual rights are fully respected and that residents can reach the highest levels of sexual health. In some cases, this will mean creating opportunities so that those who feel that sex is an important part of their life and wish to be sexually active, either with or without a partner, are allowed to do so. In other cases, this will mean giving full consideration to residents' concerns regarding the changes that they have experienced in their sexual functioning.

Reinforcing staff development and training on sexual issues appears as one of the most fundamental interventions required to achieve the goal of meeting sexual and erotic choices. Staff development sessions should involve honest discussion of conflicts and dilemmas that could be encountered so that all staff can abide by a coherent and consistent response. Residents and their families also need awareness-raising experiences that might challenge them and get them to rethink common misconceptions about sexuality, as well as to be aware of their sexual rights.

Literature in this field of knowledge has also highlighted the importance of developing formal and clear institutional guidelines on sexuality, which promote a consistent approach to sexual issues in daily practice and show the commitment of the organisation with respect of residents' rights (including those not interested in sex). Guidelines and protocols, despite their usefulness, should not be used as recipes to give automatic responses. Any decision should take full consideration of the complexity of each individual case.

Finally, improvement in this area also implies a deeper change. That is, substituting a medical-biological, task-oriented model of care for a person-centred care model. Such a model would also view older people living in L-TCFs not just as bearers of 'needs' but also as human beings with rights and full citizens and would conceive institutions as places to live in, embracing the community in which they are embedded and allow for personalisation and respect for residents' lifestyles and decisions. Addressing this issue is overdue and failure to act would mean contributing to inequality and the denial of some fundamental human rights.

References

AARP (2018) 'Maintaining Dignity: Understanding and Responding to the Challenges Facing Older LGBT Americans: An AARP Survey of LGBT Adults Age 45-Plus'. Available at: https://www.aarp.org/content/dam/aarp/research/surveys_statistics/life-leisure/2018/maintaining-dignity-lgbt.doi.10.26419%252Fres.00217.001.pdf.

Bauer, M., Fetherstonhaugh, D., Tarzia, L., Nay, R., Wellman, D. and Beattie, E. (2013) '"I Always Look Under the Bed for a Man". Needs and Barriers to the Expression of Sexuality in Residential Aged Care: The Views of Residents with and without Dementia', *Psychology & Sexuality,* 4(3): 296–309.

Bauer, M., McAuliffe, L. and Fetherstonhaugh, D. (2016) 'Older People and Sexuality in Residential Aged Care: Reconstructing Normality', in Peel, E. and Harding, R. (eds) *Ageing and Sexualities: Interdisciplinary Perspectives*. New York: Routledge, pp 119–40.

Benbow, S.M. and Beeston, D. (2012) 'Sexuality, Aging, and Dementia', *International Psychogeriatrics*, 24(7): 1026–33.

Benner-Carson, V., Vanderhorst, K. and Koening, H.G. (2015) *Care Giving for Alzheimer's Disease: A Compassionate Guide for Clinicians and Loved Ones*. New York: Springer.

Black, B., Muralee, S. and Tampi, R.R. (2005) 'Inappropriate Sexual Behaviors in Dementia', *Journal of Geriatric Psychiatry & Neurology*, 18(3): 155–62.

Bouman, W.P., Arcelus, J. and Benbow, S.M. (2006) 'Nottingham Study of Sexuality & Ageing (NoSSA I). Attitudes Regarding Sexuality and Older People: A Review of the Literature', *Sexual and Relationship Therapy*, 21(2): 149–61.

Brennan-Ing, M., Seidel, L., Larson, B. and Karpiak, S.E. (2014) 'Social Care Networks and Older LGBT Adults: Challenges for the Future', *Journal of Homosexuality*, 61(1): 21–52.

Celdrán, M., Villar, F., Serrat, R., Fabà, J. and Martínez, T. (2018) 'Policies Regarding Sexual Expression in Spanish Long-Term Care Facilities for Older People', *Journal of the American Geriatrics Society*, 66(5): 1044–5.

Davies, H.D., Sridhar, S.B., Newkirk, L.A., Beaudreau, S.A. and O'Hara, R. (2012) 'Gender Differences in Sexual Behaviors of AD Patients and Their Relationship to Spousal Caregiver Well-Being', *Aging & Mental Health*, 16(1): 89–101.

Dorsen, C. and van Devanter, N. (2016) 'Open Arms, Conflicted Hearts: Nurse-Practitioner's Attitudes Towards Working with Lesbian, Gay and Bisexual Patients', *Journal of Clinical Nursing*, 25(23–24): 3716–27.

Ehrenfeld, M., Bronner, G., Tabak, N., Alpert, R. and Bergman, R. (1999) 'Sexuality Among Institutionalized Elderly Patients with Dementia', *Nursing Ethics*, 6(2): 144–9.

Fine, M. (2015) 'Cultures of Care', in Twigg, J. and Martin, W. (eds) *Routledge Handbook of Cultural Gerontology*. Abingdon: Routledge, pp 269–76.

Furlotte, C., Gladstone, J.W., Cosby, R.F. and Fitzgerald, K.A. (2016) '"Could We Hold Hands?" Older Lesbian and Gay Couples' Perceptions of Long-Term Care Homes and Home Care', *Canadian Journal on Aging*, 35(4): 432–46.

Gardner, A.T., de Vries, B. and Mockus, D.S. (2014) 'Aging Out in the Desert: Disclosure, Acceptance and Service Use Among Midlife and Older Lesbians and Gay Men', *Journal of Homosexuality*, 61(1): 129–44.

Gewirtz-Meydan, A., Hafford-Letchfield, T., Benyamini, Y., Phelan, A., Jackson, J. and Ayalon, L. (2018) 'Ageism and Sexuality', in Ayalon, L. and Tesch-Römer, C. (eds) *Contemporary Perspectives on Ageism*. Cham, Switzerland: Springer, pp 148–62.

Gilmer, M.J., Meyer, A., Davidson, J. and Koziol-McLain, J. (2010) 'Staff Beliefs About Sexuality in Aged Residential Care', *Nursing Praxis in New Zealand*, 26(3): 17–24.

Johnson, C., Knight, C. and Alderman, N. (2006) 'Challenges Associated with the Definition and Assessment of Inappropriate Sexual Behavior Amongst Individuals with Acquired Neurological Impairment', *Brain Injury*, 20(7): 687–93.

Johnson, M.J., Jackson, N.C., Arnette, J.K. and Koffman, S.D. (2005) 'Gay and Lesbian Perceptions of Discrimination in Retirement Care Facilities', *Journal of Homosexuality*, 49(2): 83–102.

Jönson, H. and Jönsson, A. (2015) 'Baby Boomers as Future Care Users—An Analysis of Expectations in Print Media', *Journal of Aging Studies*, 34(3): 82–91.

Lichtenberg, P.A. and Strzepek, D.M. (1990) 'Assessments of Institutionalized Dementia Patients' Competencies to Participate in Intimate Relationships', *The Gerontologist*, 30(1): 117–20.

Lindau, S.T., Schumm, L.P., Laumann, E.O., Levinson, W., O'Muircheartaigh, C.A. and Waite, L.J. (2007) 'A Study of Sexuality and Health Among Older Adults in the United States', *The New England Journal of Medicine*, 357(8): 762–74.

Lindau, S.T., Dale, W., Feldmeth, G., Gavrilova, N., Langa, K.M., Makelarski, J.A. and Wroblewski, K. (2018) 'Sexuality and Cognitive Status: A U.S. Nationally Representative Study of Home-Dwelling Older Adults', *Journal of the American Geriatrics Society*, 66(10): 1902–10.

Lindsay, J.R. (2010) 'The Need for More Specific Legislation in Sexual Consent Capacity Assessments for Nursing Home Residents', *Journal of Legal Medicine*, 31(3): 303–23.

Mahieu, L. and Gastmans, C. (2012) 'Sexuality in Institutionalized Elderly Persons: A Systematic Review of Argument-Based Ethics Literature', *International Psychogeriatrics*, 24(3): 346–57.

Mahieu, L., Anckaert, L. and Gastmans, C. (2014) 'Eternal Sunshine of the Spotless Mind? An Anthropological-Ethical Framework for Understanding and Dealing with Sexuality in Dementia Care', *Medicine, Health Care, & Philosophy*, 17(3): 377–87.

Mahieu, L., Anckaert, L. and Gastmans, C. (2017) 'Intimacy and Sexuality in Institutionalized Dementia Care: Clinical-Ethical Considerations', *Health Care Analysis*, 25(1): 52–71.

Makimoto, K., Kang, H.S., Yamakawa, M. and Konno, R. (2015) 'An Integrated Literature Review on Sexuality of Elderly Nursing Home Residents with Dementia', *International Journal of Nursing Practice*, 21(S2): 80–90.

Matthews, C., Hill, C. and Frederiksen, D. (2016) 'Niche Housing as Social Prosthetic for Lesbian, Gay, Bisexual, and Transgender Seniors: Resident Motivations and Perceptions', *Journal of Interior Design*, 42(3): 29–51.

MetLife (2010) 'Still Out, Still Aging: The MetLife Study of Lesbian, Gay, Bisexual, and Transgender Baby Boomers'. Available at: https://www.asaging.org/sites/default/files/files/mmi-still-out-still-aging.pdf.

Morgan, L.A. (2009) 'Balancing Safety and Privacy: The Case of Room Locks in Assisted Living', *Journal of Housing for the Elderly*, 23(3): 185–203.

NSCLC (2011) *LGBT Older Adults in Long-Term Care Facilities: Stories from the Field*. Washington, DC: National Research Center on LGBT Aging. Available at: https://issuu.com/lgbtagingcenter/docs/storiesfromthefield.

Ostaszkiewicz, J., Dunning, T. and Streat, S. (2018) 'Models of Care for Aged Care: Social or Biomedical?', *Australian Nursing and Midwifery Journal*, 25(7): 45.

Pinho, S. and Pereira, H. (2019) 'Sexuality and Intimacy Behaviors in the Elderly with Dementia: The Perspective of Healthcare Professionals and Caregivers', *Sexuality & Disability*, 37(4): 489–509.

Putney, J.M., Keary, S., Hebert, N., Krinsky, L. and Halmo, R. (2018) '"Fear Runs Deep": The Anticipated Needs of LGBT Older Adults in Long-Term Care', *Journal of Gerontological Social Work*, 61(8): 887–907.

Quinn, C., Clare, L. and Woods, R.T. (2015) 'Balancing Needs: The Role of Motivations, Meanings and Relationship Dynamics in the Experience of Informal Caregivers of People with Dementia', *Dementia*, 14(2): 220–37.

Riveria, E., Wilson, S.R. and Jennings, L. (2011) 'Long-Term Care and Life Planning Preferences for Older Gays and Lesbians', *Journal of Ethnographic & Qualitative Research*, 5(3): 157–70.

Roach, S.M. (2004) 'Sexual Behavior of Nursing Home Residents: Staff Perceptions and Response', *Journal of Advanced Nursing*, 48(4): 371–9.

Rowntree, M.R. and Zufferey, C. (2015) 'Need or Right: Sexual Expression and Intimacy in Aged Care', *Journal of Aging Studies*, 35(4): 20–5.

Shuttleworth, R., Russell, C., Weerakoon, P. and Dune, T. (2010) 'Sexuality in Residential Aged Care: A Survey of Perceptions and Policies in Australian Nursing Homes', *Sexuality and Disability*, 28(3): 187–94.

Simpson, P., Wilson, C.B., Brown, L., Dickinson, T. and Horne, M. (2017) 'The Challenges and Opportunities in Researching Intimacy and Sexuality in Care Homes Accommodating Older People: A Feasibility Study', *Journal of Advanced Nursing*, 73(1): 127–37.

Simpson, P., Almack, K. and Walthery, P. (2018a) '"We Treat Them All the Same": The Attitudes, Knowledge and Practices of Staff Concerning Old/er Lesbian, Gay, Bisexual and Trans Residents in Care Homes', *Ageing & Society*, 38(5): 869–99.

Simpson, P., Brown Wilson, C., Brown, L., Dickinson, T. and Horne, M. (2018b) '"We've Had Our Sex Life Way Back": Older Care Home Residents, Sexuality and Intimacy', *Ageing & Society*, 38(7): 1478–1501.

Stein, G.L., Beckerman, N.L. and Sherman, P.A. (2010) 'Lesbian and Gay Elders and Long-Term Care: Identifying the Unique Psychosocial Perspectives and Challenges', *Journal of Gerontological Social Work*, 53(5): 421–35.

Syme, M.L. and Cohn, T.J. (2016) 'Examining Aging Sexual Stigma Attitudes Among Adults by Gender, Age, and Generational Status', *Aging & Mental Health*, 20(1): 36–45.

Tarzia, L., Fetherstonhaugh, D. and Bauer, M. (2012) 'Dementia, Sexuality and Consent in Residential Aged Care Facilities', *Journal of Medical Ethics*, 38(10): 609–13.

Thys, K., Mahieu, L., Cavolo, A., Hensen, C., Dierckx-de-Casterlé, B. and Gastmans, C. (2019) 'Nurses' Experiences and Reactions Towards Intimacy and Sexuality Expressions by Nursing Home Residents: A Qualitative Study', *Journal of Clinical Nursing*, 28(5–6): 836–49.

Tucker, I. (2010) 'Management of Inappropriate Sexual Behaviors in Dementia: A Literature Review', *International Psychogeriatrics*, 22(5): 683–92.

Vancouver Coastal Health Authority (2009) 'Supporting Sexual Health and Intimacy in Care Facilities: Guidelines for Supporting Adults Living in Long-Term Care Facilities and Group Homes in British Columbia, Canada'. Available at: http://www.vch.ca/Documents/Facilities-licensing-supporting-sexual-health-and-intimacy-in-care-facilities.pdf.

Victor, E. and Guidry-Grimes, L. (2019) 'Relational Autonomy in Action: Rethinking Dementia and Sexuality in Care Facilities', *Nursing Ethics*, 26(6): 1654–64.

Villar, F., Celdrán, M., Fabà, J. and Serrat, R. (2014a) 'Barriers to Sexual Expression in Residential Aged Care Facilities: Comparison of Staff And Residents' Views', *Journal of Advanced Nursing*, 70(11): 2518–27.

Villar, F., Celdrán, M., Fabà, J. and Serrat, R. (2014b) 'Staff Attitudes Towards Sexual Relationships Among Institutionalized People with Dementia: Does an Extreme Cautionary Stance Predominate?', *International Psychogeriatrics*, 26(3): 403–12.

Villar, F., Fabà, J., Serrat, R. and Celdrán, M. (2015a) 'What Happens in Their Bedrooms Stays in Their Bedrooms: Staff And Residents' Reactions Toward Male-Female Sexual Intercourse in Residential Aged Care Facilities', *Journal of Sex Research*, 52(9): 1054–63.

Villar, F., Serrat, R., Fabà, J. and Celdrán, M. (2015b) 'As Long as They Keep Away from Me: Attitudes Toward Non-Heterosexual Sexual Orientation Among Residents Living in Spanish Residential Aged Care Facilities', *The Gerontologist*, 55(6): 1006–14.

Villar, F., Serrat, R., Celdrán, M. and Fabà, J. (2016) 'Staff Attitudes and Reactions Towards Residents' Masturbation in Spanish Long-Term Care Facilities', *Journal of Clinical Nursing*, 25(5–6): 819–28.

Villar, F., Celdrán, M., Serrat, R., Fabà, J. and Martínez, T. (2018a) 'Staff's Reactions Towards Partnered Sexual Expressions Involving People with Dementia Living in Long-Term Care Facilities', *Journal of Advanced Nursing*, 74(5): 1189–98.

Villar, F., Serrat, R., Celdrán, M., Fabà, J. and Martínez, T. (2018b) 'Disclosing a LGB Sexual Identity When Living in an Elderly Long-Term Care Facility: Common and Best Practices', *Journal of Homosexuality*, 66(7): 970–88.

Villar, F., Celdrán, M., Serrat, R., Fabà, J., Genover, M. and Martínez, T. (2019a) 'Sexual Situations in Spanish Long-Term Care Facilities: Which Ones Cause the Most Discomfort to Staff?', *Sexuality Research and Social Policy*, 16(4): 446–54.

Villar, F., Serrat, R., de Sao José, J.M., Montero, M., Arias, C.J., Nina-Estrella, R., Curcio, C.L., da Cassia Oliveira, R., Tirro, V. and Alfonso, A. (2019b) 'Age-Discrepant Couples Involving an Older Adult: The Final Frontier of Ageism? Attitudes in Eight Latin American Countries', *Journal of Intergenerational Relationships*, 17(4): 430–48.

Villar, F., Serrat, R., Celdrán, M., Fabà, J., Genover, M. and Martínez, T. (2019c) 'Staff Perceptions of Barriers That Lesbian, Gay and Bisexual Residents Face in Long-Term Care Settings', *Sexualities*. doi: 10.1177/1363460719876808. Available at: https://journals.sagepub.com/doi/abs/10.1177/1363460719876808.

Wilkins, J.M. (2015) 'More Than Capacity: Alternatives for Sexual Decision Making for Individuals with Dementia', *The Gerontologist*, 55(5): 716–23.

Willis, P., Maegusuku-Hewett, T., Raithby, M. and Miles, P. (2016) 'Swimming Upstream: The Provision of Inclusive Care to Older Lesbian, Gay and Bisexual (LGB) Adults in Residential and Nursing Environments in Wales', *Ageing & Society*, 36(2): 282–306.

10

Ageing and the LGBTI+ community: a case study of Australian care policy

Jane Youell

Introduction

Sexuality and intimacy have largely been seen as a domain of the young and attractive in contemporary society (White, 2011). Assumptions persist that the over-65s should be, or are, sexually retired (Bauer et al, 2007). Ageing has traditionally been associated with decline, frailty, unattractiveness, disability and illness, and wrinkly and withered bodies (through a western cultural lens, at least), so it is easy to dispel any notion that older people would enjoy a full sexual life, and by dispelling it we fail to support and encourage it. When adding to this the sense of distaste, disgust and taboo that older age sex seems to elicit, it is easy to see why there is a dearth of research, policy and good (pro-sex) practice (Bouman et al, 2006). Increasingly, the benefits of a full sexual and intimate life are being recognised across the lifespan, although research seems to focus mostly on ageing and heterosexual sex (Sinković and Towler, 2019).

For those who are older and identify as LGBTI+, there is significantly less evidence of good practice, and greater invisibility, particularly around supporting sexuality and intimacy (McGovern, 2014; Sinković and Towler, 2019). To ignore the importance of sexuality, intimacy and relational needs does older people, especially those already marginalised, a great disservice. The physical, psychological, social and emotional benefits of intimate relationships arguably result in greater pleasure and liberation with age (Rowntree, 2014). Sex, intimacy and relational needs are fundamental to wellbeing, and with the advent of the recent Care Quality Commission (CQC) guidance, health and social care services will be required to show evidence of how they support relationships and sexuality within their services (CQC, 2019), including the LGBTI+ community. This chapter seeks to explore this much-neglected area and add to the scant literature by offering an argument for better LGBTI+ inclusive aged care provision, by reducing invisibility of older LGBTI+ people and by offering examples of good practice using an Australian case study which could be utilised in a UK context.

Context

This work comes about following my research into sexuality, intimacy and relationships affected by dementia (Youell, 2015). The findings of this research suggest that older people are poorly served in terms of their relational wellbeing. In contrast to the assumptions of sexual retirement, which act to desexualise older people, participants often reported that retirement offered opportunities for 'resexualisation' in their relationships. The lack of dependent children, retirement from work and more free time to be together often ignited a more intimate and sexual life. Participants also reported that while they wished to continue a sexual or intimate life, their relationships were often disrupted and ruptured by care plans. It became apparent that living in a relationship affected by dementia was complex. Indeed, this study also showed that some participants had to navigate challenging sexualised behaviour, that capacity and consent were sometimes ill-considered, and that caring often took precedence over loving. What was apparent in my previous research is that no one ever discussed this aspect of dementia with them. It was a privilege to be able to shed light on this often overlooked issue. On reflection, however, I felt that my work was too heterocentric. I had glibly stated in my ethics application that the study was open to all regardless of gender, sexual orientation, sexual identity or relational status. Had I actively sought out diversity in my research? How were service providers, researchers and practitioners supporting diversity in aged care, if at all?

LGBTI+ population: UK and Australia

The number of people who identify as LGBTI+ in the UK is difficult to quantify, with much ambiguity in the statistics (Peel et al, 2016). In 2004, the Department of Trade and Industry published a Final Regulatory Impact Assessment relating to the Civil Partnership Act 2004. This impact assessment quoted statistics from 2002, which suggested that, while there were no definitive figures, approximately 5–7 per cent of the general adult population identified as lesbian, gay or bisexual (LGB). This equated to between 2.35 million and 3.3 million people across the UK. In contrast, the latest figures from the Office for National Statistics (ONS) reported that an estimated 1.1 million people (2 per cent of the population) identify as lesbian, gay or bisexual (ONS, 2017) a similar percentage to the Australian General Social Survey, which suggested 3 per cent of the population identified as gay, lesbian or 'other' (Australian Bureau of Statistics, 2014). Note these UK figures do not include the trans or intersex communities. The Government Equalities Office estimates there are in the region of 200,000 to 500,000 trans people in the UK (Government Equalities Office, 2018), while Amnesty International report that around 1.7 per cent of the population are born with intersex traits (Amnesty International, 2018). In view of such speculation about the LGBTI+ population, generally, statistics regarding those over 65 are even more elusive (Age UK, 2019).

Those over 65 years old who identify as lesbian, gay or bisexual in the UK are estimated to be around 0.7 per cent of the population (ONS, 2017). In August 2019, the ONS reported a UK population of 66.4 million, which would suggest a lesbian, gay or bisexual 65+ population of 465,000 people (ONS, 2019). The ONS is recognised as the national statistical institute of the UK and therefore deemed a reliable source of information. However, figures relating to sexual orientation are estimated using data from Annual Population Surveys and therefore should be regarded with caution, as some of the estimates are based on a small sample size (ONS, 2017). Given the increasing evidence of health inequities in the UK for the older LGBTI+ community (Kneale et al, 2019), that the older LGBTI+ community are less likely to have children to support and care for them, and that they are more likely to live alone, more likely to be single and twice as likely as their heterosexual peers to rely on aged care services, it is essential that we consider how best we can support the rainbow community in older age (Stonewall, 2018; SCIE, 2015). Coming out is an ongoing process for the LGBTI+ community (Klein et al, 2015), and when considering relational needs and how best aged care services can support sexuality and intimacy in this population, these statistics offer a limited picture. While it is useful to have statistical data acknowledging that the older LGBTI+ community are likely to be entering services, it is equally important to recognise that arguments over numbers can obscure how people are regarded and treated. It is therefore necessary that the needs of the older LGBTI+ community are compassionately considered by service providers to enable the creation of safe, caring and understanding spaces.

Inclusive care for older people and the LGBTI+ community

I began to consider the heterocentric nature of my earlier research at around the time I was involved in facilitating dementia awareness training. During the course of this project, it was necessary for me to visit care homes across the south of the UK. I began to ask how many of the residents identified as LGBTI+. More often than not the response from staff was "None, dear", a finding echoed by Willis et al (2016), who argue that care homes create heteronormative spaces where 'same-sex attractions and desires are disregarded' (Willis et al, 2016, p 282). I began to question how inclusive health and social care provisions were, and what factors might need to be in place to improve inclusive services (if, indeed, inclusive services were what the older LGBTI+ community wanted). I was also interested in how these inclusive spaces would enable and support intimate relationships.

There is limited research into the components necessary to create LGBTI+ inclusive aged care and the impact this has on supporting intimate/sexual relationships. Willis et al (2016) call for staff to be more attentive to the needs of older LGB people, especially around respect and dignity, private time with partners and friends, a visibility around inclusion, such as rainbow flags, diversity in advertising, et cetera, and the ability to be comfortable and open with other residents and staff about chosen family and partners. Hopes, however, did not match expectation. Many of those who participated in Willis et al's (2016) study had kept their sexuality a secret in their youth. Most had experienced, or had friends who had experienced, discrimination. These views were, however, reflections on future care and not from those currently living in residential care.

Johnson (2013) argues that for many older LGBTI+ people, fear of discrimination and the lack of 'safe spaces', acts to desexualise and 'makes sexual expression nearly impossible' (Johnson, 2013, p 314). This lack of visibility of intimate relationships causes anxiety around care decisions, as care providers fail to recognise the importance of these partnerships, which acts to exclude partners from care decisions (Peel et al, 2016). This is a nuanced issue, as Price (2012) argues that the LGBTI+ community are 'used to the invisibility and relative safety offered by enforced segregation' and are then 'reluctant to reveal themselves to a potentially condemnatory public gaze'.

This gaze is discussed by Knauer (2011), who argues that ageism and homophobic constructions work together and result in older LGBTI+ people being overlooked or totally ignored. These many and varied intersections play out in a myriad of oppressive practices, even within the community itself, but in aged care provision more broadly. Many older gay men felt abandoned by the community as they aged, feeling increasingly invisible in a youth-focused culture (Jowett and Peel, 2009). The intersections of LGBTI+ ageing and chronic illness led to further community isolation, as those with disabilities were unable to access gay bars and clubs and many relied on heterosexual relatives for their care (Jowett and Peel, 2009). Kimmel (2014) suggests that social gerontology, in particular, has been slow to recognise the importance of LGBTI+ intimate connections and the need for 'private contact and explicit permission to show affection'. It is perhaps unsurprising, then, that the LGBTI+ community often take care of one another, and it is this community of care which creates a strong desire to 'age in place' and avoid senior housing at all costs (Knauer, 2016). How then can we create aged care services which navigate through these complexities and best meet the needs of an increasingly ageing LGBTI+ community?

With this in mind, I undertook a Churchill Fellowship, which enabled the study of LGBTI+ inclusive aged care provision in Australia and the USA. Both Australia and the USA were initially chosen as the LGBTI+ community had experienced similar histories as those of the UK. Australia, the USA and the UK had all repealed Acts which made homosexuality illegal (Noga-Styron et al, 2012), all had previously viewed homosexuality as a mental health disorder (conversion therapy still being available in all three countries, sadly) (Drescher, 2015) and LGBTI+ discrimination had been legislated against (Equality Act 2010). I felt that if the core issues across the three countries were similar, so might be the solutions. It appeared that in Australia, in particular, there was significant work undertaken in inclusive aged care, and it is the findings from the Australian part of my study which inform this chapter. What I had hoped to find, naively perhaps, was a model of LGBTI+ inclusive aged care which supported and encouraged sexual, intimate and romantic relationships. What I actually found was a strong case for legislative change, the necessity for the community itself to champion change and that there is still work to be done before we see services breaking through those assumptions which act to desexualise older adults.

Meeting key stakeholders

Interviews were conducted with key stakeholders in Melbourne, Sydney and Adelaide and interviewees were derived through purposive sampling. As contacts were made, snowball sampling meant that further relevant contacts were recommended. Participants included contacts from the care home sector, older members of the LGBTI+ community, academics, psychiatrists, learning and teaching facilitators, diversity project managers, gerontologists, psychologists, programme and policy managers, quality improvement specialists, directors of care management, researchers, advocates, government officials, community engagement programme managers, faith leaders, authors and film makers, community health workers and even a retired judge. All participants had experience and expertise in LGBTI+ inclusive aged care. This qualitative study gathered data via interviews and focus groups. All discussions were recorded and transcribed. Emergent themes and patterns in the data were sought out using thematic analysis.

An Australian case study

Three broad themes emerged from my discussions with those I met in Australia – national drive, organisational desire and community benefits and examples of good practice. Each of these themes plays an integral role in the creation of inclusive aged care for the LGBTI+ community and it is hoped that these findings add to the ongoing conversations in the UK, particularly around inclusive aged care housing and care provision.

The theme of national drive addresses the policy and proposals which were sanctioned by the federal government in Australia. The legislative changes which resulted also increased available funding, which enabled organisations to promote and support the needs of the LGBTI+ community. Examples of community benefits and good practice are also evidenced. During my time in Australia, the national plebiscite which voted on same sex marriage laws was being held. Despite travelling to witness examples of good practice and to understand how to better create inclusive aged care, the plebiscite made clear that there was still much work to be done. While the 'yes' vote won by clear majority (61.1 per cent), the rhetoric which was heard at the time created real concern, with a sense that the political climate was not dissimilar to the liberation movement of the 1960s and 70s (Australian Bureau of Statistics, 2018).

National drive: the Australian picture

This section will discuss the policy changes and proposals made by the Australian Government which influenced inclusive aged care. Many of those I interviewed felt that the origins of improving inclusive aged care began with the Productivity Commission inquiry of 2011 (Australian

Government, 2011). The purpose of the inquiry was to identify the weaknesses and gaps in care provision in the face of an ever-aging population. The inquiry made many recommendations to further improve aged care to ensure it was robust enough to meet the challenges of the next ten years. Crucially, as part of this inquiry, consideration was given to diversity within the care sector for older people. The Productivity Commission report acknowledged that some groups were identified as special needs groups. Those from Aboriginal and Torres Strait Islander communities, non-English speakers, people living in remote areas, those who were financially and socially disadvantaged, veterans, homeless people and care leavers were all included under the 'special needs' group. The Commission report recommended that, among others, the older LGBTI+ community also be classified as a special needs group.

The Productivity Commission report recognised that many older LGBTI+ people faced, or feared facing, discrimination when engaging with aged care services. The report stated that there were no accurate records or projections as to how many people might need aged care provision in the future but argued that, with an increasingly ageing population, a proportion of those accessing services would identify as LGBTI+ and, as such, service providers should recognise sexuality and gender identity and be sensitive to the needs and preferences of older LGBTI+ people. The report consulted with LGBTI+ advocacy agencies such as ACON (AIDS Council of New South Wales) and the National LGBT Health Alliance. Based on reports from these agencies, the LGBTI+ community wanted safe, LGBTI+ inclusive aged care provisions, greater recognition and inclusion of partner's views in decision making, and greater appreciation of the importance of the LGBTI+ community in the support of those who are part of that community. The report further acknowledged early training initiatives which it was hoped would be evaluated and rolled out further, and called for a specific LGBTI+ strategy which would influence policy, service delivery and quality standards.

In response, the Aged Care Act 1997 was amended, and identified the LGBTI+ community as a 'special needs group' (Australian Government, 2012a). Despite the negative connotations of the use of the term 'special needs group', the change was generally welcomed. Following the amendment came a pledge in 2012 for $244 million in funding to help older Australians who were identified as a special needs group, with a further $2.5 million to fund specific training into the needs of the older LGBTI+ community. At around the same time, the National LGBTI Ageing and Aged Care Strategy was launched (Commonwealth of Australia, 2012). This strategy recognised and promoted the needs of older LGBTI+ people, with acknowledgement to those who had lived through an age when homosexuality was illegal and considered a mental health disorder, where family, friends and careers were lost and where trauma was caused by 'curative' interventions. Understanding and appreciating these histories is important when older people might need care provision or to move into residential care.

The National LGBTI Ageing and Aged Care Strategy (Commonwealth of Australia, 2012) outlined five core principles which were designed to provide care organisations with a framework for inclusive aged care. The core principles are those of inclusion, empowerment, access and equity, quality, and capacity building. Based on this core principle framework, the National Strategy set out six strategic goals and actions: equitable access to LGBTI+ inclusive care provisions; proactively addressing the needs of older LGBTI+ people; ensuring that organisations uphold the legal protection against discrimination; ensuring that the workforce was skilled and competent in delivering LGBTI inclusive aged care; ensuring that the LGBTI+ community were actively involved in aged care policy making; and the need for research on care issues relating to older LGBTQI+ people. This reform package was part of a five-year strategy, which raised awareness and subsequent funding, although the overall impact of the strategy was hard to measure.

In August 2013, an amendment was passed by the Australian Federal Government to the Sex Discrimination Act 1984. The amendment stated that 'it was unlawful under federal law to discriminate against a person on the grounds of their sexual orientation, gender identity or intersex status' (Australian Human Rights Commission, 2013, p 1). In the amendment, exemptions were removed to ensure that aged care providers could no longer discriminate on religious grounds (Sex Discrimination Amendment, 2013). While this reform was welcomed, the exemptions did not protect employees of these facilities from discrimination, which is an important point. If we are to cater for diversity in our communities, then staff should also reflect that diversity.

While many of those I interviewed in Australia felt that this was the golden age of reform in many ways, progress was often seen to be in the balance. This is evidenced by the recently proposed Religious Discrimination Bill. The purpose of the Bill is to protect the right to religious belief in employment, education and service provision. Many see this Bill as a threat to LGBTI+ inclusive health and social care (Equality Australia, 2019).

There was a sense of disparity within the LGBTI+ community. Those I interviewed from Transgender Victoria felt that there was still too little support for the transgender community at either a state or federal level. The focus of transgender initiatives seemed to be youth-oriented. Despite the complexities of the political climate during my visit, all organisations I met with felt that the changes to the Aged Care Act helped to drive the inclusive social care which was/is still emerging. It was felt that legislative reform was the single biggest driver to bring about positive change.

Organisational desire for LGBTI+ inclusive aged care

Anxiety about needing to move into residential care or needing care provision at home was a theme heard across many of the interviews conducted. Here, a Sydney care home resident talks openly about her anxieties about moving into a Methodist home (she was Jewish) and about her identity as a lesbian:

> 'I hoped there would be some sort of level of acceptance and I kept quiet, you know and it was the reverse. When I said to the manager "Oh by the way, I've got a woman in my life", I thought I have to say it you know, it's no good her dropping in and out, you know. And she [the manager] said "Oh congratulations!" I nearly fell over, I almost was in tears I was so excited. The recreational manager said, "Do you want to go to Mardi Gras? I'll organise transport for you." Photo came back of the march and the manager said "Where do you want to hang it?" and I thought I would have to put it up in my room and she said "Oh no, we'll put it up in the corridor where everyone can see it" and it's got my name on it so … So, the good part is that I now feel I have an identity that I always used to have.' (Interview with older lesbian care home resident, Sydney, 2017)

This particular interviewee had campaigned in the 1960s and 70s – she attended the first Mardi Gras in 1978 and was a proud 78er – and was very anxious that she should "return to the closet" having lived life as an openly lesbian woman. This quote highlights the need for organisations to be LGBTI+ inclusive and the positive impact on residents when this is achieved.

The theme organisational desire highlights the need of those in leadership roles to champion LGBTI+ inclusive care within service-providing organisations. These organisations put in place interventions which would result in better cultural competency and greater, specifically LGBTI+, inclusivity. Three factors emerged from those organisations I visited, those of strong leadership, accreditation, and accountability/visibility. The majority of Australia's care provision is supplied through not-for-profit organisations, the most common providers of which are religious organisations (Australian Government, 2012b). The amendments made to the Sex Discrimination Act in 2013 prohibited faith-based discrimination in aged care service provision (Ansara, 2015). I was therefore particularly keen to understand what factors needed to be in place to create an organisational desire to become culturally competent and LGBTI+ inclusive and how this might enable intimate/sexual relationships for older residents and service users.

In all the organisations I visited, it was the Chief Executive Officers who were championing cultural change and inclusive care. They also had the power to ensure these principles were implemented across the organisation. It was not an easy transition for many of the faith-based service providers, and strong and committed leadership was crucial to navigate organisations through some challenging discussions.

Integral to cultural change are staff development opportunities (Truong et al, 2014). During the Australian part of the cross-national study, emphasis was placed on cultural competency training. Handtke et al (2019) suggest that there are many definitions of cultural competency, but one which is particularly relevant to inclusive healthcare is defined by Garneau and Pepin (2014) as 'a complex know-act grounded in critical reflection and action, which the healthcare professional draws upon to provide culturally safe, congruent, and effective care in partnership with individuals, families, and communities health experiences, and which takes into account the social and political dimensions of care' (Garneau and Pepin, 2014, p 12).

Those who I interviewed defined cultural competency as a way of scrutinising their own biases and values, particularly about intimacy and ageing, the LGBTI+ community and their own cultural backgrounds. One interviewee, an older lesbian, talked about how the fact that she had been previously married and had children led to an assumption that she must be heterosexual. She was often cared for by staff from countries where homosexuality remained illegal, was seen as 'sinful' or was socially unaccepted. These workers would assure the resident that they would 'keep her secret because they didn't want anything bad to happen'. Having an appreciation of the cultural backgrounds of both residents and staff is important in order to create a community – care homes are communities – where everyone feels valued, appreciated and celebrated.

I was particularly interested in the impact that Rainbow Tick accreditation had on cultural change within aged care organisations. Rainbow Tick had been developed by the GLHV (Gay and Lesbian Health Victoria, 2016) in response to the growing need for LGBTI+ inclusive health and social care services. The tenet of the accreditation suggests a move from being LGBTI+ friendly to being LGBTI+ inclusive. The Rainbow Tick is based on a set of standards and quality indicators (https://www.rainbowhealthvic.org.au/). In order to be awarded with accreditation, organisations are independently assessed by Quality Innovation Performance (QIP) to show evidence of their commitment to provide inclusive, quality services for the LGBTI+ community. The Rainbow Tick accreditation is aimed at all organisations but was initially rolled out in older people's services.

The Rainbow Tick programme is made up of six standards, as follows:

1. Organisational Capability
2. Workforce Development
3. Consumer Participation
4. A Welcoming and Accessible Environment
5. Disclosure and Documentation
6. Culturally Safe and Acceptable Services

Undertaking the Rainbow Tick accreditation is an ongoing process. The initial programme takes between 12 and 18 months to complete, at the end of which the organisation must offer evidence of cultural change and embeddedness in order to be audited and accredited by an independent accreditation body. Rainbow Tick accreditation is awarded for three years, at which time organisations are expected to show evidence of their long-term organisational commitment to cultural change and LGBTI+ inclusion.

The Rainbow Tick accreditation has come under some criticism – an early iteration needed more consideration to the unique populations within the LGBTI+ community, and the second iteration focused more on the transgender and intersex community. Further criticism has been levelled around the expense and the time it takes to navigate through the programme. In the organisations I met with, strong and committed leadership drove the need for inclusive aged care, but how this commitment might be affected by a leadership change was unknown.

As part of the accreditation process, organisations needed to review all internal policies, guidance and communication to ensure their literature was inclusive, using non-binary language and appropriate pronouns.

Job advertisements made it clear that organisations were LGBTI+ inclusive and inductions included mandatory LGBTI+ training. Media outputs were reviewed to ensure a representative sample of society was presented. Email signoffs included a statement about the inclusive ethos of the organisation, and care plans and assessment recognised sexual identity and orientation. Members of the LGBTI+ community were involved in all levels of decision-making, and alliances were formed. It was often time-consuming work but essential to embedding that culture of inclusion.

Community benefits and examples of good practice

The primary aim of the fellowship was to appreciate the systems in place which enable LGBTI+ inclusive care but also to speak with local members of the older LGBTI+ community to understand the impact that such systems had in practice. The theme which emerged from these interviews was the importance of relationships, as is so nicely demonstrated in the following quote: "Everlasting impact comes from good relationships. The relationship IS everything" (interview with resident services manager). Despite the legislative changes and the apparent organisational drive to become more LGBTI+ inclusive, I still met many older people who were reluctant to engage with service providers. Their anxiety lay in fears of being judged, and they often hid their relationship status, adapting the home before visits, hiding photos, books and literature which might indicate their LGBTI+ identity, essentially erasing their sexual selves. This is tantamount to desexualising the self for fear of the judgement of others. I heard accounts of traumatic personal histories which impacted on care decisions later in life. I also heard the argument that there is still stigma around older people enjoying a full sexual life and this is made more complex when considering the LGBTI+ community. This complexity is largely due to lack of understanding and engagement with the community by staff. An attitude of 'different but same' acted to the detriment of personal histories and relational needs. Sexual identity and biography is often missing from care plans, which works against the person-centred ethos embedded in care provision (Willis et al, 2016).

While I heard many examples of poor practice, I also heard many positive examples of good practice. Yarning Circles are a concept which were introduced to me during my travels. Yarning Circles are harmonious spaces in which to listen and learn from one another's stories. Yarning Circles have been used by indigenous peoples to pass on cultural knowledge and to build relationships as a collective. When considering the LGBTI+ community and other minority groups, Yarning Circles might offer an interesting way to create opportunities for greater understanding and co-operation. This quote from Geia et al (2013) about Yarning Circles also carries an important message which could be a useful way in which to better understand the older LGBTI+ community:

> This type of Aboriginal storytelling or yarning enables Aboriginal and Torres Strait Island people to reconstruct their lives in new ways while at the same time keeping their cultural integrity intact. Further, Aboriginal and Torres Strait Island yarns are rarely an individual construct; they carry within them the shared lived experience of their families, and communities. (Geia et al, 2013, p 15)

An example I witnessed in practice which echoed that of a Yarning Circle, was in a care home in a fashionable district near Melbourne. The care home was Rainbow Tick accredited, and I was keen to see what impact this had in practice. I was met with a very warm welcome in a reception which clearly displayed their Rainbow Tick accreditation and made their LGBTI+ inclusive status immediately apparent. This particular care home worked within the 'Home 2 Home' small neighbourhood care model, with wards and wings being referred to as neighbourhoods, and staff and residents were all seen as housemates, which engendered a real sense of collaborative, homely care.

Once a fortnight, a Marigold Circle was facilitated. Led by the activities co-ordinator, discussion was encouraged around a particular theme. Discussions were facilitated in a variety of ways, sometimes using pre-printed statements to discuss as a group, sometimes around a topical news article or current affairs, both local and more global. The purpose of this fortnightly meeting was to drink tea, eat cake and discuss LGBTI+ relevant issues. The meeting was open to all residents, some of whom identified as LGBTI+, some of whom had LGBTI+ children or grandchildren, and all appreciated a safe space for discussion. I was invited as a guest of honour to a special Marigold Circle hosted on the day of my visit. The discussion topic – unsurprisingly – was that of the plebiscite. There was insightful and concerned discussion about the implications of the vote, the conversation flowed and the residents expressed how much they valued the opportunity to get together and discuss their concerns and to meet with good friends.

Further examples of embedding good practice included that of a large faith-based organisation that was committed to finding 'cultural safety points' by making the organisation credible with the LGBTI+ community. To achieve this, the organisation became Rainbow Tick accredited, which, they felt, held credibility with the LGBTI+ community. They also committed to LGBTI+ workplace inclusion through the Australian Workplace Equality Index (AWEI). The AWEI is a national benchmark on LGBT workplace inclusion and drives best practice by gauging impact of inclusion initiatives (AWEI, 2015). In so doing, they created a message to both service users and staff that they were committed to being accountable for delivering high quality inclusive care. The organisation was public about its commitment, adopting the tag line 'We come out so you don't have to', which recognised the cultural safety needs of the LGBTI+ community and worked to build trust between the organisation and the LGBTI+ community.

This trust is an important aspect of building relationships with the older LGBTI+ community, as this quote from one of my interviewees highlights so well:

> 'What is on the doors, what books do you have on your shelves, pictures on the wall, the badges for staff, reception centre will have stickers on the door and a poster when you walk in, staff have a rainbow badge. That's enough that you have a leaning for that, as a gay man I want to see more. There could be lots of people behind that door that would not be ok. It can feel a bit tokenistic, but is one stage, what you can see before you speak. You can't fake it, the LGBTI community are very attuned to whether or not it is safe to say anything. It's like an innate safety antenna.' (Interview with older gay man, Melbourne, 2017)

This quote suggests that organisations must work hard to create LGBTI+ inclusive spaces and that the community is naturally sceptical of services which do not embed a culture of acceptance.

These examples of Marigold Circles and cultural safety points go some way to creating LGBTI+ inclusive services, but how do these initiatives impact on the relational wellbeing of older LGBTI+ people? I was fortunate enough to meet an older lesbian couple who were behind the 'Our Hearts are Bigger' campaign. Edie was living with dementia and Anne talked of the impact this had on their relationship. In an attempt to maintain intimate connection, Anne and Edie wrote a love letter to each other every day for seven days. While in Melbourne I contacted Anne, who welcomed me to visit her and Edie. Edie didn't say much during my visit, as her dementia had progressed. The love letters which Anne and Edie had written to each other were kept in a box with a large heart on the front. During my visit, Edie got up, went to the box, read one of the letters and smiled. It was a beautiful, poignant moment full of love. Anne spoke candidly about her concerns for future care provision for Edie but felt that the letters would always be there for them both to hold onto. This is such a simple yet beautiful intervention, which can act to hold and maintain a loving relationship even when one partner needs to move to residential care.

Conclusion

This chapter has argued that aged care provision has traditionally created a cloak of invisibility around the older LGBTI+ community. This invisibility acts as a barrier to supporting and meeting intimate relationships and calls for aged care providers to consider how best they can remove these barriers. Evidence has been offered from an Australian perspective which discusses the legislative changes which enabled inclusive LGBTI+ provision. Evidence was offered as to how organisations had implemented change and created LGBTI+ inclusive services, with strong leadership and accountability being key drivers. Examples of good practice were offered.

My hope is that other countries including the UK would adopt similar strategies to ensure that all older people's services are LGBTI+ inclusive. As has been demonstrated in this chapter, unambiguous legislation and policy, national in scope, can ensure that care services work towards LGBTI+ inclusion. With funding, organisational change and cultural humility can be achieved. However, even when these changes are in place, vigilance is required. Legislation can be rescinded and political climates change. The burden of any vigilance should not be solely the responsibility of the LBGTI+ community. LGBTI+ allies play an important supportive role. My experiences in Australia highlighted a real sense of collaborative working between care providers, members of the LBGTI+ community, legislators, regulators, educators and care facilities. While I am sure this has not been an easy path, once navigated this partnership working seems to be the foundation for change.

It is hoped that this chapter will add to the discussions of how best to support the relational needs of the older LGBTI+ community, and that care providers might utilise some of these suggestions within their services. Recognising the relational, sexual and intimacy needs of older LGBTI+ people is vital to wellbeing in old age. Understanding how care provision desexualises older LGBTI+ people means that practitioners and professionals can counter this and enable intimate, sexual and meaningful relationships within their care services.

References

Age UK (2019) 'Later life in the United Kingdom 2019'. Available at: https://www.ageuk.org.uk/globalassets/age-uk/documents/reports-and-publications/later_life_uk_factsheet.pdf [Accessed 16 December 2019].

Amnesty International (2018) It's Intersex Awareness Day - Here Are 5 Myths We Need to Shatter'. Available at: https://www.amnesty.org/en/latest/news/2018/10/its-intersex-awareness-day-here-are-5-myths-we-need-to-shatter/ [Accessed 11 January 2020].

Ansara, Y.G. (2015) 'Challenging Cisgenderism in the Ageing and Aged Care Sector: Meeting the Needs of Older People of Trans and/or Non-Binary Experience', *Australasian Journal of Ageing*, 34(2): 14–18.

Australian Bureau of Statistics (2014) '4159.0 - General Social Survey: Summary Results, Australia, 2014'. Available at: https://www.abs.gov.au/ausstats/abs@.nsf/mf/4159.0 [Accessed 15 February 2020].

Australian Bureau of Statistics (2018) '1800.0 - Australian Marriage Law Postal Survey, 2017, National Results'. Available at: http://www.abs.gov.au/ausstats/abs@.nsf/mf/1800.0 [Accessed 13 June 2018].

Australian Government (2011) 'Caring for Older Australians. Productivity Commission Inquiry Report Vol. 1'. Available at: https://www.pc.gov.au/inquiries/completed/aged-care/report/aged-care-volume1.pdf [Accessed 5 January 2020].

Australian Government (2012a) 'Explanatory Notes to the Aged Care Act 1997, Explanatory Notes: Allocation Amendment (People with Special Needs) Principles 2012'.

Australian Government (2012b) 'Residential Aged Care in Australia 2010-2011: A statistical overview'. Available at: https://www.aihw.gov.au/getmedia/ba6a7e49-6939-499e-af79-f72acc5bff56/13755.pdf.aspx?inline=true [Accessed 14 January 2020].

Australian Human Rights Commission (2013) 'Sexual Orientation, Gender Identity and Intersex Status Discrimination: Information Sheet'. Available at: https://www.humanrights.gov.au/sites/default/files/Information%20sheet%20on%20new%20protections%20in%20the%20Sex%20Discrimination%20Act%20-%20FINAL.pdf [Accessed 12 January 2020].

AWEI (2015) 'Welcome to the Australian Workplace Equality Index'. Available at: https://www.pid-awei.com.au/ [Accessed 19 January 2020].

Bauer, M., McAuliffe, L. and Nay, R. (2007) 'Sexuality, Health Care and the Older Person: An Overview of the Literature', *International Journal of Older People Nursing*, 2(1): 63–8.

Bouman, W.P., Arcelus, J. and Benbow, S.M. (2006) 'Nottingham Study of Sexuality & Ageing (NoSSA I). Attitudes Regarding Sexuality and Older People: A Review of the Literature', *Sexual and Relationship Therapy*, 21(2): 149–61.

Commonwealth of Australia (2012) 'National Lesbian, Gay, Bisexual, Transgender and Intersex (LGBTI) Ageing and Aged Care Strategy'.

CQC (Care Quality Commission) (2019) 'Relationships and Sexuality in Adult Social Care Services: Guidance for CQC Inspection Staff and Registered Adult Social Care Providers'. Available at: https://www.cqc.org.uk/sites/default/files/20190221-Relationships-and-sexuality-in-social-care-PUBLICATION.pdf [Accessed 15 February 2020].

Department of Trade and Industry (2004) Final Regulatory Impact Assessment: Civil Partnership Act 2004. Available at: https://webarchive.nationalarchives.gov.uk/+/http:/www.berr.gov.uk/files/file23829.pdf

Drescher, J. (2015) 'Out of DSM: Depathologizing Homosexuality', *Behavioural Sciences*, 5(4): 565–75.

Equality Australia (2019) Religious Discrimination Bill: Healthcare Fact Sheet. Available at: https://equalityaustralia.org.au/resources/religious-discrimination-bill-healthcare-fact-sheet/ [Accessed 14 January 2020].

Garneau, A.B. and Pepin, J. (2014) 'Cultural Competency: A Constructivist Definition', *Journal of Transcultural Nursing*, 26(1): 9–15.

Geia, L.K., Hayes, B. and Usher, K. (2013) 'Yarning/Aborginal Storytelling: Towards An Understanding of an Indigenous Perspective and its Implications for Research Practice', *Contemporary Nursing*, 46(1): 13–17.

GLHV@ARCSHS, La Trobe University (2016) 'The Rainbow Tick guide to LGBTI-inclusive practice'. https://www.rainbowhealthvic.org.au/

Government Equalities Office (2018) 'Trans People in the UK'. Available at: https://assets.publishing.service.gov.uk/government/uploads/system/uploads/attachment_data/file/721642/GEO-LGBT-factsheet.pdf [Accessed 11 January 2020].

Handtke, O., Schilgen, B. and Mösko, M. (2019) 'Culturally Competent Healthcare - A Scoping Review of Strategies Implemented in Healthcare Organisations and a Model of Culturally Competent Healthcare Provision', *PLoS ONE*, 14(7): 1–24.

Johnson, I. (2013) 'Gay and Gray: The Need for Federal Regulation of Assisted Living Facilities and the Inclusion of LBGT Individuals', *Journal of Gender, Race & Justice*, 16(2): 293–321.

Jowett, A. and Peel, E. (2009) 'Chronic Illness in Non-Heterosexual Contexts: An Online Survey of Experiences', *Feminism & Psychology*, 19(4): 454–74.

Kimmel, D. (2014) 'Lesbian, Gay, Bisexual and Transgender Aging Concerns', *Clinical Gerontologist*, 37(1): 49–63. DOI: 10.1080/07317115.2014.847310

Klein, K., Holtby, A., Cook, K. and Travers, R. (2015) 'Complicating the Coming Out Narrative: Becoming Oneself in a Heterosexist and Cissexist World', *Journal of Homosexuality*, 62(3): 297–326.

Knauer, N.J. (2011) *Gay and Lesbian Elders: History, Law, and Identity Politics in the United States*. Burlington: Ashgate.

Knauer, N.J. (2016) 'LGBT Older Adults, Chosen Family and Caregiving', *Journal of Law and Religion*, 31(2): 150–68.

Kneale, D., Henley, J., Thomas, J. and French, R. (2021) 'Inequalities in Older LGBT People's Health and Care Needs in the United Kingdom: A Systematic Scoping Review', *Ageing & Society*, 41(3): 493–515. DOI:10.1017/S0144686X19001326

McGovern, J. (2014) 'The Forgotten: Dementia and the Aging LGBT Community', *Journal of Gerontological Social Work*, 57(8): 845–57.

Noga-Styron, K.E., Reasons, C.E. and Peacock, D. (2012) 'The Last Acceptable Prejudice: An Overview of LGBT Social and Criminal Injustice Issues within the USA', *Contemporary Justice Review*, 15(4): 369–98.

ONS (Office for National Statistics) (2017) 'Sexual Orientation, UK: 2017 Experimental Statistics on Sexual Orientation in the UK in 2017 by Region, Sex, Age, Marital Status, Ethnicity and Socio-Economic Classification'. Available at: https://www.ons.gov.uk/peoplepopulationandcommunity/culturalidentity/sexuality/bulletins/sexualidentityuk/2017 [Accessed 16 December 2019].

ONS (Office for National Statistics) (2019) 'Overview of the UK population: August 2019'. Available at: https://www.ons.gov.uk/peoplepopulationandcommunity/populationandmigration/populationestimates/articles/overviewoftheukpopulation/august2019 [Accessed 11 January 2020].

Peel, E., Taylor, H. and Harding, R. (2016) 'Sociolegal and Practice Implications of Caring for LBGT People with Dementia', *Nursing Older People*, 28(10): 26–30.

Price, E. (2012) Gay and Lesbian Carers: Ageing in the Shadow Of Dementia', *Ageing & Society*, 32(3): 516–32.

Rowntree, M. (2014) '"Comfortable in My Own Skin": A New Form of Sexual Freedom for Ageing Baby Boomers', *Journal of Aging Studies*, 31: 150–8.

SCIE (2015) 'LGB&T+ Communities and Dementia'. Available at: https://www.scie.org.uk/dementia/living-with-dementia/lgbt/ [Accessed 16 December 2019].

Sex Discrimination Amendment (Sexual Orientation, Gender Identity and Intersex Status) Act (2013). https://www.legislation.gov.au/Details/C2013A00098

Sinković, M. and Towler, L. (2019) 'Review of *Sexual Aging: A Systematic Review of Qualitative Research on the Sexuality and Sexual Health of Older Adults*', *Qualitative Health Research*, 29(9): 1239–54.

Stonewall (2018) 'LGBT in Britain: Home and Communities'. https://www.stonewall.org.uk/sites/default/files/lgbt_in_britain_home_and_communities.pdf [Accessed 22 February 2020].

Truong, M., Paradies, Y. and Priest, N. (2014) 'Interventions to Improve Cultural Competency in Healthcare: A Systematic Review of Reviews', *Healthcare Services Research*, 14(99): 1–17.

White, E. (2011) *Dementia and Sexuality: The Rose That Never Wilts*. London: Hawker Publications.

Willis, P., Maegusuku-Hewett, T., Raithby, M. and Miles, P. (2016) 'Swimming Upstream: The Provision of Inclusive Care to Older Lesbian, Gay and Bisexual (LGB) Adults in Residential and Nursing Environments in Wales', *Ageing & Society*, 36(2): 282–306.

Youell, J. (2015) *'I loves her and she loves me': A Qualitative Study into the Relational Experience of Living with Dementia*. Northampton, UK: University of Northampton.

11

The role of professionals and service providers in supporting sexuality and intimacy in later life: theoretical and practice perspectives

Trish Hafford-Letchfield

Introduction

The transformation of intimacy and sexuality issues within historically and culturally dependent institutions is challenging established views about ageing (Bildtgard and Oberg, 2017). Health and social care is one such institution yet to respond fully to the growing empirical evidence on what constitutes a meaningful life for older people interacting with care services in relation to sexuality and intimacies across different sexual and gender identities. Transcending established views about the role of health and social care professionals in providing meaningful engagement and support for older people to fulfil their sexual needs requires providers to recognise opportunities for responding to the complexity of issues arising in care. Being open to the range of people's relationship situations, and making spaces within assessment and provision of care to enable information and support on sex and intimacy to be made available and to engage proactively with the topic, is beginning to be recognised within workforce development (SfC, 2017). Building on these initiatives involves developing new structures and methods of embedding sexuality within professional education, in policies and care practices and in the commissioning of, and evaluation of, services (Hafford-Letchfield et al, 2010, 2020).

This chapter engages with the literature focusing on what we know or need to know about how professionals and providers within health and social care exchange and interact around sex as a meaningful concept in the provision and quality of care. It focuses on themes that are important to initiating and supporting sexual expression in later life and addresses important transition points where older people are considered 'vulnerable' in care services and where their sexual rights are less likely to be promoted or transgressed. As we saw in Chapter 9, issues may occur in residential care for people with cognitive decline, and in this chapter we expand further on issues that may emerge at the end of life. Building further on Villar and Fabà's contribution in this volume, I highlight some of the underlying theoretical concepts that forge pathways to improved practice and point to areas in which there is good practice guidance from the current evidence available.

A shift in western societal perspectives has moved sex from being primarily situated within the context of marriage and reproduction to being a more central aspect of health and wellbeing in its own right (Hinchliff and Gott, 2011). With increasing emphasis on wellbeing in later life and on outcome-focused support, in both policy and practice (Glendinning et al, 2007), the workforce requires a culturally competent, curious and authentic approach to engaging with older people on this significant area of their personal lives. As people claim new intimate futures, a step up in the quality of support and care and leadership of these issues is beginning to emerge (Hafford-Letchfield, 2020; CQC, 2020). At the time of writing, the current cohort of older people are less likely to have had exposure to formal sex education yet they would have challenged and changed societal prescriptions of sexual expression and openness (Graf et al, 2020). The baby boomer generation (1946 to 1964), however, may be more permissive, outspoken and varied in their conceptualisations of sexuality (Heywood et al, 2019), and the expectations of these so-called 'silver splicers' and 'silver separators' (ILC-UK, 2015) have been impacted further by shifts in equality legislation and human rights in respect of diverse sexual and gender identities.

Sexuality as taboo in care: theoretical perspectives

There has been a growing body of research in health and social care about why the topic of sexuality and intimacy remains taboo or invisible. Several studies indicate that lack of knowledge, confidence and skill prevents practitioners from opening a discussion on what they perceive as a deeply personal aspect of life (Lyons et al, 2018; Taha et al, 2020). Professionals and practitioners report feelings of personal discomfort or fear of offending the person, or believe there is somebody else better placed to address the subject. The impact of this on older people has resulted in them reporting distress, disappointment, frustration, shock and fear of failure (Roney and Kazer, 2015; Drummond et al, 2013), which can lead to despair, devastation and a sense of hopelessness (Loe, 2004). Higgins and Hynes (2018) suggest that some clinical practitioners fear transgressing a medico-legal or cultural boundary, should they initiate a discussion on sexuality. Further, reluctance to discuss issues may follow a perception that it is inappropriate due to the age, gender, culture or religion of the person and wondering whether the person would consider and question sexuality as a legitimate topic for discussion, which would cause further embarrassment (Dyer and das Nair, 2013; Simpson et al, 2017). Professionals who reflected on the why and how of their communication about intimate issues with patients recognised the relationship between being able to discuss sexual issues with patients and their own life, or their lack of life experiences regarding sexuality (Hordern and Street, 2007).

Further, Hinchliff et al (2005), in a study of UK GPs, for example, found that almost half reported that they would be uncomfortable discussing sexuality issues with their lesbian and gay patients, and Taylor and Gosney (2011) suggest that GPs may recognise that many older people would prefer discussing sexual issues with a doctor of the same gender and as close as their age range as possible. A large Australian study of a thousand students in allied health (Weerakoon et al, 2004) demonstrated that over half would not be comfortable talking to clients about sexuality. Hafford-Letchfield et al's (2010) intergenerational work with social workers and social work students and older people revealed everyday double standards in ageing. They found that relatively infrequent contact with older people not in touch with services (as opposed to those who present with complex needs and problems) required active unlearning to combat stereotypes before they could begin to learn new skills to address this area of their practice. When talking about trans ageing, Riggs et al (2018) stress the importance of discussing or including intimacy within professional interactions, which enables a more rich and holistic account of transgender lives, rather than what tends to happen, which is solely focusing on negative experiences such as their mental health and/or discrimination.

All of the afore-mentioned issues are implicated in the silencing of older people. Indeed, professionals and practitioners can become even more guarded so as to avoid causing any further fear or anxieties and, consequentially, a well-meaning strategy of protecting people from their own distress (Wornell, 2014). Being familiar and confident with the relevant issues can be enhanced where professionals and practitioners are given regular opportunities to reflect on and discuss their work in ageing services (BASW, 2019). Without these processes, practice can be configured as simple and straightforward, where predominantly surface-level, structural responses to practice shortcomings fail to recognise that a more straightforward and authentic approach is vital in providing good basic care (Ruch, 2011). Further, as many of the chapters in this volume have reinforced, people also need the professionals involved with them to recognise when dysfunctional organisational and societal processes desexualise and create systems of care that impede, rather than support, recovery and wellbeing.

Theoretical perspectives

Within the theoretical traditions of health and social care, psychodynamic and systems theories together are one example of the rich and complex framework that explains this approach. Menzies' (1987) seminal work, for example, noted that care workers strive to externalise their psychic defence mechanisms through developing real aspects of the organisational 'structure, culture and mode of functioning' (p 101), such as the creation of depersonalising rituals of institutionalised care. Menzies asserted that these rituals protect carers against anxiety. Over time, an unconscious, collusive agreement among workers occurs about the form of these defence mechanisms, which then becomes part of the impersonal reality of the organisation and compounds ageism (Gewirtz-Meydan et al, 2018a). Within residential or hospital care, the use of humour (Ciccone et al, 2008; Hafford-Letchfield et al, 2010) and the constraining impact of risk-averse policies also protect against the anxiety inherent in care work. Together they minimise the possibility of emotional connection and reduce the potential for experiencing intimacy or joy in the work and people they serve. 'Services and support which do not enable older people to hold on to their unique sense of self and their humanity are therefore dehumanising, not just disempowering' (Bowers, 2009, p 45).

Twigg also talks about 'body work' in care settings, where focusing directly on 'assessing, handling, diagnosing, treating and manipulating' the bodies of others (Twigg et al, 2019, p 1) becomes the object of the practitioners' labour. This influences the contexts, the knowledge systems care workers draw upon, and the status and hierarchies they are embedded in. Body work lies on the borders of the erotic, where interventions in personal care mimic sexuality and further ambiguity. Twigg et al (2019) also talk about the emotional aspects of body work, in which empathy and sympathy can be nurtured, and, as noted earlier, emotions need to be managed positively as part of the care role.

If we understand sexual relations as social relations, however, then this necessitates thinking about the various ways in which bodies and embodiment might figure in care settings (Jackson and Scott, 2010). Jackson and Scott (2010) refer to objectified embodiment, given that bodies are perceptible entities in physical and social space and their categorisation and recognition is a social act, an act of decoding, that enables us to see a particular body as someone we know as classed, raced, gendered or disabled and aged. Furthermore, our bodies can be objects to ourselves, which enables each person not only to see his/her body as object, but also to imagine how it is seen by another and envisage engagement with the embodied actions of others. Having an appreciation of different ways of thinking is desirable within professional education, in order to be able to reflect upon how care is practised and the multiple ways in which desexualising attitudes and behaviours are enacted. As the language of 'function' and 'dysfunction' prominent in past medical discourse is being challenged to support more progressive and rights-based practice about 'normality' and sexuality as normal, this needs to be taken forward in the drive towards person-centred care in which care professionals interact with broader discourses that frame their work with older people.

Pedagogical frameworks that promote knowledge of everyday sexuality (Dunk-West, 2007), without recourse to these deviant or medical discourses, are further congruent with professional ethics and values (Dunk-West and Hafford-Letchfield, 2011, 2018) and call for learning opportunities that promote the acquisition of sensitive language and listening skills that enable older people to express doubts and anxieties towards desires and to access meaningful support. The compartmentalisation of sexuality into specialised areas of practice means that everyday sexuality remains empirically unexamined or under-examined within ageing care. It makes pathological what is a basic human need by denying acknowledgement of an individual's culture and identity. Against this backdrop, a number of studies consistently emphasise the impact of organisational policy and professional power in formulating assessment with older people and their limited involvement and participation in the process (Grenier, 2007; Sullivan, 2008; Gewirtz-Meydan et al, 2018a). Those examining the perspectives of older service users and carers portray the disempowerment resulting from the increased amount of set procedures used during professional–user interactions and the lack of choice in decision-making (Scourfield, 2007; Higgs and Hafford-Letchfield, 2018; Sullivan, 2008). Setting the terms of an assessment or provision are important aspects of professional power. It allows professionals to present with expert knowledge and to seek information from their service users in a prescriptive way (Grenier, 2007). The older person is, thus, objectified or classified to become eligible for services or support. Poststructuralist theorists like Foucault (1993) call this the authoritative gaze that objectifies the user of public services, generating power relationships between professionals and service users. Perspectives that redress this imbalance are those which draw directly on the narratives of the older service-users themselves (Hafford-Letchfield, 2016). The increasing leadership of older people in professional education is embodied in the concept of co-production (INVOLVE, 2019). Key principles involve the sharing of power, where people learning about sexuality respect and value the knowledge, skills and perspectives of those who can make a contribution, and reciprocity, where a joint understanding and consensus and clarity over roles and responsibilities underpins the fulfilment of needs in this area of personal life.

While education plays a critical role in shaping attitudes and behaviours towards diversity, self-awareness remains a powerful influence. Within practice with older people, professionals enter the encounter with a range of understandings and meanings derived from professional, personal, and organisational values. These can be reinforced through professional socialisation and extensive government policy and practice guidelines developed for working with older people. These belief systems or frames of reference frequently lead to professionally controlled outcomes in practice encounters with older people, which leaves unchallenged some important areas in the repertoire, such as intimacy and sexuality. More recently, sexuality is explicitly recognised within professional standards and frameworks, particularly in social care (SfC, 2017; RCN, 2018; BASW, 2019; CQC, 2020). I now turn to some of the key transition points in care settings where there is scope for illustrating good practice in working with older people on intimacy and sexuality.

Conceptualising desexualisation in care settings

Simpson et al's (2017) concept of erotophobia seeks to explain how and why care professionals are remiss in giving advice and support to older people on how to have pleasurable and safer sex, and the practice skills needed. Beyond this focus on sexuality and the implications for sexual health policies, societal-level understandings of later life around sexuality need to be something that older people identify with themselves. When developing institutional local policies and interventions, more research could focus on uncovering the nuances of older people's lived experiences of ageing and its impact on their sexual lives, engaging with their own voices (Gewirtz-Meydan et al, 2018a, 2018b). Providers, for example, need to understand the importance of enabling people to manage their sexuality needs. This includes making sure people have access to sex education and sexual health information to help them develop and maintain relationships and express their sexuality. Inequalities persist, deepen and widen across the life course and age discrimination (and its interaction with other areas of inequality) impacts on older people's access to age-appropriate sexual health and advice, despite this being absolutely related to contemporary public health challenges. For example, in the UK, older heterosexual people in England and Wales are getting married and divorced in greater numbers (ONS, 2017), with 92 per cent of these marriage partners aged 65 and over being divorcees, widows or widowers, with only 8 per cent getting married for the first time (ONS, 2017).

Further, women are more likely to be living without a partner because of widowhood or divorce but equally demonstrate increasing expectations concerning sexual fulfilment. Self-reported data from the English Longitudinal Study on Ageing (ELSA) of heterosexual men found that they were still sexually active into their seventies, eighties and nineties and challenging heteronormative ideas about sexual relationships (Lee and Tetley, 2017). Ševčíková and Sedláková's (2020) study of older people's perspectives on sexual activity in Czechoslovakia emphasised the role of partnered sex in their fulfilment. This is attributed to a profound change that people experience in later life, a reassurance that they will not be alone and a reorientation from knowledge-related goals to emotion-related goals. Older people were found to focus on what is most essential, which is typically meaningful relationships from which they mostly derived greater satisfaction.

Research by Public Heath England (PHE, 2019) has also reported increasing rates of sexually transmitted infections, with the largest proportional increase in gonorrhoea (42 per cent) and chlamydia (24 per cent) in people over 65. There is increasing incidence and prevalence of HIV in older people, with one in five UK adults with HIV aged over 50. This is also the consequence of both the expansion in uptake of HIV testing and diagnosis and major improvements in treatments, which are helping people with HIV to live longer. Despite these trends, sexual health clinics in England are less likely to offer an HIV test to older patients, despite a mandate to offer testing to all. These low rates can be explained by clinicians not seeing sexual health as relevant in this age group, or expecting older patients to be uncomfortable talking about sexually transmitted infections. Nash et al (2015) has reported the lack of prioritisation of older people from the perspective of the National Health Service (NHS) and local Department for Integrated Sexual Health (DISH) services in the UK.

Given the diversification of what we are learning about sexual health and wellbeing in later life, it is now clear that services need to step up to ensure that sexual health and relationship services are age friendly and even targeted for those in later life. As we saw in the detailed examination of sexuality in long-term care in Chapter 9, providers also need to understand the risks associated with people's sexuality needs and recognise and support these needs, so that they do not risk discriminating against people or breaching their human rights (CQC, 2019). This tendency towards conceptualising sexual practices as posing risk is a key site of tension in relation to state governance and surveillance (Jackson and Scott, 2010). While a fulfilling and life-enhancing activity, it can be seen as potentially problematic where the person is seen as vulnerable or disabled, where there is a danger of sexual acts being translated as those that concern sexual abuse, risk and danger. In 2019, the UK care regulator, the Care Quality Commission (CQC, 2020), reviewed 661 statutory notifications that described 899 sexual incidents or incidents of alleged sexual abuse that took place in adult social care services, which constituted 3 per cent of all notifications in a three-month period. A snapshot from this data revealed that 45 per cent of all people affected were women aged 75 and over, 46 per cent were from a residential home and 28 per cent from a nursing home, and almost half of the incidents reported were categorised as sexual assault, defined as sexually touching another person without their consent.

Moreover, most incidents were alleged to have been carried out by people who use services (60 per cent), and the vast majority of those affected were people using services. 16 per cent of alleged incidents were carried out by employed staff or visiting workers, and in 8 per cent of cases it was friends or relatives. Incidents were more likely to be carried out by men than women. The CQC noted emerging concerns about the use of social media, mobile phones and the internet in sexual abuse. What was troubling, however, was that 5 per cent of received reports of incidents involved consensual activity, indicating ignorance and potentially leading to an infringement of human rights. These findings illustrate some situations where providers' unwillingness to talk about sex can be due to uncertainty about the issue, a fear of getting things wrong, or a fear of enforcement or litigation as a result of reporting. I offer the following pointers to help to initiate conversations in practice:

- Promote positive messages about personal relationships in later life by service providers through their service information, imagery and general approach.
- Ensure that professionals are re-skilled to ensure that their knowledge is up-to-date on referral procedures and on where an older person might go to get advice and resources on sexual health.
- When talking to older people about their personal relationships, pose questions in such a way that avoids making assumptions about their sexuality, sexual or gender identity. Model this by using your own pronouns. Likewise, provide opportunities to support sharing and disclosure by affording privacy and respect.
- Ensure that staff are assessed for the knowledge and skills needed to confidently advocate for an older person regarding their sexual rights and challenge any ageist discrimination and provision to help them develop and refine these.
- Carry out active consultation with older people about issues concerning their intimate relationships, sexual health and social networks can be included in outreach and engagement work.

Older people are increasingly using the internet to find information about sexual health rather than consulting professionals. Older people might be especially susceptible if they do not have good access to wi-fi or are confined to their own homes. Those with care professionals coming into the home or living in institutionalised environments may require the opportunity to purchase various items in relative privacy, including vibrators, condoms and lubricants. Some older adults may also have difficulty differentiating between advertising, personal opinions and professional information on the internet. Clinicians can provide valuable assistance to older adults who may seek out the assistance of the internet in finding health and sex-related information. In a scoping review of barriers to older adults seeking sexual health advice and treatment, Ezhova et al (2020) reported only two interventions related to informing sexual health promotion, indicating a need to design, implement and assess effectiveness of interventions that help older adults seeking sexual health advice and treatment.

Transition and 'vulnerabilities'

In residential care homes, the accommodation, care practice and other arrangements should facilitate the operation of sexual rights, and information and guidance should be available if needed to help service users remain safe and healthy, enjoy pleasurable experiences and take appropriate decisions for themselves in this area of their lives (see Health and Social Care Act 2008 (Regulated Activities) Regulations 2014 – specifically Regulation 9: Person-centred Care; CQC, 2019, guidance on relationships and sexuality). One of the most common issues professionals encounter concern the complexities around dementia (see also Villar and Fabà in this volume). Dementia and sexuality, intimacy and sexual behaviour in care homes has been one of the subjects of taboo in long-term care, given that cognitive impairment does not erase the need for affection, intimacy and/ or relationships. The issues involved can be complex, controversial and sensitive, and may be guided by the person-centred approach to dementia care (NICE, 2018). Some people found that becoming a carer in their relationship with their partner either increased a sense of intimacy or changed how they felt about sex with the person they cared for, particularly if they had developed dementia (Drummond et al, 2013). A lack of recognition of sexuality diversity is particularly challenging in dementia care, where ageing sexualities are minimised and sexuality is seen as a behaviour rather than an identity, and seen as a risky behaviour at that, something to be managed and controlled (Bauer et al, 2013, 2014).

While the onset of a dementia or any conditions that affect cognitive ability may change the expression, form and nature of a sexual relationship, this does not mean that older people with dementia no longer have any desires of a sexual or intimate nature, and each situation and individual will be unique (ILC, 2015). Many people may wish to maintain a sexual relationship, experiencing sexual intimacy as a source of comfort, reassurance and mutual support. Identity work also operates at an embodied level, in terms of dress and appearance (Twigg, 2007). Both are significant in the context of dementia and personhood (Twigg, 2010; Twigg and Buse, 2013). People may also form new relationships in care homes, including where one or both has dementia. Even where established relationships are expected to continue in some way, some care workers and relatives may be uncomfortable and reluctant to acknowledge or support the sexual aspect of their relationship. As explored by Reynolds in this volume, the issues concern autonomy, capacity, competence and protection. The ILC (2015, p 17) offers the following advice:

- Establish the role played by the care home in supporting residents' pre-existing relationships.
- Promote a culture of acceptance, dignity and privacy for all residents and remember not all relationships will be hetero or cis-normative.

- Care home workers and managers should try to include, if possible and if volunteered, the social and sexual history of residents in care plans.
- Facilitate relationships by allowing regular visits either within the care home setting or outside.
- Promote privacy for residents and space so couples can be together: a simple "do not disturb" sign can help and provide information and advice if needed.
- Continue monitoring and assessment in terms of the resident's dementia and their mental capacity.
- Maintain good communication with the resident's partner and possibly their close family or friends.

Westwood (2016) further highlights what little attention has been given to lesbian and bisexual women with dementia and how their respective sexualities/sexual identities inform their experiences of dementia, how they are supported in that experience – both informally and formally – and how their histories, identities and preferences are (or are not) validated and reflected in dementia care provision, especially residential care. This, she suggests, impacts in several ways, leading to: under-recognition and hence less social support for carers; carer avoidance due to experiences of prejudice and discrimination; community care provision not being geared up to meet the needs of lesbians and bisexual women with dementia; and an associated increased risk of premature admission to residential care provision (Westwood, 2016, p 1502). Further, one of the central ways in which lesbians and bisexual women with dementia are differentiated from heterosexual-identifying women with dementia is that they are subject to heightened surveillance and regulation (Cronin et al, 2011), reducing the possibilities for recognition. It can also complicate possibilities for asserting one's rights in care spaces.

Matters can become more complicated when one or both of the residents may not have the 'mental capacity' to consent to sexual relations, leaving them open to being more vulnerable, and in the UK the Mental Capacity Act 2005 (MCA) will be relevant in assessing the situation. The MCA states that a person must always be assumed to have capacity unless it is established they lack capacity, and this is issue specific. The definition of incapacity is outlined in Section 2 of the MCA: 'A person lacks capacity in relation to a matter if at the material time he is unable to make a decision for himself in relation to the matter because of an impairment of, or a disturbance in the functioning of, the mind or brain.'

The MCA does not provide any mechanism to allow people to make advance decisions or have decisions made on their behalf about sexual matters, and 'best interest' decisions cannot be made in relation to a person's ability to consent to sex. This is specifically excluded in the section on 'Family relationships' in the MCA: 'Nothing in this Act permits a decision on ... consenting to have sexual relations' (Section 27(1)(b)). Depending on the circumstances, therefore, the relationship and individual involved could be in breach of the Sexual Offences Act 2003, which prohibits sexual activity with somebody who lacks capacity. The following principles can help in establishing capacity in relation to sexual activities:

- Does the person with dementia understand that they have a choice around sexual activity and that they can refuse?
- Are they aware that they can change their mind at any time leading up to, and during, the sexual act and able to act on this?
- Do they understand the mechanics of sex and the associated health and other risks?

Where it is difficult to determine a person's capacity to consent to sexual relations, professional advice must be sought, including speaking to the local safeguarding authority, and in some instances may be referred to the Court of Protection for legal determination. In summary, providers should recognise that people living with dementia will continue to express themselves sexually and enjoy intimacy with their partners and loved ones, and all steps must be taken to respect and enable expression with respect and privacy. Providers should have developed policies which reflect the values and principles of respecting diversity, equality, human rights and non-discrimination, in line with current legislation, such as the Human Rights Act 1998 and the Equality Act 2010, and that demonstrate that no person is excluded from the policy on the grounds of gender or sexual identity.

Another area of vulnerability for older people relates to sexuality and intimacy during end-of-life care or palliative care. The majority of people in palliative care belong to the older population. In a recent systematic review of the literature on patient–provider communication about sexual concerns with cancer patients, Reese et al (2017) concluded that sexuality needs are unacknowledged and unaddressed for many people, particularly women. Similarly, in the few studies involving palliative care patients, a particular concern was the failure of practitioners to provide a context or space to discuss sexuality or acknowledge the loss and grief they were experiencing because of changes to their sexual selves and their intimate relationships (Taylor, 2014). Loss and grief also have the potential to contribute to 'total pain' and total distress, and the desire for sex and intimacy has also shown to intensify for some at the end of life (Higgins and Hynes, 2018).

The benefits of sexual expression and intimacy in hospice and palliative care are understated, where the strengthening of relationships at the end of life includes sexual expression and physical intimacy as a significant part of the process. The act of pleasant physical touch, including masturbation, can release various neurotransmitters, leading to feelings of warmth, muscle relaxation, pain relief and improved quality of sleep (Redelman, 2008). One of the only available empirical studies of healthcare professionals' attitudes toward the discussion of sexuality with their patients in palliative care suggests that recognising different relationships and creating conditions for them to flourish is medicalised (Hordern and Street, 2007). Hordern and Street (2007) offer some 'opening lines' to help discuss the topic, and suggest normalising any discussion and giving maximum control to the person themselves. For example:

- 'Many of the people I see express concerns about how treatment may affect their sex lives. How has this been for you?'
- 'How has this experience affected intimate or sexual aspects of your life?'
- 'Has your role as parent, partner, spouse, or intimate friend changed since you were diagnosed or treated?'

This may include seeking permission by asking if it's the right time and place to discuss sexual issues, and whether people would like to discuss it with the professional or someone else or if they would prefer to have some written or practical information.

Stausmire (2004) recommends taking a sexual history regardless of the person's relationship status, which also helps to overcome any assumptions about the person's gender or sexual identities and who they may be in a relationship with. Cagle and Bolte (2009) also talk about the need for skills in demonstrating a warm, empathic and open attitude, providing information that dispels myths and misconceptions, speaking without technical jargon and terminology, using open-ended questions and respecting the values of the patient. Other tips include giving patients and their partners time to come up with questions, or to be able to write them down and give them to the professional, which can increase confidence and a sense of control, reinforcing the confidential nature of the professional interaction. It is essential to get permission to speak to the person's intimate partners as part of any consultation (Cort et al, 2004). These will be combined with practical challenges, such as giving advice about how medical equipment, such as indwelling catheters, IVs and oxygen masks, can pose clear obstacles to sexual activities. For example, nurses identified many possible efforts that could be made to help (for example, written information on sexuality, tactile massage, medications for sexual dysfunction, improved ostomy care and relieving fatigue). They also mentioned hygiene, so that patients can feel fresh and clean. According to the nurses, this could promote intimacy (Hjalmarsson and Lindroth, 2020). The International Council of Nurses (2012) suggests that nurses are well suited to develop, implement and evaluate best practices to include sexuality in palliative care in various global care contexts, since it aligns well with global ethical values on holistic and person-centred care (International Council of Nurses, 2012).

Conclusion

Given changes in demography, the increasing diversity of the ageing population and the evidence on what older people want in relation to maintaining their independence and continuing to have fulfilling sexual and intimate relationships as their health and care needs develop, the health and social care workforce will need to respond and develop accordingly. As professionals in health and social care move towards more integrated settings, we need to be able to advocate and support older people and continue to acquire additional skills, knowledge, values and approaches that promote awareness of the impact of diversity and generational inequalities in the area of sexuality, sexual and gender identities. There appears to be a willingness to develop and improve services, set practice standards and adapt as some of the government policy and guidance from advocacy organisations emerges. At the front line, training, supervision and reflection within services themselves should support the workforce. Care work involves consultation with older people, taking the time to listen, understand and respond to the issues, concerns and fears the older person may have, and knowing and being familiar with rights and responsibilities in relation to sexuality. Ensuring the voices of older people and their advocates are heard is essential to developing and enhancing this key area of practice, where people are supported to live as well as they can until the end of life. The medical model is still a powerful tenet in the desexualisation of older people in care settings. Health and social care professionals have a lot to offer, given their knowledge and skills in enablement and engagement. Professional training that encourages a strengths-based approach and evidence-based practice will support the recognition of issues impacting on sexuality, such as trauma in earlier life, underlying or unresolved problems including unhealthy or unsatisfactory relationships, and adapting to health, disabilities and adjustments to changes in lifestyle (Higgins and Hynes, 2018). The move towards service integration, and an interdisciplinary approach, will draw upon other expertise to develop more holistic and person-centred care alongside advocacy, underpinned by a clearly articulated anti-discriminatory and anti-oppressive stance. This will further support the development of tailored and inclusive services based upon older people's own desires and needs.

References

BASW (British Association of Social Workers) (2019) *Professional Capability Statements for Working with Older People*. London: BASW.

Bauer, M., Fetherstonhaugh, D., Tarzia, L., Nay, R., Wellman, D. and Beattie, E. (2013) '"I Always Look Under the Bed for a Man". Needs and Barriers to the Expression of Sexuality in Residential Aged Care: The Views of Residents with and without Dementia', *Psychology & Sexuality*, 4(3): 296–309.

Bauer, M., Nay, R., Tarzia, L. and Fetherstonhaugh, D. (2014) '"We Need to Know What's Going On": Views of Family Members Toward the Sexual Expression of People with Dementia in Residential Aged Care', *Dementia*, 13(5): 571–85.

Bildtgard, T. and Oberg, P. (2017) *Intimacy and Ageing: New Relationships in Later Life*. Bristol: Policy Press.

Bowers, H., Clark, A., Crosby, G., Easterbrook, L., Macadam, A., MacDonald, R., Macfarlane, A., Maclean, M., Patel, M., Runnicles, D., Oshinaike, T., Smith, C. (2009) *Older People's Vision for Long-Term Care*. York: Joseph Rowntree Foundation.

Cagle, J.G. and Bolte, S. (2009) 'Sexuality and Life-Threatening Illness: Implications for Social Work and Palliative Care', *Health & Social Work*, 34(3): 223–33.

Ciccone, A.A., Meyers, R.A. and Waldermann, S. (2008) 'What's So Funny? Moving Students Towards Complex Thinking in a Course of Comedy and Laughter', *Arts and Humanities in Higher Education*, 7(3): 308–22.

Cort, E., Monroe, B. and Oliviere, D. (2004) 'Couples in Palliative Care', *Sex Marital Therapy*, 19(3): 337–54.

CQC (Care Quality Commission) (2019) 'Relationships and Sexuality in Adult Social Care Services: Guidance for CQC Inspection Staff and Registered Adult Social Care Providers'. London: CQC.

CQC (Care Quality Commission) (2020) 'Promoting Sexual Safety Through Empowerment: A Review of Sexual Safety and the Support of People's Sexuality in Adult Social Care'. London: CQC.

Cronin, A., Ward, R., Pugh, S., King, A. and Price, E. (2011) 'Categories and Their Consequences: Understanding and Supporting the Caring Relationships of Older Lesbian, Gay and Bisexual People', *International Social Work*, 54(3): 421–35.

De Vocht, H., Hordern, A., Notter, J. and van de Wiel, H. (2011) 'Stepped Skills: A Team Approach Towards Communication About Sexuality and Intimacy in Cancer and Palliative Care', *Australasian Medical Journal*, 4(11); 610–9.

Drummond, J.D., Brotman, S., Silverman, M., Sussman, T., Orzeck, P., Barylak, L. and Wallach, I. (2013) 'The Impact of Caregiving: Older Women's Experiences of Sexuality and Intimacy', *Affilia: Journal of Women & Social Work*, 28(4); 415–28.

Dunk-West, P. (2007) 'Everyday Sexuality and Social Work: Locating Sexuality in Professional Practice and Education', *Social Work & Society*, 5(2). Available at: http://www.socwork.net/2007/2/articles/dunk.

Dunk-West, P. and Hafford-Letchfield, T. (eds) (2011) *Sexuality and Sexual Identities in Social Work: Research and Reflections from Women in the Field*. Farnham: Ashgate.

Dunk-West, P.and Hafford-Letchfield, T. (eds) (2018) *Sexuality, Sexual and Gender Identities Research in Social Work and Social Care: A Lifecourse Epistemology*. London: Routledge.

Dyer, K. and das Nair, R. (2013) 'Why Don't Healthcare Professionals Talk About Sex? A Systematic Review of Recent Qualitative Studies Conducted in the United Kingdom', *Journal of Sexual Medicine*, 10(11): 2658–70.

Ezhova, I., Savidge, L., Bonnett, C., Cassidy, J., Okwuokei, A. and Dickinson, T. (2020) 'Barriers to Older Adults Seeking Sexual Health Advice and Treatment: A Scoping Review', *International Journal of Nursing Studies*. DOI: 10.1016/j.ijnurstu.2020.103566

Foucault, M. (1993) *The History of Sexuality*. New York: Pantheon.

Gewirtz-Meydan, A., Hafford-Letchfield, T., Ayalon, L., Benyamini, Y., Biermann, V., Coffey, A., Jackson, J., Phelan, A., Voß, P., Geiger, M. and Zeman, Z. (2018a) 'How Do Older People Discuss Their Own Sexuality? A Systematic Review of Qualitative Research Studies', *Culture, Health & Sexuality*, 21(3): 293–308.

Gewirtz-Meydan, A., Hafford-Letchfield, T., Benyamini, Y., Phelan, A., Jackson, J. and Ayalon, L. (2018b) 'Ageism and Sexuality', in Ayalon, L. and Tesch-Römer, C. (eds) *Contemporary Perspectives on Ageism*. New York: Springer. Available at: https://link.springer.com/chapter/10.1007/978-3-319-73820-8_10.

Glendinning, C., Clarke, S., Hare, P., Kotchetkova, I., Maddison, J. and Newbronner, L. (2007) *SCIE Knowledge Review 13: Outcomes-Focused Services for Older People*. Leeds: Social Care Institute for Excellence.

Graf, I.S. and Johnson, V. (2020) 'Describing the "Gray" Area of Consent: A Comparison of Sexual Consent Understanding across the Adult Lifespan', *The Journal of Sex Research*. DOI: 10.1080/00224499.2020.1765953

Grenier, A. (2007) 'Constructions of Frailty in the English Language, Care Practices and the Lived Experience', *Ageing & Society*, 27(3): 425–45.

Hafford-Letchfield, T. (2016) *Learning in Later Life: Challenges for Social Work and Social Care*. London: Routledge.

Hafford-Letchfield, T. (2020) 'Intimacy, Sex and Relationships', in *Ageing Well – Care and Support for a New Generation. Practice Guide*. Totnes: Research in Practice.

Hafford-Letchfield, T., Couchman, W., Webster, M. and Avery, P. (2010) 'A Drama Project About Older People's Intimacy and Sexuality', *Educational Gerontology*, 36(7): 1–18.

Heywood, W., Minichiello, V., Lyons, A., Fileborn, B., Hussain, R., Hinchliff, S. and Dow, B. (2019) 'The Impact of Experiences of Ageism on Sexual Activity and Interest in Later Life', *Ageing & Society*, 39(4): 795–814.

Higgins, A. and Hynes, G. (2018) 'Sexuality and Intimacy', in MacLeod, R.D. and van den Block, L. (eds) *Textbook of Palliative Care*. Cham, Switzerland: Springer, pp 1–21.

Higgs, A. and Hafford-Letchfield, T. (2018) '"At What Cost? the Impact of UK Long-term Care Funding Policies on Social Work Practice with Older People": A Literature Review', *Ethics and Social Welfare*, 12(3): 229–43.

Hinchliff, S. and Gott, M. (2011) 'Seeking Medical Help for Sexual Concerns in Mid- and Later Life: A Review of the Literature', *Journal of Sex Research*, 48(2–3): 106–17.

Hinchliff, S., Gott, M. and Galena, E. (2005) '"I Daresay I Might Find It Embarrassing": General Practitioners' Perspectives on Discussing Sexual Health Issues with Lesbian and Gay Patients', *Health & Social Care in the Community*, 13(4): 345–53.

Hjalmarsson, E. and Lindroth, M. (2020) '"To Live Until You Die Could Actually Include Being Intimate and Having Sex": A Focus Group Study on Nurses' Experiences of Their Work with Sexuality in Palliative Care', *Journal of Clinical Nursing*, 29(15–16): 2979–90. DOI: 10.1111/jocn.15303

Hordern, A.J. and Street, A.F. (2007) 'Constructions of Sexuality and Intimacy After Cancer: Patient and Health Professional Perspectives', *Social Science Medicine*, 64(8): 1704–18.

ILC-UK (International Longevity Centre, UK) (2015) 'The Rise of the Silver Separators: Divorce and Demographics in Later Life', *Population Seminar Series*. London: ILC-UK. Available at: https://ilcuk.org.uk/wp-content/uploads/2018/10/The-rise-of-the-silver-separators.pdf [Accessed 14 July 2020].

International Council of Nurses (2012) 'The ICN Code of Ethics for Nurses'. Available at: https://www.icn.ch/sites/default/files/inline-files/2012_ICN_Codeofethicsfornurses_%20eng.pdf [Accessed 17 February 2020].

INVOLVE (2019) *Co-production in Action: Number One*. Southampton: INVOLVE.

Jackson, S. and Scott, S. (2010) *Theorising Sexuality*. New York: Open University.

Lee, D.M. and Tetley, J. (2017) '"How Long Will I Love You?" – Sex and Intimacy in Later Life'. London: ILC-UK.

Loe, M. (2004) 'Sex and the Senior Woman: Pleasure and Danger in the Viagra Era', *Sexualities*, 7(3): 303–26.

Lyons, A., Mikolajczak, G., Heywood, W., Fileborn, B., Minichiello, V., Hinchliff, S. and Brown, G. (2018) 'Sources of Information-Seeking on Sexually Transmitted Infections and Safer Sex by Older Heterosexual Australian Men and Women', *Educational Gerontology*, 44(2–3): 186–95.

Menzies, I.E. (1987) 'A Case-Study in the Functioning of Social Systems as a Defence Against Anxiety: A Report on a Study of the Nursing Service of a General Hospital', *Human Relations*, 13(2): 95–121.

Nash, P., Willis, P., Tales, A. and Cryer, T. (2015) 'Sexual Health and Sexual Activity in Later Life', *Clinical Gerontology*, 25(1): 22–30.

NICE (National Institute for Clinical Excellence) (2018) 'Dementia: Assessment, Management and Support for People Living with Dementia and Their Carers', NICE guideline [NG97]. London: NICE.

ONS (Office for National Statistics) (2017) Census data. Available at: http://www.ons.gov.uk/ons/guide-method/census/2011/census-data/index.html.

PHE (Public Health England) (2019) 'People Urged to Practise Safer Sex After Rise in STIs in England'. Available at: https://www.gov.uk/government/news/people-urged-to-practise-safer-sex-after-rise-in-stis-in-england.

RCN (Royal College of Nursing) (2018) 'Older People in Care Homes: Sex, Sexuality and Intimate Relationships. An RCN Discussion and Guidance Document for the Nursing Workforce'. Available at: https://www.rcn.org.uk/professionaldevelopment/publications/pub-007126.

Redelman, M. (2008) 'Is There a Place for Sexuality in the Holistic Care of Patients in the Palliative Care Phase of Life?', *The American Journal of Hospice & Palliative Care*, 25(5): 366–71.

Reese, J.B., Sorice, K., Beach, M.C., Porter, L.S., Tulsky, J.A., Daly, M.B. and Lepore, S.J. (2017) 'Patient-Provider Communication About Sexual Concerns in Cancer: A Systematic Review', *Journal of Cancer Survivorship*, 11(2): 175–88.

Riggs, D., von Doussa, H. and Power, J. (2018) 'Transgender People Negotiating Intimate Relationships', in Dunk-West, P. and Hafford-Letchfield, T. (eds) *Sexuality, Sexual and Gender Identities and Intimacy Research in Social Work and Social Care: A Lifecourse Epistemology*. London: Routledge, pp 86–100.

Roney, L. and Kazer, M.W. (2015) 'Geriatric Sexual Experiences: The Seniors Tell All', *Applied Nursing Research*, 28(3): 254–6.

Ruch, G. (2011) 'Where Have All the Feelings Gone? Developing Reflective and Relationship-Based Management in Child-Care Social Work', *British Journal of Social Work*, 42(7): 1315–32.

Scourfield, P. (2007) 'Social care and the Modern Citizen: Client, Consumer, Service User, Manager and Entrepreneur', *British Journal of Social Work*, 37(1): 107–22.

Ševčíková, A. and Sedláková, T. (2020) 'The Role of Sexual Activity from the Perspective of Older Adults: A Qualitative Study', *Archives of Sexual Behavior*, 49(3): 969–81. DOI:10.1007/s10508-019-01617-6

SfC (Skills for Care) (2017) 'Supporting Personal Relationships: Supporting People Who Need Care and Support to Have Meaningful Relationships'. Leeds: SfC.

Simpson, P., Brown Wilson, C., Brown, L., Dickinson, T. and Horne, M. (2017) ' "We've Had Our Sex Life Way Back": Older Care Home Residents, Sexuality, Intimacy and Erotophobia', *Ageing & Society*, 73(1): 127–37.

Stausmire, J.M. (2004) 'Sexuality at the End of Life', *American Journal of Hospice and Palliative Medicine*, 21(1): 33–9.

Sullivan, M.P. (2008) 'Social Workers in Community Care Practice: Ideologies and Interactions with Older People', *British Journal of Social Work*, 39(7): 1306–35.

Taha, S., Blanchet-Garneau, A. and Bernard, L. (2020) 'Une revue de la portée sur la pratique infirmière auprès des personnes âgées issues de la diversité sexuelle et de genre', *Recherche en soins infirmiers*, 140(1): 29–56.

Taylor, A. and Gosney, M. (2011) 'Sexuality in Older Age: Essential Considerations for Healthcare Professionals', *Age and Ageing*, 40(5): 538–43.

Taylor, B. (2014) 'Experiences of Sexuality and Intimacy in Terminal Illness: A Phenomenological Study', *Palliative Medicine*, 28(5): 438–47.

Twigg, J. (2007) 'Clothing, Age and the Body: A Critical Review', *Ageing & Society*, 27(2): 285–305.

Twigg, J. (2010) 'Clothing and Dementia: A Neglected Dimension?', *Journal of Aging Studies*, 24(4): 223–30.

Twigg, J. and Buse, C.E. (2013) 'Dress, Dementia and the Embodiment of Identity', *Dementia*, 12(3): 326–36.

Twigg, J., Wolkowitz, C., Cohen, R.L. and Nettleton, S. (2019) 'Conceptualising Body Work in Health and Social Care', in Twigg, J., Wolkowitz, C., Cohen, R.L. and Nettleton, S. (eds) *Body Work in Health and Social Care: Critical Themes, New Agendas*. Chichester, UK: Wiley Blackwell.

Weerakoon, P., Jones, M. and Kilburn-Watt, E. (2004) 'Allied Health Professional Students' Perceived Level of Comfort in Clinical Situations That Have Sexual Connotations', *Journal of Allied Health*, 33(3): 189–93.

Westwood, S. (2016) 'Dementia, Women and Sexuality: How the Intersection of Ageing, Gender and Sexuality Magnify Dementia Concerns Among Lesbian and Bisexual Women', *Dementia*, 15(6): 1494–1514.

Wornell, D. (2014) *Sexuality and Dementia: Compassionate and Practical Strategies for Dealing with Unexpected or Inappropriate Behaviors*. New York: Demos Medical Publishing.

12

Final reflections: themes and issues arising from the volume on desexualisation in later life

Paul Simpson, Trish Hafford-Letchfield and Paul Reynolds

Given that the desexualisation of older people emerged as a dominant theme in the first volume (addressing diversity) in this book series, this volume was created specifically to probe this subject further and, in doing so, provide a coherent and critical overview of it as a possible basis for critique and action.

This volume has showcased a variety of work by emerging and established scholars (based in Argentina, Britain, Sweden and Spain). As such, it has featured a mix of theoretical and theoretically-informed empirical work that reflects theorising from social gerontology, social psychology, structuralism, poststructuralism and feminism and some combinations thereof. In various ways, all contributors have addressed the intersecting influences that help to make up later life sexuality. If the first volume in the book series addressed influences of age combined with gender, sexual identification, race and class, this volume has focused a bit more on age as it enmeshes with gender (see the chapter by Clare Anderson), with sexual identification (see the chapter by Jane Youell) and with disability/ableism (see the chapters by Susan Gillen and Paul Reynolds and by Linn J. Sandberg).

Moreover, the main foci of this volume have concerned the cross-cutting physical/embodied, relational, cultural, structural and policy and practice-related constraints on older people's intimate and sexual self-expression. Although such theorising indicates a fairly wide purview, this volume has presented key examples rather than a comprehensive survey of accounts of desexualisation. Nevertheless, it does provide considerable insight and critical reviews of the state of current scholarship on the subject of desexualisation in later life and prompts ideas for further research.

To avoid a simple recap of key points in individual chapters, this concluding section attempts more of a synthesis of overarching themes and issues that the chapters point to, though, inevitably, we refer to individual authors. Subsequently, we move to discuss what this volume indicates about the state of scholarship in an emerging field of knowledge and how this suggests an agenda for research and serves as a precursor to a future volume addressing the resexualisation of the older self. Indeed, the agentic capacities of older people as sexual beings are visible in chapters in this volume, and the subject of resexualisation, often in the face of significant obstacles, appears to be much overlooked in analysis (Simpson et al, 2018).

Overarching themes relating to the desexualisation of older people

Reading across the ten substantive chapters that make up this volume, several overarching themes become evident. Chapter 1 has already noted how risk/control serve as structuring conditions of ageing sexuality, though, perhaps unsurprisingly, 'ageist erotophobia' (also flagged in the book series introduction) cuts across all chapters in various ways. The concept was particularly salient in the chapter by Simpson, who identified its workings at (overlapping) macro-societal, meso-institutional and micro-interpersonal levels. Related to ageist erotophobia, chapters in this volume also point to themes that involve respectively how changes involved in growing/being older are considered synonymous with loss (see the chapter on aesthetics and ageing sexuality) and how various policy and practice issues contribute to desexualisation. Taken together, ageist erotophobia, change as loss and the policy and practice issues discussed in this volume have much to tell us about a lack of awareness of the diverse lived experiences, realities and sexual needs of older people. In effect, sexual activity and erotic desires are commonly seen as irrelevant to radically changed older people's identities, their sense of belonging and of (sexual) citizenship (Hafford-Letchfield, 2008; Villar et al, 2014). When older people's sexuality does find a modest degree of legitimacy in the form of the 'sexy oldie' (see Gott, 2004), such a figure (often female) is indicative of ideas of 'successful ageing', which themselves can reflect ageist assumptions, indexing just how much any 'success' is dependent on the ability to produce a youthful appearance.

Being old = multiple changes = loss

Because ageist erotophobia has been amply discussed, we move to our theme that concerns the equation of age with loss and how this can work in various ways. This is particularly visible in Anderson's chapter, which explores discourses that conflate the menopause with decline in physical capacity/vitality, in emotional stability and, putatively, in attractiveness. The latter is also abundantly clear in the chapter by Iacub and Villar on the aesthetics of sex in later life. Further, older women's sense of loss can involve degendering and desexualisation (see also Sandberg on dementia and Reynolds on the complexification of consent). Although a sense of loss might register visibly at a biological level, like the menopause itself, ageing and the menopause ramify particularly as cultural constructs familiar to late modern/consumerist societies that practically make it a moral imperative for older women to avoid looking old(er). Again, this resonates with the chapter by Iacub and Villar on how aesthetics can work discursively to exclude older people from the sexual imaginary.

The broader issue here adverts to the notion of older women as made to stand for a failed (feminine, sexual) subjectivity. The idea of a failed socio-sexual subjectivity applies not just to older females but more generally to other ageing subjects, though in different ways and with different consequences. For instance, failed sexual subjectivity also featured in the chapters by Reynolds addressing consent and by Gillen and Reynolds addressing compromised capacity, as well in the chapters by Villar and Fabà and by Sandberg. The latter concerns older people with a dementia but here signifies both loss of sexual capacity *and* excess of a pathological sexuality (where disinhibition might be involved), which positions individuals outside of contemporary legitimate ('western') sexual subjectivity.

Diversity in desexualisation

Just as the first volume on diversity in this book series commonly invoked desexualisation, so this volume on desexualization has invoked diversity in reported experiences of exclusion from the sexual and intimate imaginary.

Such diversity is apparent not just in the various discussions of intersectional influences on desexualisation, but is further explored in the chapter by Sandberg, which has drawn attention to the importance of recognising the diversity of responses to sex and intimacy in the context of a dementia. Such responses, which illustrate historic gender inequalities of caring, also afford insight into the varied, complex and challenging forms of love and of emotional labour that range from practical caring, adaptation to a radically changed person, a sense of disconnection, a felt lack of reciprocation and recuperation of the person and the (long-term) relationship.

Of course, the principle just outlined could apply to *all* older subjects. Indeed, in their chapter on sexuality and older residents in long-term care facilities, Villar and Fabà describe how residents might not only represent a failed (sexual) subjectivity – they also indicate how staff/ care settings' policies (or lack thereof) and practices can contribute to the notion of older people's/residents' sexuality as a *problem* and thus to be contained or managed rather than represented as human need and a question of rights. Besides, such issues would have particular resonance for those made to stand for non-normative forms of gender and sexuality, as implicit in Reynolds' chapter and as discussed in the one by Youell addressing LGBTI individuals (in an urban, Australian context). In the latter case, a failure of recognition of sexual and gender difference can ramify in terms of multiple exclusion and deficits in self-esteem and mental health. Such factors also contribute to the construction and exacerbation of a failed subjectivity in relation to ageing sexuality.

Furthermore, implicit in this same chapter is the notion that the double jeopardy of heteronormative and cisgender discourses, intersecting with ageism and predominating in care spaces, combine to desexualise and by removing opportunities for self-expression, especially for those understood as different. Reflecting concerns amply voiced in the chapter by Villar and Fabà, Youell also raises the issue of deficits in wellbeing that can result from a felt obligation to 're-closet' oneself on entry to a care home given that fellow residents' generationally shaped attitudes tend to be less approving of sexual and gender difference.

Policy and practice issues

If we are serious about equality and justice, when considering how to theorise desexualisation in later life, one is never far from considering how our thought and practice can restrict others and thus thinking about how such challenges can be addressed. Indeed, all chapters in this volume have, in various ways and to varying degrees, indicated the need in policy and professional practice to challenge and move beyond thinking and structures that render older people's sexuality problematic. Many of the issues identified also ramify in terms of an agenda for further research.

The kind of critical thinking about older people's sexuality just mentioned is particularly evident in the Villar and Fabà chapter. This chapter is also important for its synthesis of the various institutional and interpersonal barriers to the expression of sexuality and intimacy. The obstacles identified are suggestive of how ageist erotophobic discourse is manifest in practice and material form in a lack of the privacy that is prerequisite for intimacy and sexual activity. The barriers identified here also reflect broader social and generationally formed attitudes, and organisational cultures that lack policy and knowledge and that veer towards paternalism and control/management rather than the enablement of older residents' sexuality. In this regard, Villar and Fabà point up the need for clear inclusion policies addressing diverse sexual needs and development opportunities for diverse staff that encourage critical reflection on the provenance of deeply habitual ways of thinking of sex, intimacy and sexual identification. Commonly, such ways of thinking involve notions of more and less acceptable expressions of sexuality on the grounds of age and of sexual and gender identification. Also of interest here is thinking that cultures of care need to be shifted from biomedical concerns and knee-jerk approaches to safeguarding onto concerns of rights that centrally involve older people, or their proxies if capacity to understand consent is seriously impaired.

In a similar vein, the chapter by Sandberg suggests the need for professional support for all concerned (including family/significant others adapting to radical change) in relation to understanding sex and intimacy in the context of a dementia. The chapter by Youell adopts a similar stance in relation to staff awareness of and competencies in supporting older individuals identifying as lesbian, gay, bisexual, trans and intersex or (LGBTI) with personal and sexual self-expression. It is also worth including, as Villar and Fabà suggest, all care home residents in events that are designed to encourage critical examination of anti-LGBT+ prejudices. Such measures would also need to be underpinned by organisational policies that establish inclusion and accreditation criteria and active engagement with LGBT+ voluntary/support groups.

More specifically, some contributors' thinking adverts to the need for a staff development resource that aims to encourage frontline care staff to *discuss* how they can support all residents' choices concerning sexuality and intimacy (see the chapters by Simpson, by Villar and Fabà, by Youell and by Hafford-Letchfield). Of course, this would include the right to define oneself as asexual or even no longer sexual, though we are all probably intimate (physically and/or emotionally) in various ways short of being sexual. The process of supporting sexuality and intimacy would inevitably involve confronting the challenges presented by the need to differentiate how sexual and intimate lives can be enabled in line with intersecting cultural differences and the personalisation of support. Again, such ideas are at least implicit in all chapters. Besides, there is a resource that has been developed by the Older People's Understandings of Sexuality (OPUS) research team, which aims to raise care home staff awareness of older residents' sexuality and intimacy needs. This was considered necessary because, in the UK, official and practitioner guidance is either unknown or ignored, and, arguably, because much of it does not fit well with care staff needs and organisational realities (Simpson et al, 2018).

The state of research on desexualisation and possible future directions

This volume has addressed various, intersecting constraints on older people's sexuality. As such, it could be considered indicative of the state of largely European research in more economically developed countries on a set of uses that have been relatively neglected in scholarship. The book series is committed to at least two further volumes exploring aspects of ageing sexuality in cultures beyond the imaginary of the 'West' or the 'Global North'. However, no matter the geo-political focus, we might conclude that scholarship – and, indeed, political struggles – over ageing sexuality are relatively novel and that social change in the direction of normalising older people as sexual and intimate beings will be, as ever, a long haul. Indeed, much remains to be done to build on the vibrant scholarship that has emerged more recently and to effect change in how people think and how truly holistic care, involving sexuality and intimacy needs, is delivered.

In more practical terms, an agenda for research on desexualisation is apparent in several contributions, such as those by Iacub and Villar, Sandberg, Villar and Fabà, Youell and Hafford-Letchfield, whose chapters have indicated the need for studies exploring the different factors that contribute to autonomy and resexualisation of the older self. It seems there is urgent cultural-political work to be done on the aesthetics of later life sex and intimacy and widening beyond ageist erotophobia what we can see as beautiful and pleasing, et cetera. Any studies of desexualisation might well have resexualisation in mind as political goals, and could include focus on older people *and* those supporting them, whether as significant others or as care professionals. As regards the latter, knowledge of older people's sexuality and their legitimacy as sexual citizens could be advanced by placing emphasis on rights-based approaches to enabling older people's sexual and intimate self-expression in preference to safeguarding approaches that resort instinctively to (over-)protection or even prevention of sexual, intimate or erotic experience. The afore-mentioned authors also underscore the value of foregrounding the voices of older people themselves (or proxies in the case of people with severe dementia) and might stress the value of working *with* older people as research partners, which could include co-production research (see Willis et al, 2018).

In all chapters in the book, we gain some insight into how older people can exercise agency in terms of their challenges to ageist erotophobia and desexualisation. After much emphasis on desexualisation and constraint, it seems only fair and fitting that the sexual and intimate agency of older people should be a focus of further research. A start has already been made on this particular issue, and indeed use of 'the resources of ageing' has been extant for some time in the work of Heaphy (2007) and that of Simpson (2015). Such resources involve accumulated knowledges – emotional, cultural, social and political – that undergird capacity to question or avoid compliance with dominant social expectations of putatively sexless older people (Simpson et al, 2018).

However, agency is never a quality of super-aware, asocial, atomised and purely voluntaristic individuals unfettered by social structures and discourses. It is contingent on the (often hidden) influences of class structure and institutions, dominant ways of thinking (generally and in particular contexts) and interpersonal relations. Capacities for agency and deployment of the resources of ageing are not equally distributed and need to be linked to further explorations of intersectional and relational ageing. With more collective, institutional/organisational issues in mind, the chapter by Youell has drawn attention to the significance of good practice by voluntary support groups, government and care service providers in enabling agency in relation to older LGBTI individuals' sexuality in healthcare settings. Again, assertion of sexual and intimate autonomy is largely consonant with social positioning informed by cross-cutting social differences working in particular contexts.

Earlier we spoke of the need for change in policy and practice in relation to healthcare and support services, but such considerations could be integrated into an agenda for research. Studies of inclusion policies in relation to healthcare come immediately to mind – something prompted by Youell's chapter. Indeed, all contributors have discussed, in various ways, the need to challenge dominant ideas that construct ageing/later life automatically as loss and as sexual/intimate loss in particular. Indeed, taking our cue from Butler and Scott (1992), rescuing subjects from pathologised forms of sexuality/intimacy will require widening discourse to enable newer articulations of legitimate sexuality and viable sexual/intimate identities to emerge. A step in this direction has been made by the UK-wide Sex and Intimacy in Later Life Forum (SILLF), which has brought together public health officials, voluntary sector campaigners, service providers and academics to co-ordinate research designed to inform policy and practice. SILLF is working on two campaigns: one focused on promoting via social media and established/'mainstream' media a bigger societal conversation about older people as valid sexual citizens; and the other focused on developing age-inclusive sexual health services. The latter was motivated by the increase in sexually transmitted infections among those aged 50 and over in UK contexts (Davis/Department of Health, 2016; Poynten et al, 2013): one of the more negative indicators that older people are still 'doing it'!

In summary, this volume has explored cross-cutting biological/ embodied, relational, cultural, structural and policy and practice-related constraints on older people's intimate and sexual self-expression. While it may reflect a vibrant and diverse scholarship, this book marks a beginning of studies on the desexualisation of older people, though it also suggests an agenda for research, and significant within this agenda are the conditions under which older people can exercise autonomy in relation to sexual, erotic and intimate matters. To ignore older people's sexual agency would be to homogenise them and render them a great disservice. To avoid such a one-sided account, sexual agency and resexualisation of the older self will be the subjects of a forthcoming volume in this book series.

References

Butler, J. and Scott, J. (1992) 'Contesting Grounds', in Butler, J. and Scott, J. (eds) *Feminists Theorise the Political*. New York: Routledge.

Davis, S./Department of Health (2016) 'Department of Health Annual Report of the Chief Medical Officer 2015 on the State of the Public's Health. Baby Boomers: Fit for the Future'. London: Department of Health. Available at: https://www.gov.uk/government/publications/cmo-annual-report-2015-health-of-the-baby-boomer-generation.

Gott, M. (2004) *Sexuality, Sexual Health and Ageing*. London: McGraw Hill Education.

Hafford-Letchfield, T. (2008) '"What's Love Got to Do with It?" Developing Supportive Practices for the Expression of Sexuality, Sexual Identity and the Intimacy Needs of Older People', *Journal of Care Services Management*, 2(4): 389–405.

Heaphy, B. (2007) 'Sexualities, Gender and Ageing: Resources and Social Change', *Current Sociology*, 55(2): 193–210.

Poynten, I.M., Grulich. A.E. and Templeton, D.J. (2013) 'Sexually Transmitted Infections in Older Populations', *Current Opinion in Infectious Diseases*, 26(1): 80–5. DOI:10.1097/QCO.0b013e32835c2173

Simpson, P. (2015) *Middle-Aged Gay Men, Ageing and Ageism: Over the Rainbow?*. Basingstoke: Palgrave Macmillan.

Simpson, P., Brown Wilson, C., Brown, L., Dickinson, T. and Horne, M. (2018) '"We've Had Our Sex Life Way Back": Older Care Home Residents, Sexuality and Intimacy', *Ageing & Society*, 38(7): 1478–1501.

Villar, F., Celdrán, M., Fabà, J. and Serrat, R. (2014) 'Barriers to Sexual Expression in Residential Aged Care Facilities (RACFs): Comparison of Staff and Residents' Views', *Journal of Advanced Nursing*, 70(11): 2518–27.

Willis, P., Hafford-Letchfield, T., Almack, K. and Simpson, P. (2018) 'Turning the Co-production Corner: Reflections from a Community-based Action Research Project to Promote LGB&T Inclusion in Care Homes for Older People', *International Journal of Environmental and Public Health*, 15(4): 695–711. DOI:10.3390/ijerph15040695.

Index